Filipino American Faith in Action

Filipino American Faith in Action

Immigration, Religion, and Civic Engagement

Joaquin Jay Gonzalez III

NEW YORK UNIVERSITY PRESS
New York and London

NEW YORK UNIVERSITY PRESS
New York and London
www.nyupress.org

Library of Congress Cataloging-in-Publication Data
Gonzalez, Joaquin Jay.
Filipino American faith in action : immigration, religion, and civic engagement / Joaquin
Jay Gonzalez III.
p. cm.
Includes bibliographical references and index.
ISBN-13: 978-0-8147-3196-3 (cl : alk. paper)
ISBN-10: 0-8147-3196-1 (cl : alk. paper)
ISBN-13: 978-0-8147-3197-0 (pb : alk. paper)
ISBN-10: 0-8147-3197-X (pb : alk. paper)
1. Filipino Americans—Religion. 2. Filipino Americans—California—San Francisco Bay
Area. 3. San Francisco Bay Area (Calif.)—Religious life and customs. 4. United States—
Emigration and immigration. 5. Philippines—Emigration and immigration. I. Title.
BR563.F53G66 2009
277.94'60830899921—dc22   2008039037

New York University Press books are printed on acid-free paper,
and their binding materials are chosen for strength and durability.
We strive to use environmentally responsible suppliers and materials
to the greatest extent possible in publishing our books.

Manufactured in the United States of America
c 10 9 8 7 6 5 4 3 2 1
p 10 9 8 7 6 5 4 3 2 1

Contents

Acknowledgments   vii

1   Introduction: Calling in San Francisco   1

2   Resurrecting Christian Faith   33

3   Praying, Then Delivering Miracles   63

4   Gathering Souls with Food   82

5   Converting Bowling to Civic Involvement   100

6   Blessing Passion and Revolution   123

7   Reconciling Old and Young Spirits   149

8   Conclusion: Embracing New Bonds and Bridges   178

Notes   185

References   189

Index   203

About the Author   221

Acknowledgments

Embarking on this book project led to an exciting personal and professional journey. As a first-generation immigrant to the United States, I have found new networks and friends essential. The research introduced me to many cherished ones to whom I am most grateful.

First, what started as The Religion and Immigration Project (TRIP) co-investigators later became my generous TRIP gang: Lois Lorentzen, Kevin Chun, and Hien Duc Do. Gathering and organizing a treasure trove of migrant narratives would have been impossible without the help of TRIP research associates and fellow Filipino American sojourners, Andrea Maison, Dennis Marzan, and Claudine del Rosario. The research assistance from Glen Andag and Cristina Cortes was also invaluable. Thanks to my wonderful politics and Philippine studies students who patiently administered surveys.

Second, I wish to thank the pastors and congregations from Saint Patrick's Catholic Church, Iglesia ni Cristo, Saint Augustine's Catholic Church, the Daly City United Methodist Church, and many other San Francisco Bay Area churches who shared with us their stories but most of all their hearts, minds, and spirits. They inspired me to no end.

Third, I am grateful for the varying forms of institutional and funding support from the University of San Francisco's College of Arts and Sciences, the Center for the Pacific Rim, the Politics Department, the Maria Elena Yuchengco Philippine Studies Program, the Asian American Studies Program, and the Asian Studies Program; Golden Gate University's Mayor George Christopher Chair in Public Administration and the Edward S. Ageno School of Business; the PEW Charitable Trusts; the Jesuit Foundation; the Kiriyama Fellowship; Westbay Pilipino Multi-Services Center; the Filipino Education Center; the Veterans Equity Center; the San Francisco Immigrant Rights Commission; and the Philippine Consulate General of San Francisco.

Fourth, I thank my growing circle of friends, family, and colleagues who had to "excuse" me from gatherings, conversations, e-mails, phone calls, and meetings simply because "I'm busy with my book!" Michelle Hong, Elise Gonzalez, and the rest of the Gonzalez and Lucero clans, as well as Rhacel Parreñas, Malou Babilonia, Marylou Salcedo, Barbara Bundy, Gerardo Marin, Jenny Turpin, Eileen Fung, David Kim, Rob Elias, Shalendra Sharma, Brian Weiner, Patrick Murphy, James Taylor, John Nelson, Lorraine Mallare, Lisa Yuchengco, Efren Padilla, Dan Gonzales, Edith Borbon, Sid Valledor, Leo Paz, Bong and Cathy Bengzon, as well as Ed and Rica Campos, were most understanding, patient, and supportive. There are many more.

Finally, I am grateful to Jennifer Hammer at New York University Press and two anonymous reviewers for being piercing but collegial in their comments, feedback, and suggestions.

1

Introduction

Calling in San Francisco

One Sunday more than a century ago, an elegantly dressed Peter Burnett and his wife, Harriet, walked two blocks from their home to the Sunday school where their daughter taught. As they crossed the street, a young gentleman respectfully tipped his black top hat as he recognized Burnett, who was the first governor of California. The Bible study groups at the Sunday school were organized by members of the University Mount Presbyterian Church, who came from the wealthy families of European descent living in nearby Portola Valley. In attendance were affluent first- and second-generation Italian migrants as well as a few French and German families. Some had moved to San Francisco from South and North Carolina but still considered themselves citizens of the Old World—Sicilian and Maltese, for example. These families established homes and businesses around San Francisco's Visitacion Valley. As their numbers grew, and undeterred by the battering of the great 1906 earthquake, they built Saint James Presbyterian Church on Leland Street. However, in the 1960s and 1970s, the pull of suburbia and the influx of African, Latino, and Asian imigrants changed the demographic makeup of the busy neighborhood. For various reasons, newcomers to the area were not drawn to Saint James. Attrition took its toll on the once-vibrant church membership, and by the 1980s, Saint James faced closure by the presbytery. By 1990, however, instead of closing its doors, historic Saint James Presbyterian Church was opening them wider to receive an eager group of Protestants from across the Pacific. Unlike the church's founding members, these new parishioners liked to hear the word of God in a mix of the Philippine dialect Tagalog and English (or Taglish). Many originated from Cavite Province, but in all, the membership represented numerous regions throughout the Philippines. As part of a rehabilitation plan established with the Presbytery, the new Filipino membership recruited the Reverend Jerry Resus, who was then pastor of the First Presbyterian Church in Pasig, Metro Manila. Together with a few remaining descendants of the founders of the church, they formed a new multiracial congregation that remains active today.

Currently, the San Francisco Bay Area is home to many thousands of Filipino migrants. Filipino Americans have become the second-largest Asian American population–numbering more than Japanese Americans and Korean Americans combined. Not surprisingly, many existing religious sites have become their spiritual homes. Like the Filipino Presbyterians at Saint James, Filipino migrant Witnesses, Methodists, Baptists, Iglesia ni Cristo (INC) members, Aglipayans, Episcopalians, Mormons, Adventists, and others are also repopulating many of San Francisco's other declining churches.

From these new spiritual homes, Filipino migrants have built "bonds" and "bridges" with religious, civic, governmental, business, and social institutions within their new San Francisco communities. They have done so by means of (1) transnational influence, (2) adaptive spirit, and (3) intergenerational cohesion.

By showing how Filipino migrant faithful Filipinize elements of the cultural, political, and economic arenas within the San Francisco Bay Area cities and towns in which they have settled, this book will tell a new kind of migration saga—one that is enriched with descriptions of transnational, adaptive, and intergenerational *kasamahan* (bonding Filipinization) and *bayanihan* (bridging Filipinization).[1] I will discuss these terms in greater detail later in this chapter.

A New Migration Story

I tell this story about the civic engagement of Filipino migrants through religion from my perspective as a scholar, church member, activist, and migrant. Growing up in the Philippines, I was very familiar with the central role of the church in practically all aspects of life. But I never dreamed that as a parishioner of historic Saint Patrick's Catholic Church in the South of Market (SoMa) neighborhood, the civic spirit of the church's Irish Catholic founders (who concurrently served in San Francisco's city hall) would one day descend upon me and awaken my own civic sensibilities—this time for my new homeland.[2]

Let us think back to September 11, 2001. On that day, terrorists pierced America's financial and military arteries, prompting a wave of fear that stimulated anti-immigrant sentiment. Soon thereafter, Congress hurriedly passed the Patriot Act in an effort to protect the United States against further attacks, but at the expense of certain civil liberties. The San Francisco immigrant community acted swiftly to voice its concerns. Encouraged by Saint Patrick's highly energetic Filipino pastor, Monsignor Fred Bitanga, the Filipino American community became the first ethnic group to take a collective stand on this and other political issues that emerged after the tragedy. After all, Saint Patrick's had to live up to its role as a voice for social justice, as well as a spiritual fount. As the so-called Vatican of all Filipino American Catholic churches, with Monsignor Bitanga as the figurative "pope," Saint Patrick's sees political activism as part of its responsibility to its congregation. One by one, Filipino American, Latino American, Chinese American, Indian American, Native American, Arab American, and African American religious and community leaders, young and old, joined the vigil. They called and prayed for the maintenance of peace, for a stop to violence against Arab and Muslim Americans, and for the United States to take a step back and examine its foreign policies as a possible motivation for the terrorist attacks. Several speakers proposed that America's hegemonic role in the global economy was a motivating force for would-be terrorists. At the end of the gathering, more than 200 voices joined together in singing John Lennon's peace anthem "Imagine." The church was filled with emotion.

As if timed by fate, my cell phone buzzed while I was saying goodbye to the ever-smiling monsignor. The call was from San Francisco's city hall. Mayor Willie Brown's appointment secretary was asking if I would be willing to serve on the Immigrant Rights Commission of the City and County of San Francisco. There was no time to think or to pray for guidance about this important request. I looked at the fearless leader of my church. He winked his blessing, and I nodded my head in thanks. So like Governor Burnett of Saint James Presbyterian Church, I, Commissioner Gonzalez of Saint Patrick's Catholic Church, led a life of religious worship and civil service. While performing my volunteer city hall duties, I found other community-focused Filipino migrants like me who belonged to other local churches: the Jehovah's Witness Kingdom Hall in the Excelsior District, Saint Francis and Grace United Methodist Church in the Sunset neighborhood, the Salvation Army Chapel on Broad Street, the Sixth Church of Christ the Scientist in ritzy Pacific Heights, the San Francisco Tabernacle Seventh-Day Adventist Church in the Mission District, and the Geneva United Methodist Church on Geneva Street. Like me, some attended services at more than one church and had multiple volunteer and civic duties. The focus of their work included local and "Filipino issues," such as the rights of Filipino veterans of World War II and employees at San Francisco International Airport, but also national concerns, such as immigration and health care reform. As my list of churches grew, so did my collection of business cards from fellow Filipino migrant faithful who served both God and their new country. Some of them had even run for public office. Others were simply political activists and advocates. I became more intrigued not with the churches' varying spiritual dogma but with the ways in which Filipinos utilize religious places as new migrants and new Americans, and the influence they are having—as mediated through these places—on the historical, cultural, and political aspects of their San Francisco Bay Area communities. Given the strong ties that many Filipino migrants maintain to their home country, I also became curious about the continuing impact that Filipino migrants in the United States have on their families and hometowns in the Philippines.

From the day of that prayer vigil onward, I began to view the Filipino spiritual experience in San Francisco as a useful lens through which to consider the social, political, and cultural integration of migrants from the Philippines into San Francisco society. Doing so renders visible the crucial but often unseen influence of Filipino migrants on their new homeland. Given the deep-seated and omnipresent religious traditions of Filipinos, I believe that the best places to observe the unique interplay of their integration and influences are the San Francisco church spaces that Filipino migrants have come to occupy. More than simply attending churches in the Bay Area, Filipino migrant groups have actually saved several religious spaces—ranging from modest storefronts to grand architectural edifices—from closure, or else taken them over from earlier migrant Catholic and Evangelical congregations, including German Lutherans, Italian Catholics, Irish Protestants, and many others.

Consequently, this book exposes an important facet of Filipino migration history to the United States. In the chapters that follow, I will discuss the migration of Filipinos to the San Francisco Bay Area in a new way, that is, through several local church sites.

Why Is the Filipino Migrant Religious Experience Important to America?

The Filipino migrants' sociocultural integration experience, as it occurs through their churches, challenges and builds on two of the most prominent paradigms of American social history: *assimilation theory* and *multicultural theory*. Assimilation theory assumes that to do well in American society, migrants have to fully assimilate into the dominant population or blend in with the predominantly European American majority. Multicultural theory, however, points out that while this "melting pot model" may be relevant to the assimilation experience of early European immigrants to the United States, it might not adequately represent the experiences of newcomers in the late twentieth century and early twenty-first century, and particularly minority populations, like African American, Asian American, and Latino American migrants. The Filipino migrants' integration experience builds on the notion that a melting pot dilutes the cultural particularities that new Americans bring to a diverse, multicultural society. Instead, multiculturalism allows the unique qualities of its component communities to emerge, ultimately improving the larger society.

My observations of Filipino migrant faithful from San Francisco align with those of multiculturalist scholars Min Zhou and Carl Bankston. In *Growing Up American* (1998), they highlight the excellent educational performance of Vietnamese migrant youth in Louisiana, which they attribute to the strong kinship support structure and network provided by Vietnamese American neighborhood-based organizations. Zhou and Bankston argue that the nonassimilation of Vietnamese led to their societal mobility and success. According to their findings, the indigenous social capital created within the Vietnamese community is what enables mobility for those who do not assimilate. Interestingly, the local church had been the central avenue for the creation of social capital in the community studied by Zhou and Bankston. However, they did not examine closely the site's spritual dynamics, but instead only addressed certain social outreach activities, such as helping with homework. Similarly, the multiculturalist writings of Asian American scholars like Yen Le Espiritu (2003) in *Home Bound: Filipino American Lives across Cultures* and Rick Bonus (2000) in *Locating Filipino Americans: Ethnicity and the Cultural Politics of Space*, among others, illuminate how churches have been used as sites to meet and recruit key informants and interviewees from the Filipino migrant communities in order to expose interactions among themselves and others, in community centers and cultural events as well as at their homes and family gatherings. They were not focused on the significance of the church itself.

In their pioneering works that question the assumptions of assimilation theory, Zhou, Bankston, Espiritu, Bonus, and others analyze the inwardly focused ethnic bonds that Asian American migrants have developed through the community centers, hometown associations, Internet Web pages, ethnic enclaves, and colorful festivals that they have established in the United States. But because these scholars were not focused on examining deeply the connections between church and civic engagement, their writings do not tell the story of the many outwardly focused, action-oriented, civic "bridges," and the ways in which these connections have allowed migrants to span two homelands, blend American and Asian cultures, and form alliances between young and old. This omission in the foundational writings on Filipino migration provides an opportunity to examine the church sociologically, especially the ways in which it facilitates the integration of migrants into the United States and enables them to influence their new American homeland. This analysis reconciles some of the diverging assumptions between the assimilationist and multiculturalist paradigms by showing how new Filipino migrants have managed to align with the rest of American society without having to disengage themselves from either their Filipino cultural practices or their families and communities in the Philippines. These two competing views are the real philosophical underpinnings of the immigration debate in the United States. Understanding their divergence and then recasting U.S. immigration policy to reflect this conciliatory "Filipino American way," spurred by Filipino American churches, provides a possible way of working out this long-standing U.S. sociopolitical concern.

The steady influx of Filipino Christian migrants over the past century into the San Francisco Bay Area has increased attendance at local Christian churches, many of which had been mostly or entirely abandoned by earlier Christian migrants. These American Christian churches and their congregations have helped Filipino migrants cultivate allegiances to their new homeland. But these churches are also learning that to many new Filipino members, being faithful to God in America and becoming an American Christian does not necessarily mean discarding either their Filipino ways of worshiping or their obligations to their Philippine homeland. Observing a mix of first- and second-generation Filipino American migrant faithful in San Francisco kiss and then wipe the foot of a Filipino saint in church prior to joining the civil rights marches on Market Street draped in a Philippine flag testifies to the fact that it is certainly possible for migrants to integrate into America while asserting their ethnicity, protesting human rights abuses in the Philippines in the name of the U.S. War on Terror, or exposing the environmental exploitation of U.S. corporations, since this is what American liberal democracy is all about. Having recognized the necessity and benefits of catering to this new migrant group, dominant institutional structures in California like government and corporations have developed services and products tailored to Filipino American taxpayers and consumers. Moreover, although some may participate in mainstream American organizations such as Lions Clubs, the Red Cross, United Way, the Young Women's Christian Association (YWCA), and the Parent-Teacher Association (PTA), a large majority of Filipino Americans, especially first-generation immigrants, tend to connect to American society primarily through their California-based Filipino hometown, religious, political, business, social, alumni, and professional veterans' groups, as well as their Filipino consulates, casinos, groceries, bingo tournaments, restaurants, media, parades, rallies, fund-raisers, auctions, dances, beauty pageants, concerts, nightclubs, and fiestas. It is through these familiar institutions that Filipino migrants contribute to American society. To examine this phenomenon more intensely, I focus in this book on an institution that earlier studies have failed to recognize adequately—the church. San Francisco's many spiritual sites treat their Filipino American worship communities as *barangay* residents. A *barangay* is a traditional Philippine village, barrio, district, or neighborhood. A *barangay* is composed of family clusters and is considered to be the smallest political unit in the Philippines. A group of *barangays* makes up a town, city, or municipality. Filipinos see their church as a key community gathering space in their new American *barangay*. Churches therefore become sites where the familiar social structure of the *barangay* can be practiced. Seen in this way, church spaces are the most obvious places in the San Francisco Bay Area to observe Filipino migrants cultivating their ethnicity while at the same time becoming American citizens, consumers, volunteers, taxpayers, and voters.

Broadly speaking, the influx of Filipinos is subtly Filipinizing segments of the larger American society. *Filipinization* refers to varying degrees of Filipino cultural, political, culinary, financial, or spiritual influence, support, ownership, or control. There are several notable examples of the Filipinization of American media and popular culture, both in the San Francisco Bay Area and nationally. The podcast section of the online *San Francisco Chronicle* (www.sfgate.com) includes the popular "Pinoy Pod." One can watch Filipino news, talk, and drama on KTSF 26 all over the San Francisco Bay Area. Meanwhile, televised twenty-four hours a day all over the United States and Canada is TFC (The Filipino Channel). In music, the Grammy Award–winning hip-hop group the Black Eyed Peas have included two Tagalog-language songs in their last two chart-topping albums, courtesy of Allan Pineda Lindo, a member of the group who is also Filipino. When disc jockeys throughout the San Francisco area play the Black Eyed Peas' "Bebot" and "APL Song" on popular radio stations, they not only increase the circulation of Tagalog but also help to mainstream it in this American locale. Of course, it also helps that many San Francisco DJs are themselves Filipino. This demographic particularity of the San Francisco Bay Area prompted the Oakland Raiders football team to develop a Tagalog-language page on its Web site (www.raiders.com/Tagalog) for its thousands of Filipino American and Philippine-based fans. On national television contests, Filipino Americans called in en masse to help their *kababayan* (country-woman/countryman), singer Jasmine Trias, become a finalist in FOX's highly rated *American Idol* and helped propel Filipina American dancer Cheryl Bautista-Burke into the winner's circle twice in ABC's hit show *Dancing with the Stars*. These singular examples from popular culture reflect the presence of a large and influential Filipino American population. English training in the Philippines has always enabled many Filipinos to enter the American workforce with relative ease. A recent trend has been for districts with teacher shortages to recruit teachers from the Philippines for their public schools. School systems in California, New York, Maryland, Florida, and Nevada are currently among those hosting migrant elementary, middle school, and high school teachers from the Philippines. Many other Filipino Americans have served and continue to serve the United States in the uniformed services—military, police, and fire. And, of course, one is hard-pressed to find a hospital in the United States without Filipino doctors or nurses.

The extensive presence and influence of Filipinos nationwide has prompted the development of specialized media. Philippine and Filipino American newspapers and magazines are now often found side by side with mainstream and ethnic media outlets in San Francisco, Los Angeles, Seattle, Honolulu, and New York. Inside these mass publications are gigantic Tagalog-language advertisements enticing Filipino consumers to switch to AT&T and send money back to the Philippines through Western Union. Given the pervasiveness of Filipinos in the United States, it is not surprising that Tagalog has become the second most spoken Asian language and sixth most used non-English language in the United States, according to language-learning software giant RosettaStone. Even Costco, the largest wholesale warehouse club chain in the world, mainstreams Philippine mango products (dried fruit and mango juice) through its 389 stores in the United States and Puerto Rico. These illustrations of various forms of Filipinization, particularly in the influential mass media, big business, and language-learning markets, indicate that while the phenomenon is strong in San Francisco and California in general, it extends to other parts of the United States as well.

The Filipino American community, a growing and influential segment of the U.S. population, has the highest median household income, along with Asian Indian Americans, compared with all ethnic groups, according to the 2000 census. This is the case in spite of the social, political, and cultural barriers that many Filipinos have encountered in their new homeland. There may be lessons to be learned from the process of adaptation and integration that Filipinos have developed, in which they form both *bonds* and *bridges* that create social and cultural capital, which in turn enable them to contribute to American society. *Kasamahan* (community organization) and *bayanihan* (community action) are forms of bonding and bridging social capital that need replenishment in American society.[3] *Kasamahan*, or bonding Filipinization, refers to the inward-focused kinship and ethnic ties and relationships that Filipino American churches help to establish and nurture. Cultivating formal and informal groupings through the church—such as Filipino-language choirs, Bible study groups, or masses; rosary crusades, youth groups, blessed singles groups, or Couples for Christ groups; Marian devotional activities, bingo socials, mahjong groups, and Filipino provincial and town associations—leads to feelings of togetherness, companionship, fraternity, sisterhood, solidarity, pride, and competitiveness. By contrast, *bayanihan*, or bridging Filipinization, describes the church-inspired, outward-oriented linkages and networks that Filipino American groups use to engage and contribute to

U. S. and Philippine society. These linkages encompass a broad array of activities, including volunteer activities, civic involvement, community partnerships, political advocacy, protest marches, cleanup drives, sending money, military service, government work, overseas mission work, donating food, Peace Corps and AmeriCorps work, and fund-raising. Together, both modalities of Filipinization help strengthen America's diverse societal base as well as refurbish the nation's larger supply of social capital and civic involvement—the bedrock of American democracy. In this book, we will see how Filipino migrant faithful build *kasamahan* bonds and *bayanihan* bridges through transnational influence (integration through a continuous back-and-forth movement of people, symbols, finance, and food), employing an adaptive spirit (cultural traits, behavior, or practices that facilitate adjustment and acculturation), and intergenerational cohesion (collaboration across generations, old and young, or first, second, and third generations).

Filipino American Faith in Action provides a contrarian case to the prevailing assumption that religion and spirituality are diminishing in the rich developed countries of the world (which incidentally are major migration destinations) and flourishing only in poor developing countries of the world (which interestingly are major migration countries of origin). Based on the empirical evidence gathered during the research for this book, it seems that religion and spirituality in rich developed countries, like the United States, are being boosted by new migrant faithful from poor developing countries, like the Philippines. This is especially true with the influx of Filipino Christians to San Francisco Bay Area churches. More important, this book provides religion and migration scholars with the first academic volume solely on the intersections of Filipino migration, civic engagement, and faith. Scholarly ethnographic works have explored the contemporary effects of and issues associated with Filipino and Filipino American transnational migration, globalization, and diaspora.[4] However, none of these books have ventured into the Filipino migrants' religious socialization, their civic contributions, and the transpacific societal, economic, and political implications of their spirituality, even though churches are the spaces where Filipinos are most visible ethnographically.

Given these gaps, this book makes a unique and important contribution to religious studies, migration studies, political studies, Filipino studies, Asian American studies, and Asian studies by doing the following:

1. Drawing on the intersections of a number of academic disciplines, including history, sociology, political science, economics, American studies, ethnic studies, public policy, and religious studies. In other words, interdisciplinary theories underpin the research. These include concepts drawn from studies of the political economy of migration, immigration, the sociology of religion, transnationalism, globalization, assimilation, diaspora, revisionist histories, state-civil society relations, as well as class and structural analyses.

2. Blending theoretical and conceptual frameworks to understand the role of religion and politics in new migrant communities, particularly Filipino migrant communities. The book brings together scholarly literature that is seldom in dialogue, most especially with regard to the Filipino diaspora.

3. Implementing community-based ethnographic and survey research techniques that illuminate how religion is intertwined with the everyday lives of new Filipino migrants, and how these migrants are influencing the practice of spirituality in America well beyond the Filipino migrant community. The large-scale migration and faith community survey discussed in chapter 3 is unprecedented because it measures data on the financial contributions of Filipinos to both the Philippine and the American economy, providing richer information than the U.S. census and other official sources.

4. Going beyond most studies on Filipinos and their churches, which still deal primarily with Roman Catholicism and its offshoots, such as El Shaddai. This book brings together research on Filipino Catholic, Protestant, and Independent churches. This denominational breadth is unprecedented in Philippine and Filipino studies, both locally and internationally. In many spaces we entered, my fellow Filipino team members and I were the first outsider scholars allowed entry, and were given permission to write voluminous field notes about the sociology of these churches and congregations. It is notable that in spite of being ethnic insiders, we were not immediately accepted and had to build trust over the many years of the study.

5. Giving voice to pastors, ministers, lay workers, church members and nonmembers, religious women and men, veterans, youth, families, the elderly, gays and lesbians, activists, students and others— all in all, a wide array of new Filipino migrants.

How Is This Book Organized?

This book consists of eight chapters, which are subdivided into three major themes: (1) transnational influence, (2) adaptive spirit, and (3) intergenerational cohesion. Each theme has a chapter illustrating bonding Filipinization (*kasamahan)* and bridging Filipinization (*bayanihan).*

Chapter 2, "Resurrecting Christian Faith," focuses on the transnational influence flowing to and from church spaces in the Philippines and San Francisco. Supplementing library information with archival research and interviews with key informants, I delve first into the Americanization of Philippine churches and Christianity and then the Filipinization, later on, of San Francisco congregations and religious spaces. This migratory phenomenon has facilitated the creation of *kasamahan* bonds with Filipino prayers, pastors, icons, rituals, and migrant faithful easily moving back and forth among San Francisco and Philippine spiritual homes and gatherings. This transnational movement not only facilitates the influence of Filipinos on San Francisco communities but also helps them integrate with the broader, multicultural American society.

Chapter 3, "Praying, Then Delivering Miracles," is an analysis of the large-scale San Francisco Bay Area Religion and Remittance Survey, which measures the extent of transnational praying (homeland to hometown) then sending of money by Filipino faithful. Based on the results, I argue that migration brings not only a transnational influence of Filipino faith into American congregations and churches but also a transnational Filipino faith-based *bayanihan* to San Francisco. Their economic situation, enhanced in America, has empowered Filipino Catholics, Protestants, and Independent church members to socioeconomically influence not only their San Francisco communities but also their Philippine hometowns. The survey and follow-up focus group meetings revealed that besides congregating and praying for relatives back home from their churches in the United States, Filipino faithful deliver on their promises to help with their families' health, retirement, and education needs, as well as community social and economic development programs and disaster relief projects in both the San Francisco Bay Area and hometowns in the Philippines. Knowing that all is well with their families back home gives Filipinos in the United States the necessary peace of mind to concentrate on their adaptation to life in America.

Chapter 4, "Gathering Souls with Food" focuses on the role of food in the religious life of migrants. It expounds on the ways in which the adaptive spirit of faithful Filipino migrants helps them negotiate the complexities associated with migration to multicultural San Francisco. This chapter also demonstrates how the American, Latino, and Asian elements embedded within Filipino culture facilitate migrants' absorption and accommodation of San Francisco's culturally diverse environment. Adaptive *kasamahan* in two sites—Iglesia ni Cristo in Daly City and Saint Patrick's Catholic Church in downtown San Francisco—illustrates how the blending of Filipino and American culinary traditions creates opportunities for camaraderie and religious conversion.

Chapter 5, "Converting Bowling to Civic Involvement," provides evidence from San Francisco disputing the premise of Robert Putnam's critically acclaimed book, *Bowling Alone: The Collapse and Revival of American Community*, that social capital, especially the bridging variety, has declined all over the United States. I present evidence that describes how the Filipino migrants' adaptive spirit, mediated through San Francisco churches, allows them to balance the competing social and civic responsibilities of new migrants, which include religious obligations and civic duties in both the United States and the Philippines. Thereafter, I use two *bayanihan* case studies to illuminate more clearly how the adaptive spirits (or esprit de corps) of migrant faithful at Saint Patrick's Catholic Church in San Francisco and the Iglesia ni Cristo in Daly City are cultivated and channeled for the betterment of American society.

Chapter 6, "Blessing Passion and Revolution," explores the dynamics of intergenerational *kasamahan*. I begin by discussing the respect filled interactions we observed between youth and their elders in homes and Filipinized churches, and then explore what university students in San Francisco—particularly children of Filipino migrant faithful who attend spiritual schools—learn about social justice, community organizing, and counterhegemonic actions vis-à-vis the church. Then I explore how these students use their classroom and library learning to foster a passion for justice within themselves and then release this passion as revolutionary action to challenge injustices in American society. Thereafter, using an in-depth case discussion of Saint Augustine's Catholic Church in South San Francisco, I elaborate on four conditions, following the development of intergenerational respect, that are necessary for transforming passionate energy and revolutionary spirit into intergenerational *kasamahan*.

Chapter 7, "Reconciling Old and Young Spirits," demonstrates how ardent Filipino American youth, many socialized in faith-influenced family relations and schooling, have joined forces with their parents' and grandparents' generations to tackle certain social injustices. This chapter focuses on the critical role played by Filipino faithful and their spiritual communities in the pursuit of justice for Filipino World War II veterans and around extrajudicial killings in the Philippines. It will discuss the strategies these Filipino American youth used to convince the larger American public and the global community to join them in planning and launching intergenerational counterhegemonic activities, or *bayanihan* initiatives. These activities have included protest marches, letter-writing campaigns, testifying before Senate and House committees, and candle-light vigils.

Chapter 8, "Embracing New Bonds and Bridges," ends the book with two compelling narratives that summarize and integrate key research findings. These two stories bring us to the conclusion that San Francisco society has in many ways embraced both bonding and bridging Filipinization.

Where Is Religion Situated in the Life of a Filipino Migrant?

A majority of Filipino migrants make a conscious effort to place religion at the center of their lives, wherever they sojourn. Unlike their counterparts from other Asian countries, contemporary Filipino American migrants in San Francisco do not center their lives in highly visible ethnic business and linguistic enclaves like Chinatown, Japantown, or Little Saigon. For Chinese Americans, Japanese Americans, and Vietnamese Americans in San Francisco, these enclaves play a major role in their social networking with civic connections to American society. They seek to draw other members of American society into their "Asiatowns" for business and social purposes. Conversely, the Filipino migrant centers for cultivating *kasamahan* and *bayanihan* in San Francisco are much more dispersed. Most would rather blend in with whatever ethnoscape they face (*kahit ano*: whatever; *bahala na*: leave it to God), especially since Filipino migrants are, in a sense, Latino, Asian, and American rolled into one. Ethnically, Filipinos are a product of hundreds of years of Chinese, Malay, and Indian migration and intermarriages, and thereafter close to four centuries of Spanish and American racial and cultural exchanges.

In San Francisco Bay Area cities with large Filipino populations, most of the Filipino residences, community centers, restaurants, and churches are interspersed with mainstream commercial, governmental, and residential areas, not clustered as a dense enclave. Additionally, given their advanced English communication skills, it is relatively easy for Filipino Americans to learn the nuances of American social interactions and to get along with others (*makisama*). After the destruction of San Francisco's Manilatown in 1974, a more dispersed but connected web of social and civic networks grew out of Filipino churches (*simbahan*) and other places of worship (*sambahan*) in and around San Francisco. These are located in the centers of the American *barangays*, where Filipino immigrants gather together as one community (*bayan*) for Sunday or weekday worship (*samba*). Filipinos believe that God's presence reaches beyond the physical church. Scattered somewhere outside their spiritual focal points are their other San Francisco Filipino community meeting and gathering places: supermarkets, Asian grocery stores, businesses, schools, parks, restaurants, senior centers, performing art and visual art studios, recreational and social halls, shopping malls, city halls, and the Philippine consulate. The supermarket and grocery store might not be Asian or sell Filipino products but could still be considered a favorite place (*suki*) to get Vietnamese fish sauce and Chinese bok choy (from Pacific Supermarket) and beef shank (from Safeway), which Filipinos will mix together to create *nilaga*, a Filipino stew. To remind them of the centrality of religion in their lives, most formal social events held in these meeting and gathering places might begin with a spiritual invocation or ecumenical prayer.

Filipino migrants come to the United States from a vibrant spiritual environment in the Philippines. After all, the Philippines is an Asian country with a large Christian majority: 84 percent are Roman Catholic, 8 percent are Protestant (mostly Evangelical/Pentecostal), 3 percent are Iglesia ni Cristo, 3 percent are Muslim, and 2 percent belong to other religions and denominations. El Shaddai, which emerged in the Philippines, is one of the fastest-growing Catholic charismatic groups in Asia. The 1991 and 1998 International Social Survey Program went so far as to declare Filipinos the most religious people in the world. In the Philippines, it is common to see worship, devotion, and prayer in many forms, being performed by community leaders and ordinary citizens on the streets, in offices, and in homes. Catholic masses are held in airports, in shopping malls, in parks, at home—almost everywhere, with no restrictions. Events and meals, big or small, generally begin with a prayer or invocation. Sunday is a religious day of obligation for Filipino Catholics, Protestants, and Independent churches (with certain exceptions like the Seventh-Day Adventists, who attend Saturday services). For most Filipino Catholics, attending additional masses during the week is also important. If at all possible, many attend mass daily; given that religious services are widely and frequently available, it is not hard to find a mass and to make time in one's busy schedule for it. Because of the prevalence of religious practices in everyday life, daily discourse, verbal and written, is also influenced by religion.

In the Philippines, many individuals follow the Christian liturgical calendar alongside their calendars for work and school. Moreover, many religious holidays are also official national holidays, like Christmas, All Saints' Day, All Souls' Day, and Holy Week. On Sundays and religious holy days, all roads literally lead to churches. In America, Filipino migrant faithful echo the religious practices in their homeland by going to mass every Sunday and strictly observing major religious holidays, like Christmas and Holy Week. The Christmas celebration in the Philippines is easily the most significant event of the year and is not complete without Simbang Gabi, a nine-day, early morning novena service leading up to Christmas Day. Simbang Gabi is now commonly celebrated in Filipinized Catholic churches in the United States. Migrant faithful often ask visiting Catholic priests from the Philippines to say masses for them and lead Bible studies and rosary sessions in homes and hotels, at private parties, and so on. Fasting and abstinence are common to Filipino Catholic migrants during the Lenten season, which begins with the placement of ashes on their foreheads during Ash Wednesday, extends through Holy Thursday, Good Friday, and Black Saturday, and ends on Easter Sunday. In the Philippines, Holy Week (Cuaresma or Semana Santa) entails daily church visits (*bisita Iglesia*), readings of the Passion of Christ (*pagbasa ng pasyon*), Passion plays (*sinakulos*), and public displays of atonement for sins—in certain parts of the country, some extremist devotees even go so far as to self-flagellate, whipping themselves on the back as they walk, bloodied, down the street. A few even have themselves crucified, literally impaled at their hands and feet, and hang briefly on the cross before descending to receive medical attention. Many of these traditions and rituals have been transplanted to the United States; the gory spectacles of self-flagellation and crucifixion, however, remain localized in particular regions of the Philippines.

In the Roman Catholic calendar consulted by Catholic Filipinos, there is a saint's feast day for every day of the year; sometimes there are even two saints listed on one day. Each person is born into the feast day of a saint, which in some cases influences the naming of a child as well as a place. Each town has a feast day based on its patron saint that is celebrated with a town fiesta. For instance, Santa Ana, Manila, where I grew up, celebrates the feast of Our Lady of the Abandoned (or Nuestra Señora de los Desamparados) every May 12. Usually, a special service is held, followed by a townwide procession, and then feasting in people's homes. Migrants to the United States from Santa Ana get together and commemorate this important feast day even though—or perhaps because—they are away from their hometown. The feast days of other towns are also celebrated in America by their former residents. For instance, I have seen Bicolanos in the San Francisco Bay Area celebrate the feast of Our Lady of Peñafrancia, while former residents of Lucban, Quezon, still host a version of that town's traditional Pahiyas harvest festivals. There are also numerous devotions and venerations to various saints and Mother Marys (Our Ladies or Nuestra Señoras) that have been exported to the United States from the Philippines. Performing traditional Filipino celebrations and devotions such as these in the United States is a way that migrants have been able to make home away from hometown.

Religious persons, personifications, icons, images, objects, and symbols abound in Filipino religious life. They remind worshipers to always pray and be thankful, that God is constantly present, and of the need to be morally upright and just. Rosaries, crucifixes, Bibles, pendants, and various items bearing images of the Santo Niño (Christ Child), Jesus Christ, Virgin Mary, the holy family (Jesus, Mary, and Joseph together), and patron saints are commonly found among the possessions of Filipinos. In the Philippines, these religious objects and symbols are displayed freely in both private and public places. The symbols are tattooed on bodies, painted on vehicles, and posted on walls; there is no law prohibiting their public display. Filipino migrant faithful in the United States have had to adapt to the religious diversity of their new communities and have limited the display of these items to private spaces such as homes and cars. In the Philippines, some statues of the Virgin Mary are so strongly venerated that they are transported weekly among devotees' homes. The migration of Filipinos to the United States has expanded the range of these icons accordingly. Some even travel internationally, between hometowns and churches in the Philippines and homes and churches in the United States. San Lorenzo Ruiz (the first Filipino saint) and the Santo Niño de Cebu (Christ Child from the Cebu Province), are widely worshiped, usually in the form of figurines or photographs. During the Christmas season, the traditional Filipino *parol* (Christmas lantern) and *belen* (Nativity scene) also appear in Filipinized American churches and homes.

Religious power and political power, although separated by a constitutional provision in the Philippines, are still very much intertwined in practice. From birth, most Filipinos are taught to see the church as the "fourth branch of government." Citizens are expected to be not only law-abiding but also God-fearing. This holds true whether one belongs to a Catholic, Protestant, Iglesia ni Cristo, El Shaddai, Charismatic, Evangelical, or any other spiritual congregation.[5] Catholic, Protestant, and Independent church leaders generally ask their members to exercise their right to vote on election day by supporting particular candidates who have been sanctioned by the church. Some large, independent groups, such as El Shaddai and the Iglesia ni Cristo, are wooed by candidates for their bloc votes. The late Jaime Cardinal Sin, the powerful former Catholic archbishop of Manila, was often quoted in national headlines as saying "Not to vote is a sin." This appeal to the conscience of voters directly from the pulpit was found to increase election turnout rates to an impressive 90 percent. By contrast, in the November 2006 elections, San Francisco had a 60 percent voter turnout. Though comparatively low, this was one of the highest voter turnouts in the United States.

High-ranking Catholic priests and Christian pastors in the Philippines rank high socially, alongside town mayors and rich businesspersons. Priests, pastors, nuns, brothers, missionaries, and other religious persons are accorded a high amount of respect. They are treated as "holy persons" and never called simply by their first name. Instead, a title such as "Father," "Sister"," "Brother"," "Pastor," or "Kapatid" (Brother/Sister) is usually placed in front of the name as a sign of respect. Filipino migrants bring with them this same degree of reverence for religious authorities. They tend to place high value on the advice and opinion of religious persons, the mere presence of whom is seen as a blessing from God. Hence, priests, pastors, and religious men and women are often invited to (literally) bless anniversaries, birthdays, graduations, or any other special family occasion with their presence. Many Filipino faithful believe that miracles and divine interventions are logical explanations for events, such as the healing of illnesses. Personal testimonies about the power and influence of God are common in everyday conversation.

For Filipino Catholics in the Philippines, who constitute 84 percent of the national population, congregating as a group for prayer daily is made very convenient by the frequency of mass services, offered every day of the week from early morning to late evening. These attract large numbers of people, both young and old. Requests for baptisms (*binyag*), confirmations (*kumpil*), weddings (*kasal*), wakes (*lamay*) and burials (*libing*), and funeral services, as well as vehicle, office, and home blessings (*bendisyon*) are numerous. At 13 percent of the population, Filipino Protestants and Independents experience this same vigorous spirituality on their days of worship. Filipino Muslims, who constitute 3 percent of the population, are also known to be quite devout. Hence, from the perspective of a new Filipino migrant to the United States, the church is the most important point of contact and acculturation. By bridging the Philippines to the United States using religion, churches facilitate the establishment of a migrant's roots in his or her new American *barangay*. To many, their new church in the United States might even be considered more critical to their adjustment than the new bank, supermarket, school, or office. There may be many Filipinos or no Filipinos at all at the new church. But eventually, this new church becomes a part of the migrant family's weekly routine. The church ultimately becomes one of the most important focal points of a migrant's life, marking all significant milestones, from the birth of new babies to the death of elders.

Behaviorally, then, religion greatly influences the way Filipinos respond to the situations they face daily, whether in the Philippines or anywhere else in the world. Because of this influence, Filipino migrant faithful have a strong tendency to exhibit these religion-reinforced Filipino traits, values, and actions: *samba* (worship), *dasal* (prayer), *panata* (vow), *bahala na* (leave up to God), *utang na loob* (debt of gratitude), *makisama* (get along with others), *pasalamat* (thankful), *damay* (sympathy), *galang* (respect), *awa* (mercy), *patawad* (forgiveness), *sakripisyo* (sacrifice), *tulong* (help or contribution), *lingkod* (serve), *pagmamahal* (care), *pagbigay* (giving), *maintindihin* (understanding), and *hiya* (shy or embarrassed). When practiced by Filipino migrant faithful in everyday life, these have led to varying manifestations of *kasamahan*, and thereafter *bayanihan*, for the benefit of church and community, as well as San Francisco society and Philippine hometowns.

How Should Filipinization Be Understood in San Francisco History?

San Francisco's Filipinization and its embedded spirituality and religiosity begin with 82 million Filipinos in the Philippines, plus another 10 million who are a part of the Filipino global diaspora to close to 200 countries.[6] Of this number, 2.4 million call the United States their home. As we have seen, over the course of just 100 years of migration, Filipinos have become the largest Asian American population in San Francisco and the United States (if Chinese Americans are disaggregated by their countries of origin—Taiwan, Hong Kong, Singapore, Macau, and China). Filipino Catholics, Protestants, and Independents combined are the largest Asian Christian group in the San Francisco Bay Area, in California, and in the United States. Many Filipino Americans vote and get involved in political concerns, and make solid contributions toward making San Francisco's economy one of the most vibrant in the United States and California's economy the seventh largest in the world. These actions are largely informed by a strong Filipino spirituality.

Today, San Francisco and Manila are sister cities, which is a natural outgrowth of the two cities' long-standing connection. San Francisco and the Philippines have a long, shared history as colonial territories of Spain. Hence, it is not a surprise that Filipinos first landed on the Pacific Coast during the period of Spanish empire building and foreign conquest (see Borah 1995). As a matter of fact, on Coleman Park in Morro Bay (a city halfway between San Francisco and Los Angeles) is a historic marker that describes this linkage:

> During the Manila-Acapulco Galleon Trade era from 1565 to 1815 Spanish galleons crossed the Pacific between the Philippines and Mexico. On October 18, 1587, the Manila Galleon *Nuestra Señora de Esperanza* commanded by Pedro de Unamuno entered Morro Bay near here. A landing party was sent to shore which included Luzon Indios, marking the first landing of Filipinos in the continental United States. The landing party took official possession of the area for Spain by putting up a cross made of branches. The group was attacked by native Indians two days later, and one of the Filipinos was killed. Unamuno and his crew gave up further exploration of this part of the coast.

On November 6, 1595, another Spanish galleon in transit to Acapulco, the *San Agustin,* was shipwrecked near Point Reyes at the mouth of the San Francisco Bay, forcing the disembarkation of Filipino seamen to the shore (Nolte 1995). These are the very first recorded instances of Filipinos landing on Californian soil.

In 1776, Spanish priest Francisco Palon founded a Catholic mission on the peninsula, which was named San Francisco de Asis after the founder of the Franciscan religious order. Incidentally, it was from this mission that the city of San Francisco received its name. It was not long before the name of a Filipino Catholic sailor appeared in a local church's registry. On August 10, 1779, Blessed Father Junipero Serra administered the rite of confirmation to Vicente Tallado, "*indio de la Panpangua en Philipinas, marinero.*" This event was recorded in the confirmation records of California's Monterey mission, less than 100 miles from San Francisco.

In the early nineteenth century, even before the formal annexation of the Philippines by the United States in 1898, Filipinos had already been trickling into the ports of San Francisco on board merchant ships. One of these sojourners was the Philippine national hero Dr. Jose Rizal, who inspired his countrymen to revolt against Spain by writing novels exposing the atrocities and abuses of Spanish authorities. On April 29, 1888, while Rizal was on board the SS *Belgic* and trying to get into San Francisco, his U.S. port of entry, he was held up by immigration officials. To keep himself busy during the long bureaucratic delay, Rizal penned a letter to his parents, stating:

> Here we are in sight of America since yesterday without being able to disembark, placed in quarantine on account of the 642 Chinese that we have on board coming from Hong Kong where they say smallpox prevails. But the true reason is that, as America is against Chinese immigration and now they are campaigning for the elections, the government, in order to get the vote of the people, must appear to be strict with the Chinese, and we suffer. On board there is not one sick person.[7]

Rizal's disdain for America's discriminatory immigration policies was palpable. When he was finally allowed to disembark, Rizal stayed at the classy Palace Hotel on Stockton Street. A metal plaque on the wall outside of that hotel (now the Sheraton Palace Hotel on Market Street) attests to his passing through on the way to New York.

Still reeling from their protracted struggle with their Spanish colonizers, Philippine revolutionaries found themselves fighting a bloody war
against the United States, their new colonizer. The mighty Presidio of San
Francisco and many other nearby military installations became launching pads for American troops who were deployed to the Philippines to
carry out the "civilization and Christianization of those savage Filipinos" under President William McKinley's Manifest Destiny and benevolent assimilation policies (see Karnow 1989). Congress officially declared
that the "Philippine insurrection"—not war—ended on July 4, 1902,
although fighting continued until 1913. U.S. general Franklin Bell estimated that more than 600,000 Filipinos died in this war of annexation
(Agoncillo 1990; Constantino 1989).

In 1903, to commemorate the formal annexation of the Philippines,
a ninety-seven-foot Corinthian column topped with a bronze Goddess
of Victory was erected at the center of San Francisco's Union Square.
Surrounded then by the distinguished residences of the fashionable and
wealthy, a brown marker proudly hailed: "Erected by the Citizens of
San Francisco to commemorate the Victory of the American Navy under
Commodore George Dewey at Manila Bay." San Franciscans may have
built the monument out of pride in Dewey's flagship, the protected cruiser
USS Olympia, which had been built and launched from San Francisco,
along with many of America's other battleships. Whatever the reason,
this majestic pillar and its well-heeled neighbors celebrated the expansion of the American empire to Asia.

Between 1903 and 1934, Filipino pensionados, students on all-expenses-
paid U.S. government scholarships, were recruited to study at American
universities. They were being trained to become the next generation of
entrepreneurs, civil servants, and teachers. Many of them transited through
San Francisco on the way to the best midwestern colleges. Some stayed on
to study at prestigious San Francisco Bay Area universities, including the
University of San Francisco, a Catholic Jesuit school. Beginning in 1906,
Hawaii's booming sugar plantation economy also brought in thousands of
Filipinos as "special noncitizen U.S. nationals." They became the first generation of manongs (elders). During their summer breaks, many pensionados
worked alongside their manongs in the agricultural fields, fruit orchards,
and fish canneries. Many who got tired of toiling on Hawaii plantations,
and in California crops and Alaskan canneries, or who simply wanted to
retire, flocked to cities on the West Coast. Their destinations included San
Francisco, which enjoyed an economic boom following the gold rush.

The migratory waves that came from the Philippines after its 1898 annexation by the United States led to the steady growth in the attendance of Filipino migrant workers at local Catholic and Protestant churches. Between 1920 and 1929, a total of 31,092 Filipinos entered California, more than 80 percent of them through the port of San Francisco (California Department of Industrial Relations 1930). However, the 1940 census counted only 3,483 Filipinos living in the city of San Francisco.

Up until the 1930s, most Filipinos were hired in farming communities south of San Francisco to perform agricultural work, but many also worked in downtown San Francisco as domestic helpers and manual laborers in the area's numerous hotels, restaurants, and ports. Many had been told of the wealth of opportunity in cities like San Francisco while still in the Philippines. According to Dioscoro R. Recio Sr., a Watsonville, California, farmworker originally from Banga, Aklan Province, in the Philippines, "Missionaries came to the *barangay* and told us about America. They said there were many jobs and opportunities there" (Recio 2000, 1).

Located on Lake Street in the Richmond District and, later, Sutter Street near Union Square, the Philippine Consulate General in San Francisco was established immediately after the Philippines gained independence from the United States in July 1946. The consulate's mission was to serve the needs of Filipino migrants not just in San Francisco but also in the rest of Northern California, Alaska, Utah, Wyoming, Colorado, Oregon, northern Nevada, Idaho, Washington, and Montana. Like the church, the consulate became another important community center for migrants. Today, among its many duties, it administers oaths for dual citizenship and acts as the polling place for Philippine elections.

The end of World War II, the passage of the U.S. Immigration Act of 1965, and the declaration of martial law in the Philippines in 1972 intensified the conditions that drew Filipinos to U.S. cities like San Francisco. Many Filipinos who had served in the U.S. military during World War II as soldiers and civilians decided to follow the promises of a productive postmilitary life to San Francisco and its growing suburbs. Joining these soldiers were beneficiaries of the Immigration Act of 1965, which encouraged highly skilled professionals such as doctors, nurses, engineers, and accountants to move to the United States. Many brought their immediate families (spouses and children) and, upon gaining U.S. permanent residency status or U.S. citizenship, petitioned to bring more of their extended relations (parents, siblings, and their families) (see Cordova 1983; Takaki 1987, 1995). The booming industrial, business, financial, and health care sectors of the San Francisco Bay Area garnered a large share of this new pool of Filipino professional migrants. According to the 1960 U.S. census, there were 12,327 Filipinos in the city of San Francisco. This number increased to 24,694 in 1970 and 38,690 in 1980.

The deplorable state of the Philippine economy in the 1970s and 1980s also forced a mass exodus of migrants to San Francisco. Some came to the United States on nonimmigrant visas (as tourists, students, or exchange visitors) and later overstayed their short-term visitor visas. These illegal immigrants are popularly known as "TNTs," or *tago ng tago* (literally, "hide and hide"). Some married American citizens to legalize their stay, while others paid for "green card" marriages. Later, the 1986 general illegal immigration amnesty enabled many TNTs to legalize. Filipino migrants who became illegal or undocumented after the 1986 amnesty have been insulated from federal scrutiny by San Francisco's "INS Raid-Free Zone" and "City of Refuge" resolutions and most recently by a sanctuary city ordinance. For current TNTs, both their churches and their city are their safe havens.

The dot-com boom in the vast Silicon Valley south of San Francisco in the late 1980s also increased the numbers of highly skilled Filipino migrants to the San Francisco Bay region with an expanded working visa (H-1) category. Interestingly, the dot-com bust did not decrease immigration but instead brought a new population of Filipino migrants, since the health care industry had successfully lobbied the U.S. Congress to allow more health care professionals, particularly nurses, to migrate with their families as U.S. permanent residents. Filipino nurses are helping to alleviate an acute nursing shortage that has been exacerbated by an ever-growing number of elderly Americans requiring medical care. Thus, San Francisco's hospitals, assisted living centers, hospices, and clinics are staffed with highly trained and caring Filipino migrant nurses.

From about 1910 to the 1970s, a ten-block stretch of Kearny Street, from California Street to Columbus Avenue, was informally referred to by locals as "Manilatown," a dense Filipino settlement in downtown San Francisco. During its peak in the 1920s and 1930s, more than 20,000 *manongs* lived, worked, and relaxed there. After all, wages in San Francisco were much better than on the plantations in Hawaii. Also, Manilatown had Filipino-owned barbershops, pool halls, restaurants, and other businesses. Many *manongs* worked seasonal jobs on farms, and in canneries and factories. During the off-season, they lived in the many single-room occupancy (SRO) residential hotels in Manilatown, including the Columbia, the Temple, and the Palm. Since many of these men remained single, these residential hotels were important social centers where the *manongs* could support one another spiritually, emotionally, and sometimes financially.

The most popular of these was the red brick, three-story International Hotel (popularly known as the I-Hotel). In 1977, the owner of the I-Hotel sold it to a wealthy developer, sparking a battle that united a wide range of Filipino activists, from leftists to those on the Religious Right. In August of that year, the sheriff and his deputies forcibly evicted the I-Hotel's elderly Filipino and Chinese bachelor tenants. The eviction spelled death for Manilatown. The *manongs*, who at that time were in their sixties and seventies and had little money, had no choice but to move away from their old, familiar neighborhood and relocate to other inexpensive accommodations in the South of Market and Tenderloin areas and the suburbs, including Daly City. Ironically, after the demolition of the I-Hotel, the lot on which it stood remained empty for twenty-five years, until a broad-based coalition of individuals, community groups, and foundations, including the Catholic Archdiocese of San Francisco, pitched in and bought the property from its Thai owner. It has become a fully functioning community space called the International Hotel Manilatown Center, joining the other Filipino places in San Francisco: Bayanihan Center, Filipino Cultural Center (inside Bloomingdale's), and Bindlestiff Studios (Estrella 2004; Sobredo 1998).

The late twentieth century brought peoples from all geographic regions of the world to San Francisco, from Latin America to South Asia. New Filipino migrants now arrive on Philippine Airlines A300 airbuses at the San Francisco International Airport instead of on ships at the ports of San Francisco or Oakland. They are inspected by uniformed U.S. Immigration and Naturalization Service (INS) officials who, in the post-9/11 era, have been renamed Immigration and Customs Enforcement (ICE) officers and are part of the powerful U.S. Department of Homeland Security. The massive influx of migrants to San Francisco has made ICE one of the most visible public agencies in the Bay Area. As a result, the terms "INS," "ICE," and "green card" have been mainstreamed into the local discourse of San Franciscans. Nonetheless, and in keeping with its progressive politics, its mayor and board of supervisors uphold the city's status as a sanctuary for all migrants, as well as a "language access city"

TABLE 1.1
Filipino Population in the San Francisco Bay Area, by County

COUNTY	NUMBER OF FILIPINO RESIDENTS
Santa Clara	76,060
Alameda	69,127
San Mateo	59,847
San Francisco	40,083
Solano	36,576
Contra Costa	34,595
Sonoma	2,697
Napa	1,759
Marin	1,389
Total	322,133

Source: U.S. Census 2000

for native speakers of Spanish, Chinese, Russian, and Tagalog, and those with limited English proficiency.

The results of the millennium census (U.S. Bureau of the Census 2000) showed significant demographic shifts, particularly in the ethnic distribution of U.S. residents. The American-born white population of San Francisco shrank to less than half of the total number. African Americans represented less then 8 percent of the total population. The numbers of both racial groups showed a rapid decline from the 1990 census. Meanwhile, Asians, Pacific Islanders, and Hispanics made up close to 50 percent of all San Francisco residents. Including those in San Francisco, the U.S. Census Bureau counted close to 1 million potential Filipino food consumers in California. This is surely why there are so many Filipino fast-food restaurants in the Golden State. In 2008 these included nine Jollibee, fifteen Goldilocks, and seventeen Red Ribbon restaurants—all franchises of Philippine-based restaurants.

Filipinos in Northern California have come a long way from the days when they were referred to as "Luzon *indios*." Estimated at more than 320,000 by the 2000 U.S. census (table 1.1), the Filipino community in the San Francisco Bay Area is a major part of the larger diasporic migration to the United States. Because of this large-scale Filipinization, San Francisco (like Los Angeles, San Diego, New York, and Honolulu) has in some ways become a "provincial area" of the Philippines. The growing affluence of Filipino migrants led them to move from crowded Bay Area cities, such as Oakland (6,407), to more suburban areas such as San Jose (48,149), Daly City (32,720), Vallejo (24,215), Hayward (12,755), Union City (12,587), Fremont (11,782), South San Francisco (9,987), and Milpitas (9,381) (U.S. Bureau of the Census 2000). These suburban areas experienced Filipino population growths of between 20 and 80 percent between the 1990 and 2000 census and have become figurative *barangays*.

The destruction of the I-Hotel in the late 1970s was the last nail in the coffin of the old Manilatown bachelor community. The neighborhood known as South of Market (SoMa), catering mostly to Filipino families, has since emerged as a new *barangay*. At SoMa, Filipino newcomers and old-timers live side by side in rent-controlled Victorian and Edwardian-style apartments on narrow Natoma, Minna, Clementina, and Kipling streets. Besides these apartments, there are high-rise buildings such as the Bayanihan House (former Delta Hotel), Ed De La Cruz Building, 957 Mission, and the Mint Mall. Aside from being a residential building, the Mint Mall is also home to businesses and organizations serving the local Filipino American community. Surrounded on each side by streets named after Filipino heroes (Mabini, Bonifacio, Tandang Sora, Rizal, and Lapu Lapu) is the San Lorenzo Ruiz Senior Housing Complex. And unlike the old Manilatown, the new Filipino *barangay* in SoMa has its share of dispersed Filipino eateries, grocery stores, barbershops, video rental stores, and tailors. Even the local elementary school, Bessie Carmichael Elementary School, is more than 50 percent Filipino and has had Filipino principals (see Canlas 2002; Reyes 2004).

Because of its Filipino population base, SoMa has become home to a number of community organizations, businesses, and institutions that cater to that population. These include the Filipino Education Center, the only bilingual, bicultural Filipino program in Northern California; Bindlestiff Studio, the epicenter of Filipino performing arts in the San Francisco Bay Area; the Veterans Equity Center, Northern California's largest social service agency for Filipino World War II Veterans; Arkipelago Bookstore, the only Filipino American bookstore in California; West Bay Pilipino Multi-Services Center, the oldest Filipino social service agency in Northern California; and Saint Patrick's Catholic Church. As in the Philippines, this Irish-turned-Filipino church occupies the center of the *barangay*, with a "plaza" extending from the front of the church to the majestic waterfall of Yerba Buena Gardens across the street.

The post-1965 mass migration of Filipino professionals brought to the United States a group of persons who were able to quickly earn and save money. Many started out renting in the South of Market area and other districts of San Francisco, but once they had enough savings, they moved to the outlying suburbs, buying homes and setting up businesses in nearby Daly City. In a single decade, Daly City gained 7,628 Filipino residents. This rapidly changed the suburb's ethnic makeup. At 43 percent of the total population, Filipinos in Daly City now comprise the largest concentration of Filipinos outside of the Philippines. The effects of this increased migration are visible in the suburb's educational system. For example, in the 1997–1998 school year, 29 percent of the students in the Jefferson Union High School District of Daly City were ethnically Filipino. With this shift, Daly City's Serramonte Mall became the center of yet another Filipino *barangay* in the San Francisco Bay Area.

How Did I Select the Churches and Informants in This Study?

It is a well-known fact that following Los Angeles and New York, San Francisco is one of the country's most ethnically diverse cities, serving as one of several "gateway" cities for new migrants to the United States. Hence, I did not have to look far from where I lived, worked, and volunteered. A first-generation Filipino American Catholic rooted in San Francisco, I could attest to the important role of religion for new migrants. I know that the hundreds of spires and domes, mosques, temples, and storefront churches that meld into the milieu of the San Francisco Bay Area are important repositories of migrant stories. But my formal research for *Filipino American Faith in Action* only began with the formation of The Religion and Immigration Project (TRIP) and consequent financial support provided by the Pew Charitable Trusts, the Jesuit Foundation, the University of San Francisco, and Golden Gate University. The larger TRIP project encompassed Chinese, Filipino, Vietnamese, Mexican, and Salvadoran migrant communities to assess how religious groups and communities encourage the participation of recent migrants in the political, civic, and associational life of San Francisco and the United States, while maintaining their involvement with political and social systems in their societies of origin. TRIP analyzed the role of religion, religiosity, and religious communities as part of a transnational migration paradigm and a multidimensional approach to understanding political and cultural identities.

As co-investigator, I led the Filipino TRIP team with research assistance from Andrea Maison, Dennis Marzan, and Claudine del Rosario, all Filipino Americans who were also keen bilingual and bicultural observers. Andrea has mixed-race parentage; Dennis and I were born in the Philippines; Claudine was born and raised in the United States. Our disciplinary perspectives also differed but complemented each other: Andrea is an art history scholar, Dennis majored in history and political geography, Claudine is trained in psychology and Asian American studies, and I am a political scientist. Because of their assistance, at times the writing perspective in the book switches from "I" or "my" to "the Filipino team," "our," or "we" to recognize our collective work. Besides our migrant backgrounds, another trait we all shared was our dedication to faith, knowledge, and community service.

Like the other Asian and Latino teams, we embarked on our fieldwork guided by the following broad research questions: (1) How do migrant religious groups encourage and support or reject participation in the political, civic, and associational life of San Francisco and of the larger U.S. political and civic scene? (2) In what ways do religious congregations foster the transnational character of new immigration? (3) What social services do religious congregations provide for new migrants? (4) Do religious congregations actively attempt to preserve the culture of new migrants? (5) What is the relationship between migrant family relations, religion, and incorporation?

The Filipino TRIP team undertook a long-term ethnographic study of Filipino Catholic, Protestant, and Independent churches and their roles in incorporating new Filipino migrants to American life. We also examined how the churches help new migrants deal with acculturative stress. The Filipino TRIP Team began by attending services, activities, and meetings at the following ten religious sites with Filipino migrant populations:

1. Saint Patrick's Catholic Church (San Francisco)
2. Saint Augustine's Catholic Church (South San Francisco)
3. Iglesia ni Cristo (Daly City)
4. Daly City United Methodist Church
5. Jehovah's Witnesses (San Francisco)
6. Faith Bible Church of San Francisco
7. San Francisco Filipino American Seventh-Day Adventist Church (Pacifica)
8. Saint Francis and Grace United Methodist Church (San Francisco)
9. Saint James Presbyterian Church (San Francisco)
10. Saint Boniface Catholic Church (San Francisco)

We also met with pastors from the Philippine Independent Church (Aglipayan), Corpus Christi Church, All Souls Church, and Saint Ignatius Church. We did archival research in the basement of Saint Patrick's Catholic Seminary in Menlo Park and talked with Noemi Castillo, then director of ethnic ministries at the Catholic Archdiocese of San Francisco. The overall reception to the team by the church leaders and members in the prospective sites was warm and friendly. We conducted preliminary interviews on church histories and collected some informational materials. We were granted permission to attend worship services and other group activities. Because of time and resource constraints, the Filipino team decided to limit its in-depth ethnographic study to three churches—Saint Patrick's Catholic Church in San Francisco, the Iglesia ni Cristo in Daly City, and Saint Augustine's Catholic Church in South San Francisco. These were the three religious sites with the largest Filipino congregations in the area.

The first site, Saint Patrick's Catholic Church, is located in the South of Market area of San Francisco, which has the highest density of Filipino migrant residents in the city. This Filipino community includes people of all ages—from toddlers to seniors, and both single adults and large, extended families. Saint Patrick's refers people to the many Filipino-oriented social and welfare service agencies close to its doors. These agencies provide basic social services, as well as extras, including after-school care, Tagalog classes, computer training, and tutoring services. There are also numerous other Filipino businesses nearby. Saint Patrick's follows conventional Roman Catholic doctrines and theology as defined by the catechism of the Roman Catholic Church, which in itself is the accumulation of doctrine derived from both scriptural teaching and ecclesiastical tradition. Though the parish's congregation is predominantly Filipino, Filipino Catholicism is known for its strict adherence to orthodox Roman Catholic theology and teaching. Nevertheless, many adaptations of indigenous folk practices have become part of the Filipino practice of Roman Catholicism; these adaptations are discussed throughout this book.

The second site is the Iglesia ni Cristo–Daly City locale, located in the former Jefferson public high school complex. This complex straddles a residential and commercial neighborhood in Daly City, a suburb just to the south of San Francisco. The Iglesia ni Cristo (INC) is neither Catholic nor Protestant but an independent Christian church that originated in the Philippines. This independence is manifest in its Bible-based lessons and in the original hymns sung during worship services and missionary events. In claiming administrative and theological independence, the INC seeks to distance itself from what it sees as corruption, hypocrisy, and ineffectuality in both the Catholic and Protestant churches in the Philippines. Nevertheless, the INC does not claim to be born out of these perceived shortcomings. Instead, the church believes that its founder, Felix Manalo, was called upon by God to establish the INC. It is for this reason that the Iglesia ni Cristo sees itself as an independent church.

The third site, Saint Augustine's Catholic Church, is located in the city of South San Francisco. Like Daly City, South San Francisco is a suburb of the city and county of San Francisco with a large population of first- and second-generation Filipinos. Based on congregational size, Saint Augustine's is the largest Roman Catholic parish in the vast Catholic Archdiocese of San Francisco, which is composed of San Francisco, San Mateo, and Marin counties. The membership, which is more than 90 percent Filipino, is responsible for the lively atmosphere every weekend at Saint Augustine's, which is reminiscent of a *barrio fiesta* (village festival). Parishioners come from South San Francisco and nearby Daly City, Colma, Burlingame, and Pacifica. The church has five masses on Sundays and three services on Saturdays to accommodate the more than 4,000 families that are registered parishioners, which means that the church is bustling with activity all weekend. After each of the masses, many parishioners remain at the church for an hour or two, socializing with friends. This illustrates the degree to which Saint Augustine's functions as a social as well as a religious center for its Filipino members.

The Filipino TRIP team compiled three years' worth of weekly field notes from these three sites. We also organized the first-ever interdenominational conference of San Francisco Filipino migrant religious leaders at the Catholic University of San Francisco and invited pastors and congregants from Filipino migrant churches throughout the Bay Area. It is notable that in spite of the religious theme and the Jesuit Catholic school setting, the attendees willingly looked past the differences in their belief systems and joined us in examining the valuable contributions of emerging Filipino migrant congregations to the ideas, beliefs, morals, and institutions that mold and shape contemporary San Francisco culture and society. We also presented at local and international conferences, at sites as close as Berkeley and as far away as Europe.

The Filipino TRIP team also conducted extensive fieldwork in the Philippines, in the cities and provinces of Manila, Quezon City, Laguna,

Cavite, Cebu, Tagaytay, and Bohol. In the Philippines and the United States, we wrote extensive field notes, took hundreds of photographs, and shot hundreds of hours of video on the Filipino religious and spiritual terrains. We observed and participated in rites and rituals at convents, seminaries, schools, monasteries, temples, grottos, and, of course, churches. We also participated in Bible studies, prayers, meditations, outreach events, picnics, masses, baptisms, weddings, confirmations, house blessings, and funerals. For a time, we practically lived our lives around this research, eating *almusal* (breakfasts), *tanghalian* (lunches), *hapunan* (dinners), and *merienda* (snacks) with our research subjects. The teams that conducted the community survey described in chapter 3 were composed of enthusiastic Golden Gate University and San Francisco State University Filipino American graduate students, as well as University of San Francisco Philippine studies and politics students. They administered the remittance surveys in churches and other sites all over the San Francisco Bay Area.

The Filipino TRIP Team shared our research findings with the ethnic community that we served. We have published articles in *Philippine News, Manila Bulletin USA, Filipinas Magazine*, and *Call of Nature*, all publications with predominantly Filipino American readerships. Our research was also referenced in *Pasugo*, the Iglesia ni Cristo's official global publication. *Filipino American Faith in Action* brings together our collective experiences and research, providing an overview of the ways in which Filipino Americans use their religious spaces and activities to enact their civic engagement.

2

Resurrecting Christian Faith

The Friday evening in May 2001 was glorious—crystal clear skies with a smooth, gentle breeze. In a small, unassuming neighborhood elementary school just outside of cosmopolitan San Francisco, California, Catholic priests, nuns, and lay workers were gathering for what appeared at first to be a quiet meditation or evening prayers. But as they slowly trickled into the brightly lit cafeteria, the noise sounded more and more like a *handaan* (food feast) than a meditative encounter among respected spiritual leaders. Listening to them laugh and banter in a mix of English, Tagalog, Ilocano, Bicolano, Cebuano, Kapampangan, Waray, Boholano, and other Philippine dialects, one could tell they were not your ordinary American clergy. All sixty-three participants were migrants from various parts of the Philippines, and that night was an unprecedented assembly. They all knew that their mission in the United States was not just to quench the spiritual thirst of the hundreds of thousands of Filipino Catholics who had resettled here but also to minister to the larger, multicultural Catholic communities in Marin, San Francisco, and San Mateo counties. Between alternating mouthfuls of crunchy *lechon de leche* (roasted suckling pig), tasty *adobong manok* (chicken soy stew), and luscious *lumpiang sariwa* (fresh vegetable egg rolls), men and women of the cloth exchanged animated stories of ministering not only to an "overseas Filipino flock" but also, according to one young priest from a parish in Marin—"mga puti at iba pa" (white persons and others). They harped on the multitude of "American and Filipino issues" for which their Philippine seminary or convent education never prepared them. From a corner of the room, an elder pastor whom they jokingly nicknamed "Bishop" quipped loudly that one approach he definitely "imported from home" was "how to raise consciousness and rally in the streets, when needed, on social problems—whether American or Filipino." Silence filled the room. Then a young nun piped up in Taglish (mixed Tagalog and English) from the back: "Bishop, gamitin na ang People Power[1] sa America!" (Bishop, use that

People Power in America!). There was a brief pause, and then everyone laughed—apparently, in agreement.

As at this gathering, Filipino migrant religious leaders and the spiritual sites they manage are primary sources of transnational *kasamahan* (bonding Filipinization) at many towns and cities in the San Francisco Bay Area. This continuous transmigratory connection is not unusual between former mother country and colony, between new homeland and old hometown. After all, more than a century of transnational relations (from 1898 to the present) between the Philippines and the United States have seriously affected both countries economically, militarily, environmentally, and politically. Moreover, cross-cultural exchanges and transnational influences between the two countries have also forged the creation of new, adaptive social and cultural practices.

Unlike other transnational studies that have concentrated heavily on the broad sociocultural outcomes that emerged from immigration (Pido 1985; Posadas 1999; San Juan 1998), this chapter revisits the historical roots of the intersection of American and Filipino spiritualities. Moreover, it moves away from the unidirectional emphasis on America's contributions to religious life in the Philippines, especially the Protestant churches (see, among others, Apilado 1999; Kwantes 1998; Maggay 1989; Miller 1982) by focusing on Filipino transnational influences upon a broad range of church denominations in the San Francisco Bay Area.

As I mentioned in chapter 1, the turn of the millennium brought a plethora of scholarly works exploring the intersecting issues associated with Filipino transnational migration and globalization (see, among others, Choy 2003; Espiritu 2003; Ignacio 2005; Manalansan 2003; McKay 2006; Parreñas 2001, 2005). But, ironically, none have ventured into the Filipino religious contexts and their transpacific societal implications, even though churches are the spaces where Filipinos' ethnicity is most visible overseas. The Filipinization of faith locations as a transnational cultural phenomenon gained greater relevance as waves of Filipino migrants started flowing into the major gateway cities of the United States beginning in the early 1900s. Manalansan (2003) alluded to this in discussing the Filipino queer community and its important role in the annual Santacruzan parade and celebration hosted by the Filipino American community in New York City. And yet, while a number of recent studies on Asian Americans and their religious spaces and encounters have emerged from scholars of transnationalism (e.g., Carnes and Yang

2004; Jeung 2004; Min and Kim 2002; Yang 2000), the Filipino American migrants' transnational experience vis-à-vis their faith and churches has remained understudied.

Although known largely for their economic contributions to their old and new homelands, as alluded to in chapter 1, modern-day Filipino sojourners also bring with them their religiosity, which is embedded in their Hispanic, Anglo-Saxon, and indigenous religious belief systems and spiritual practices. This is, of course, a result of Spanish and American colonization, American neocolonization, and globalization. Through the church, a societal institution with which they are comfortable, new Filipino migrants are able to deal effectively with acculturative stress, assimilate politically, and contribute social energy to the communities with which they come into contact. But at the same time, their Filipinized American churches have also become safe spaces for negotiating and challenging identity, ethnicity, and nationalism (see Cordova 1983; San Buenaventura 1999). Filipinized locations are where Filipino migrants have been allowed, and even encouraged by church leaders (some who are Filipino and some who are not but are willing to accommodate new styles to replenish membership numbers), to express Filipino-style Catholic, Charismatic, Evangelical, Masonic, Independent, and even indigenous (*babaylan*) spiritual practices. Therefore, Filipino migrants are helping to shape a new, transnational American faith not only by taking over empty churches, but also by influencing American religious practices. As generations of Filipino parents, grandparents, children, siblings, grandchildren, and other relatives go back and forth, religious practices, symbols, and songs also move back and forth from their hometown churches in the Philippines to their San Francisco churches.

This circular transnational movement between the Philippines and San Francisco of prayers, pastors, icons, practices, and people has cultivated bonding Filipinization through the *kasamahan* spirit and the organizations that are flourishing on both sides of the Pacific Ocean. In this chapter, I elaborate on the origins of these transnational influences, exchanges of practices, and congregational formations by piecing together archival data and key informant interviews on (1) the Americanization of many Christian practices in Manila with the arrival of American Protestant and Catholic missions, which also inspired the founding of Filipino independent churches, and (2) the subsequent Filipinization later on of some of San Francisco's Catholic, Protestant, and Independent congregations and religious spaces.

The Americanization of Christianity in Manila

The emergence of the United States as the new global powerhouse at the end of the nineteenth century brought forward international economics and security as key starting points for negotiating power relations between and among nation-states. Many scholars have noted that the tenor of American political rhetoric regarding the Philippines at this time was typically focused on the economic and military benefits of controlling the archipelago and its inhabitants (Banlaoi 2002; Baviera and Yu-Jose 1998; Delmendo 1998; Fast and Richardson 1982; Schirmer and Shalom 1987; Williams 1926).

For example, in a stirring speech to U.S. Congress in 1900, Senator Albert Beveridge outlined the economic imperative for the United States in colonizing the Philippines, in the following statement:

> The Philippines are ours forever . . . and just beyond the Philippines are China's illimitable markets. . . . The Pacific is our Ocean. Where shall we turn for consumers of our surplus? Geography answers the question. China is our natural customer. The Philippines will give us a base at the door of all the East. No land in America surpasses in fertility the plains and valleys of Luzon: rice, coffee, sugar and coconuts, hemps and tobacco. The wood of the Philippines can supply the furniture of the world for a century to come. (Lyon and Wilson 1987, 62)[2]

Meanwhile, speaking from a military standpoint, General Arthur MacArthur (father of Douglas) highlighted the importance of the Philippines to America's security:

> The Philippines are the finest group of islands in the world. Its strategic location is unexcelled by that of any other position in the globe. The China Sea, which separates it by something like 750 miles from the continent, is nothing more nor less than a safety moat. It lies on the flank of what might be called a position of several thousand miles of coastline: it is in the center of that position. It is therefore relatively better placed than Japan, which is on a flank, and therefore remote from the other extremity; likewise India, on another flank. It affords a means of protecting American interests, which with the very least output of physical power has the effect of a commanding position in itself to retard hostile action. (quoted in Bello 1983, 53)

Scholarly critical analyses of the relations between the United States and the Philippines have duly emphasized these key areas, especially the dysfunctional economic and political effects of the colonial and neo-colonial linkages between the two countries (Brands 1992; Delmendo 1998; Golay 1998; Pomeroy 1970; Shalom 1981). As the relationship deepened, many researchers from both sides of the Pacific also began to discuss the converging sociocultural experiences between the two countries (see Shaw and Francia 2003). However, very few scholars actually mention that the transnational links that developed between colonizer and former colony also had an interesting religious dimension—one that would actually usher in a resurrection or revitalization of the Christian faith in Catholic Philippines with the arrival of evangelical Christians.

Just like the United States' economic and security imperatives for colonizing the Philippines, which were trumpeted by leaders in Washington, its religious calling was announced from the highest political pulpit in the land. In 1898, President William McKinley, a devout Methodist, proclaimed that there was a burning need for the "benevolent assimilation" of the Philippine Islands. McKinley elaborated on this political revelation with the following remarks to a delegation of Methodist church leaders who called on him at the White House:

> I walked the floor of the White House night after night until midnight, and I am not ashamed to tell you, gentlemen, that I went down on my knees and prayed to Almighty God for light and guidance more than one night. And one late night it came to me this way—I don't know how it was, but it came . . . *that there was nothing left for us to do but to take them all, and to educate the Filipinos, and uplift and civilize and Christianize them, and by God's grace do the very best we could by them, as our fellow men for whom Christ also died.* (quoted in Schirmer and Shalom 1983, 22; emphasis mine)

To many of his astonished guests, it seemed that the president had forgotten that the country to which he was referring was already very Christian after more than 300 years of evangelization by Spanish Catholic religious orders. Nonetheless, as his tirade continued, it became apparent that what McKinley really meant was that his fellow Methodists should spread the word of an American brand of Christianity to what he perceived as wayward Filipino Christians. His visitors left the White House with McKinley's civilize and Christianize mantra still ringing in their ears—the church must go where America chooses to go!

Arrival of American Protestant Churches

Like its European colonial predecessors, the United States used the church to effectively and efficiently make the Filipinos embrace the behavior patterns that were part of the colonizers' culture. Although at first hesitant to support what seemed to be the beginning of American imperialism, church leaders in the United States would eventually stand behind their president's appeal. In the years to follow, many American Christian missionaries boarded the same ships that carried business-men, civil servants, teachers, and military officers who were going to the Philippines for commercial, governmental, educational, and security rea-sons. Initially concentrating their religious activities in the capital city of Manila, American Methodists, Congregationalists, Presbyterians, Luther-ans, Baptists, Adventists, Anglicans, Episcopalians, Mormons, Witnesses, and other Christian missions came to convince Filipinos to embrace American Protestant teachings. They also ministered to the thousands of American Protestants who had gone with them to the Philippines to work in America's "Asian colony."

The missionaries from the United States were very effective, since unlike their Spanish religious counterparts, who discouraged the masses from learning Spanish and banned the reading of the Bible, American Protestant Christian missionaries immediately began teaching English and set up many mission schools, especially for the poor. They also encouraged the translation of the Bible into various Philippine languages and dialects. American Protestants believed that there was a need to reform the Spanish-style practice of Christianity, which was not strongly Bible-based and was tainted with folk beliefs, idolatry, as well as the ven-eration of saints and the Virgin Mary.[3]

Shortly after America's annexation of the Philippines in 1898, the first missionaries arrived as soldiers deployed to fight in the Spanish-Amer-ican War. Records indicate that Methodist chaplain George C. Stull of the First Montana Volunteers held the first Protestant service in the Phil-ippines in August 1898. By that time, two American YMCA workers, Charles A. Glunz and Frank A. Jackson, were evidently already actively ministering to U.S. soldiers in downtown Manila. Later that year, two artillery batteries arrived from Utah with Mormon missionaries Wil-liam Call and George Seaman.[4] On two Sundays in March 1899, Bishop James M. Thoburn of the Methodist Episcopal Church led a worship service at a rented theater in Manila. In April 1899, the Reverend James

Burton Rodgers established the Philippine Presbyterian Mission, the first permanent American Protestant mission in the country. Reverend Burton stayed for forty years to help guide the work of the Presbyterians. Following the lead of the Presbyterians, the American Bible Society arrived that same year. Men and women working for the American Bible Society put themselves to the task of translating and printing thousands of Bibles into local dialects.

America's insistence on its manifest destiny of colonizing the country led to the Philippine-American War, a struggle that began in 1899 and supposedly ended in 1902 with the capture of Philippine general Emilio Aguinaldo. During the war, many Philippine towns were burned to the ground. Persons who collaborated with Filipino revolutionaries were tortured. Not even churches were spared the destructive wrath of the American army. More than half a million Filipinos died in the conflict. These acts of war were performed by American troops both in the name of God and as part of the white man's burden (see Agoncillo 1990; Constantino 1989). While this destruction was occurring in areas outside of Manila, American missionaries proceeded with their religious work in the capital city as if nothing unusual were happening.

In January 1900, the Methodist Church formally established its Philippine presence when the Reverend Thomas H. Martin of Halina, Montana, started missionary work in Manila. By March of the same year, Nicolas Zamora, the first Filipino Methodist deacon, was ordained by the authority of the South Kansas Conference. Concentrated largely in Manila and its environs, the Methodists held regular meetings at Rosario, Pandacan, San Sebastian, and Trozo. Following the ordination of Reverend Zamora, the first Methodist Church was established in Pandacan, Manila. On May 9, a second American Methodist missionary arrived.

The beginning of the twentieth century also brought the American Northern Baptist Church to the Philippines. Encouraged by positive reports from the foreign missions regarding the first batch of American Protestant Churches, an annual influx of other Christian congregations arrived to claim a share of the evangelical bounty in the new colony. These included the United Brethren, the Disciples of Christ, and the Protestant Episcopals in 1901, and the Congregationalists in 1902. Harassment from local Catholic clergy and their staunch supporters evidently did not deter these missionary pioneers from their work.

The Seventh-Day Adventist Church sent its first mission to the Philippines in 1905, after the Philippine-American War.[5] The following

year, Adventists J. L. McElhany and his wife arrived and began working among the American soldiers, businessmen, and teachers living in
Manila. The work of the Jehovah's Witnesses also began in the Philippines, when American Charles T. Russell, president of the Watchtower
Bible and Tract Society in New York, gave a lecture entitled "Where Are
the Dead?" at the Manila Grand Opera House on January 12, 1912.
Russell's talk was attended by close to 1,000 persons, including General
J. Franklin Bell, the commander in chief of the 20,000 American troops
stationed in the Philippines at that time. To spread the gospel, organized
missionary work followed in the years to come with Bible literature
provided by the headquarters of the Seventh-Day Adventist Church in
Brooklyn, New York. More than two decades after Russell's pioneering visit, a Philippine branch of the church was formally established in
Manila.

In October 1914, more than thirty years before the founding of the
ecumenical World Council of Churches, Philippine-based Presbyterians,
Methodists, and Disciples of Christ decided to form the Union Church
of Manila. The union of these Protestant churches was formally established at a liturgical service officiated by Bishop Charles Henry Brent of
the Episcopal Church, Reverend George W. Wright of the Presbyterian
Church, and Reverend Edwin F. Lee of the Methodist Church. The Union
Church of Manila congregation eventually grew to comprise twenty-two
denominations, including Baptist, Congregationalist, Disciples of Christ,
Lutheran, Episcopalian, Federated churches, United Brethren, Church
of God, Latter-day Saints, Greek Orthodox, Hebrew, Dutch Reformed,
Evangelical, Mennonite, Nazarene, and Roman Catholic. Union Church
has historically been the premier place of worship for expatriate Americans and Europeans based in Manila. At this church, they were able to
interact with persons from their U.S. hometowns, organize picnics and
socials, and maintain a familiar, predominantly Western atmosphere
while based in the Philippines. Members also used Union Church to
channel contributions to Philippine charities as well as to alleviate poverty both in their home countries and elsewhere in the world.

The early Filipino converts from Catholicism and other Christian
faiths were very helpful in spreading the gospel. But many lay expatriate
American citizens—nonmissionaries, who were simply serving in official
military and civilian functions such as setting up businesses and teaching
in Manila and other parts of the Philippines—were also responsible for
promoting Protestant Bible and gospel teachings. Canadian and Euro-

pean Protestant missions also supplemented the work of the Americans. In the decades to come, Protestant missionaries would spread the word to all the regions of the country. They built not only churches but also seminaries, schools, hospitals, publishing houses, shelters, and social service agencies in all the major cities and towns, even reaching hinterland areas that the Spanish Catholic friars had not covered.

The Americanization of the Spanish Catholic Church Regime

Many scholarly works have been written about the systematic religious conversion of native Filipinos to Catholicism by Spanish religious orders, or friars. It is well known that the Order of Saint Augustine sent the first Catholic priests to the Philippines. They came with the conquistador Miguel Lopez de Legazpi's expedition of 1565. The Augustinians were followed by the Franciscans in 1577, the Jesuits in 1581, the Dominicans in 1587, and then the Recollects in 1606. In the second half of the nineteenth century, the first batch of Spanish religious groups was joined by: the Sons of Saint Vincent de Paul in 1862, the Sisters of Charity in 1862, the Capuchins in 1886, and the Benedictines in 1895. For more than three centuries, these religious orders of women and men facilitated the conversion of more than 85 percent of the population (or 6.5 million out of an estimated 8 million Filipinos) to Catholicism.

The new American governmental administrators had no choice but to get involved early on in the religious situation in the Philippines, since the Philippine Revolution of 1896 spurred popular outrage not only against the Spain's provincial government in the islands but also against the entrenched friar establishment. At the outbreak of hostilities, thousands of friars were able to flee to the safe confines of Manila. But some who were not lucky enough to reach the capital city were taken prisoner, while others were beaten or killed. Not only fearing for their lives but also concerned about the sequestration of their vast properties, the friar leadership ensured that the terms of surrender between Admiral George Dewey and the Spanish authorities—as well as the Treaty of Paris, which formally ceded the Philippines to the United States—included provisions that guaranteed American army protection for their churches and "ecclesiastical lands." The Vatican had no objection to this arrangement. The honeymoon between the United States and the Philippines ended swiftly when American military Governor-General Elwell Otis, created controversy when he allowed Archbishop Nozaleda of

Spain, a friar who was widely disliked by the Filipino public, to replace the Filipino pastor at Paco Church in Manila. Made without their involvement, these policies and actions angered many Filipinos, especially the clergy, who began to suspect that their battle to gain control and influence over their own church and state had not ended with the ousting of their Spanish conquistadors. Instead, it was becoming clear that American religious authorities and the American government were now their new enemies.

The changeover to American rule in 1898 and Washington's formal ending of Philippine-American hostilities in 1902 brought many American and other non-Spanish, European Catholic orders and congregations to the Philippines. These included the Redemptorists (1906), the Benedictine Sisters (1906), the Congregations of San Jose (1906), the Fathers of the Divine Word (1907), and the Missionaries of the Immaculate Heart (1907). The Franciscans, Jesuits, and Dominicans also made adjustments to their Philippine organizations by sending more American priests. Because of local Filipino resentment against the historic abuses and excesses of the Spanish friars, the American religious orders tried to create a new image of the Roman Catholic clergy. The Americans also tried very hard to show the local populace that even though they were Catholic, they were different from the Spanish friars, whom the Filipinos disliked universally. They also opened public schools to everyone as a gesture of goodwill and to appease Filipinos' apprehensions. Naturally, the person who was put in charge of U.S. educational initiatives was a Catholic priest, Reverend Father William D. McKinnon, the chaplain of the First California Volunteers. He was directed by Governor-General Otis to organize and construct primary and secondary institutions in Manila. Father McKinnon's rapport with the Philippine Catholic laity, the predominantly Catholic population, and his knowledge of Spanish contributed heavily to his initial successes at setting up an American educational system in the capital city.

During this period, some changes were also implemented within the Catholic Church hierarchy in the Philippines. Unlike the Spanish military personnel and government officials, Spanish priests were not expelled. Nevertheless, given the strong Filipino resentment against them, many decided to go back to Spain or seek reassignment. Immediately after the American takeover, high-ranking positions held by the Spanish clergy were assumed by American priests, many of whom were of Irish descent. One such priest was Missouri native the Reverend Father Jeremiah

James Hart, who became the first American archbishop of Manila in 1903. Many parishes with Spanish pastors were redistributed to diocesan priests from Ireland, Germany, Belgium, and France. Religious societies of monks, brothers, and sisters from America and Europe also established missions, monasteries, convents, and schools all over the country. Just five years after the American takeover, the number of Spanish friars in the Philippines had been reduced from a peak of more than 1,100 in 1896 to a mere 246. In 1904, the last Spanish bishop left the Philippines, and almost all the high positions in the Catholic Church were occupied by American bishops, to the disdain of Filipino clergy. To them, history seemed to be repeating itself.

These new Christian leaders tried to create an American-style church regime beginning with the firm promotion of the separation of church and state and the freedom to believe in any religion. These attempts to promote American liberal democracy through religion in the Philippines were actively supported by both American Catholic and Protestant church leaders. Many Filipinos also warmly received this change, which compared favorably to the centuries of intrusion and intimidation by the Spanish Catholic church in all aspects of life, from governmental to personal.

The American Roman Catholic orders agreed with some of the observations of American Protestant Christians that there was a need to reform the Spanish-style practice of Christianity. Apparently, both were after the creation of a more Anglo-Saxon-Teutonic culture in the practice of religion. Again, however, it was through religion that America began an effective campaign to win the hearts and minds of the Filipino people. Language served as an important vehicle for the U.S. incursion into Philippine culture and society. English was made the language of the church, education, government, military, and business.

The Establishment of Filipino Independent Congregations

The Spaniards used the Catholic Church to secure positions of power in Philippine society, and the Americans utilized the Protestant Church to do the same. Many Filipino nationalists noticed this and concluded that the American modus operandi was likely to be no different from Spain's. For instance, just as in the running of government, very few Filipino religious leaders were granted positions of influence in Protestant and Catholic church hierarchies during the early American period. Besides, Americans controlled the military, and American firms held monopolies in certain industries and received subsidies and preferential treatment. Tired of this same disadvantageous socioeconomic situation, many Filipino leaders decided to lobby and fight for their political, social, and economic rights, while Filipino spiritual leaders were emboldened to organize their own indigenous and independent Christian churches.

The most significant breakaway group from the Philippine Catholic Church was the Philippine Independent Church (known as the PIC, Iglesia Filipina Independiente [IFI] or Aglipayan Church). Although founded largely as a response to the total dominance of Spanish friars in the Catholic Church hierarchy, the PIC did not anticipate that any serious organizational changes would accompany the arrival of American Catholic clergy. Hence, in August 1902 (just one month after U.S. president Theodore Roosevelt declared the end of the Philippine-American War), in a meeting of the General Council of the Union Obrera Democratica (UOD), its head, Isabelo de los Reyes Sr., announced the establishment of the Philippine Independent Church with Reverend Gregorio Aglipay as *obispo maximo* (supreme bishop). De los Reyes and Aglipay convinced many Filipino priests to join their cause-oriented religious sect and sequestered Roman Catholic churches "in the name of Filipinos." A year after the PIC's founding, it was believed to have amassed 1.5 million members, which was roughly 25 percent of the population of the Philippines at the time. Although rejected by the Vatican, the PIC did not see fit to align with the Protestant churches despite numerous talks with Methodist, Presbyterian, and American Bible Society leaders and missionaries. The PIC's membership grew slowly but steadily to more than 3 million globally by 2000.[6]

An independent Filipino Christian church that emerged during the American occupation was the Iglesia ni Cristo (INC). This independent church was founded by Brother Felix Y. Manalo, who was born and baptized a Catholic. As a teenager, Manalo left the Catholic Church, reportedly drawn by the Bible teachings of various American Protestant Christian denominations that arrived in the Philippines. In order to learn more about their views of the gospel, Manalo joined the Methodist Episcopal Church and studied at the Presbyterian Ellinwood Bible Training School in Manila. He later ventured to the American-inspired Christian Mission and the Seventh-Day Adventist Church. However, according to Manalo, exposing himself to these Bible teachings only left him dissatisfied with what he perceived to be doctrinal contradictions

*Figure 2.1. (above)
Every day, thousands of
Filipinos light candles at
their favorite Philippine
churches praying for a
family member or seeking
divine intervention for an
opportunity to live and
work overseas.
Photo credit: Jay Gonzalez*

*Figure 2.2. (left) A migrant
praying to San Lorenzo
Ruiz, the first Filipino
saint at San Francisco's
historic Saint Patrick's
Catholic Church, now a
joint ethnic Filipino and
Irish American church.
Photo credit: Jay Gonzalez*

and inconsistencies within both Catholicism and its Protestant "alternatives." Manalo is seen by INC members as a messenger of God who established a new Church of Christ in response to divine command. According to church history, in 1913, after praying, fasting, meditating, and seeking the guidance of God, Manalo began the work of forming a new and independent church. He developed an integrated set of teachings and an administrative organization based on the various American Christian faiths he had studied (Reed 1990; Tuggy 1978). Today, the INC is the largest non-Catholic Christian church in the Philippines and wields tremendous political power, as I will discuss later.

Attempts by Filipino Protestant and Independent church leaders to challenge the administrative powers of their American counterparts contributed to the creation of the United Evangelical Church in 1929, the Philippine Methodist Church in 1933, and the Evangelical Church in 1943. These loose alliances of Filipino-led independent Protestant churches were precursors to an umbrella organization called the United Church of Christ of the Philippines established in 1948—four years after the United States granted the Philippines its independence.

Other notable Filipino indigenous Christian sects and Masonic organizations that blossomed during the American period were the Benevolent Missionaries Association led by Ruben Ecleo; the Confradia de San Jose headed by Apolinario de la Cruz; Felipe Salvador's Santa Iglesia Guardia de Honor de Maria; and the Rizalistas (which are organized into the following subgroups: Samahang Rizal, Iglesiang Pilipinas, Watawat ng Lahi, and Iglesia Sagrada Filipina ng Sinco Vulcanes).

Kasamahan *in San Francisco's Churches*

Unknown to President McKinley, a revitalization of Christianity was already under way in America, even before the Philippines became a U.S. colony in 1898. Unlike the American Catholics and Protestants, whose arrival in the Philippine Islands was driven by the imperative to civilize and Christianize others, the earliest Filipino Catholic and Protestant migrants reached the shores of what would become parts of the United States as forced sea laborers on Spanish galleons, as alluded to in the previous chapter. The Manila-Acapulco galleon trade brought precious commodities to Spanish settlements in what are now California, Mexico, and Louisiana. Because of the harsh treatment and low pay they received in the service of the Spanish crown, many Filipino seamen jumped ship and settled in the pueblos of Acapulco and bayous of Louisiana. Mostly Catholics, these men blended with Mexican and American Christian church congregations wherever they went. In the Louisiana marshes, they set up Filipino settlements on stilts and introduced shrimp-processing techniques. They also brought with them to these new lands their religious faith, devotions, and prayers. While many Americans were busy administering and missionizing their one and only prized colony in the Far East, the first three decades of the twentieth century saw successive waves of Filipinos leave the Philippines for the United States.

San Francisco was the gateway city for the majority of these Filipino migrants, who brought with them distinctive cultures that eventually blended with the diverse cultural mix that already characterized the Bay Area. Filipino food, dances, languages, and other cultural products were slowly integrated into the local scene. But perhaps the most significant and visible contributions that generations of Filipino migrants have made to San Francisco society are the active roles they play in the city's churches at all levels. This mass exodus of Filipinos from their motherland is an integral part of the movement of Christianity from poor developing countries to rich developed nations.

After all, before 1965, many San Francisco Catholic and Protestant churches had been experiencing serious declines in active memberships. Low attendance rates had led to low financial contributions. With mounting maintenance costs, many of these churches had to rent out space to other groups, including other interested religious congregations, in order to survive. Some were simply forced to close and sell their properties. A factor in this downward shift was the commercial growth at this time in the downtown neighborhoods, which reduced the number of residences in the areas around churches. Earthquakes and fires further contributed to closures and migration away from San Francisco and into suburban areas. Interestingly, many religious centers affected by these natural disasters and population shifts have since been "saved" by new migrant groups, including, not surprisingly, Filipino Christians. Nowhere is Filipino Christianization in the United States felt more than in California, which is home to more than a million Filipino migrants of Catholic, Protestant, and Independent church backgrounds.

The Filipinization of San Francisco's Catholic Institutions

Coming from the only predominantly Catholic country in Asia, most new Filipino migrants were and still are socialized in the Roman Catholic faith and its traditions. Hence, the growing number of Filipino migrants to the United States over the past century increased church attendance rates, especially among Catholic churches in the major gateway cities of San Francisco, Honolulu, Los Angeles, Seattle, New York, and Chicago. The biggest beneficiaries of this Filipino inflow were San Francisco Catholic churches in the area of town then known as "Happy Valley." These historic churches included Saint Patrick (founded in 1851), Saint Joseph (founded in 1861), and Saint Rose (founded in 1878). Another favorite among Manilatown and Chinatown Filipino residents was Old Saint Mary's Cathedral (founded in 1854).

During this early period, close to 90 percent of Filipino migrants were single males, between eighteen and thirty-four years old. Building a family was difficult, since few women had migrated from the Philippines. The 1930 census estimated that there were only 1,640 women of Filipino descent in the entire United States at that time—309 single, 1,258 married, 53 widowed, and 16 divorced. To further complicate matters, antimiscegenation laws prohibited Filipino men from marrying Caucasian women. Ironically, this was not the case for Caucasian men who wanted to marry Filipino women. In fact, one of the first recorded baptisms in San Francisco was held on November 8, 1914, when Isaac Braan, originally from Raleigh, North Carolina, and his Filipina wife, Gregoria Pena, brought their infant daughter, Erminda Celeste, to Saint Patrick's Church. The Braans would later bring their two other children, born in 1916 and 1917, to Saint Patrick's to receive the same religious sacrament. Church records also indicate that a few other children of Filipino migrants were baptized in the years that followed.

To combat the restlessness of the largely male Filipino migrant group and encourage them to channel their socioemotional energies toward morally appropriate activities, the leaders of the Diocese of Seattle and San Francisco sponsored the creation of Catholic Filipino Clubs, which were established in those two cities in 1922 (Burns 2001). Around 600 farmworkers from Seattle registered and availed of the services of their club. In San Francisco, Archbishop Edward J. Hanna and the Community Chest were active supporters of the popular local Catholic Filipino

Club, which became the hub of social activities for the estimated 5,000 Filipino residents of the city. Two other Filipino Catholic organizations—the Catholic Filipino Glee Club and the Catholic Filipino Tennis Club—were also established. Other Filipino groups made use of club space by advertising activities and recruiting new members.[7]

Several fraternal orders were also set up by Filipino migrant faithful during this period. In the mid-1920s, Pedro Loreto established the Caballeros de Dimas Alang, a Masonic-style religious brotherhood, in San Francisco. Four years later, another fraternity called the Legionarios del Trabajo was formed in Stockton and San Francisco. Other famous fraternal groupings were the Gran Oriente Filipino and the Knights of Rizal. Many Filipino Catholics joined these quasi-Masonic Filipino organizations, since they felt discriminated against in the Caucasian-dominated Catholic churches. Besides, some of the new migrants had brought with them to America their negative attitudes and corresponding revolutionary thoughts about the Catholic Church.

As explained earlier, the end of World War II and the passage of the Immigration Act of 1965 further increased immigration to the United States, and thus further filled Catholic churches in the vast Archdiocese of San Francisco (which encompasses the counties of San Francisco, San Mateo, and Marin). By the 1960 census, 12,327 Filipinos resided in the city of San Francisco alone. This figure more than tripled by the 1990 census. According to the 2000 census, more than 300,000 Filipinos lived in the three counties covered by the archdiocese. Using Philippine demographic breakdowns as its basis, the Catholic Church then extrapolated that 84 percent, or roughly 250,000, of them are Filipino Catholics. The archdiocese then estimated that one out of every four Catholics in their area of jurisdiction is of Filipino descent.[8]

One example of a church that has been heavily influenced by Filipinos is Saint Patrick's Catholic Church, once the national place of worship for Irish Americans. Its dynamic Filipino pastor, Monsignor Fred Bitanga, once proudly proclaimed that "Filipino parishioners practically saved the historic church from serious demise." Saint Patrick's is staffed by Filipino priests, nuns, deacons, and lay workers. Daily noon services are popular among Filipino workers in the surrounding downtown area, while Sunday services draw loyal parishioners not just from the city but from all over the Bay Area.

New Filipino migrants to San Francisco usually attend services at Saint Patrick's and then move on to other Catholic churches once they feel comfortable with American life and can afford homes outside the city. Some continue to go to Saint Patrick's even after moving out of the area, especially to attend the two o'clock Tagalog mass the first Sunday of each month. The noon daily mass is also a favorite among Filipino migrants who live outside the city but work in San Francisco.

Saint Patrick's architecture is typically Gothic Revival and features the tall, narrow windows and spires that characterize this European style. However, its interior has been slightly Filipinized with statues and images of saints and the Virgin Mary. Some of them are indigenous Filipino folk figures, such as the Santo Niño (or Christ Child) and San Lorenzo Ruiz (the first Filipino saint). Visiting statues of the Virgin Mary from the Philippines are also accorded a special place in the church. For instance, when a statue of Our Lady of the Most Holy Rosary from Manila visited Saint Patrick's, it was displayed in a spot that gave parishioners optimal access. As in the Philippines, Filipino parishioners lined up to touch, kiss, and wipe their handkerchiefs on the statue. Many non-Filipino parishioners and visitors have also learned to venerate in this Filipino way to conform to the culture of praise and worship that they encounter in Saint Patrick's. Moreover, they may be motivated by Filipino parishioners who testify that such practices have caused miracles—a common claim.

Many other Catholic churches have filled up with devoted Filipino parishioners, especially south of San Francisco and across the bay in the neighboring Diocese of Oakland. Saint Andrew's Church and the Our Lady of Perpetual Help Church in Daly City, and Saint Augustine Church in South San Francisco all have Filipino priests preaching to memberships that are more than 80 percent Filipino. Tagalog masses are held at Saint Patrick's Church and Saint Boniface Church in San Francisco, as well as at Holy Angels Church in nearby Colma. Filipino American choirs and devotions to the Santo Niño, San Lorenzo Ruiz, and Mother Mary are very common at these sites. Seven parishes celebrate the Simbang Gabi, while Flores de Mayo and the Easter Salubong are slowly being integrated into regular church activities.[9] Popular Filipino Catholic groups such as El Shaddai, Jesus Is Lord Movement, Bukas Loob sa Diyos (Open in Spirit to God), Couples for Christ, Singles for Christ, Banal na Pagaaral (Holy Study), and Divine Mercy have also gone forth and multiplied rapidly among Filipino brothers and sisters in the United States. The U.S. Catholic Bishops Conference in Washington, D.C., estimates that there are more than 500 Filipino priests, deacons, and religious men and women serving all over the United States.

Reverend Fathers Bantigue (Mission Dolores Basilica), Antonio Rey (Our Lady of Perpetual Help Church), Max Villanueva (Holy Angels Church), and Fred Bitanga (Saint Joseph and Saint Patrick's churches) are some of the first Filipino Catholic priests in the Archdiocese of San Francisco. Father Bantigue began pastoral work in San Francisco as early as the 1950s. Since then, fourteen Philippine-based religious congregations of men (including diocesan priests) have sent members to serve in San Francisco parishes and dioceses all over the United States. The demand for Filipino priests continues to increase as fewer Americans enter the priesthood and more Filipinos immigrate to the United States. American theological seminaries have even started recruiting students from the Philippines to replenish the diminishing ministerial pool. Filipinos already make up a significant part of the leadership of San Francisco Bay Area Catholic churches. In 2002, there were 39 priests, 12 full-time deacons, 5 sisters, and 30 lay workers of Filipino descent in the 52 parishes of San Francisco. Additionally, the powerful Council of Priests in the archdiocese was once chaired by the Reverend Father Eugene D. Tungol—a Filipino pastor.[10]

Notably, some of the earliest Filipino Catholic missionary congregations to work in San Francisco and other parts of the United States were religious organizations of Filipino women. In December 1955, the Benedictine Sisters of Ilocos Sur came and helped with the needs of Filipino agricultural workers and their families in the Salinas area. The sisters opened a religious class for preschoolers. They were also instrumental in creating the Legion of Mary and Our Lady of Antipolo Society, popular devotions to the Virgin Mary practiced in the Philippines. In 1959, the Manila-based Religious of the Virgin Mary started their overseas mission in the Sacramento area, followed by Honolulu in 1972 and then San Francisco in 1982. Today, they assist with the spiritual needs of parishioners in Saint Patrick's Church and Our Lady of Mercy Church. Starting with an overseas mission in Hawaii in 1964, the Dominican Sisters of the Most Holy Rosary from Molo, Iloilo Province, in the Philippines later moved to the mainland and established a San Francisco presence in 1982. The Dominican Sisters have made an impact by helping run Catholic schools and by assisting in devotions and services at Saint Charles Borromeo Church and Holy Angels Church. By the late 1990s, thirty-two Philippines-based congregations had religious sisters working in the United States.[11]

Aside from Catholic churches, Catholic clubs, and Catholic religious organizations of men and women, other major beneficiaries of the

Filipino inflow to San Francisco were the archdiocese's many Catholic schools. As early as September 1963, thirty-eight of the forty-five elementary schools in the city reported a total of 680 Filipino children in attendance. The schools with the largest numbers were Sacred Heart Elementary (78), Saint Paul (42), Star of the Sea (41), Saint Peter (38), and Saint Monica (28).[12] In the 1980s and 1990s, San Francisco's religious elementary and high schools experienced surges in Filipino enrollment as the children of migrants from the 1960s and 1970s reached school age. New arrivals and their families also contributed to the increase. By 2000, the student body of Corpus Christi Elementary School was more than 75 percent Filipino. Several other elementary schools have student populations that are close to 50 percent Filipino; these include the Church of the Epiphany, Church of the Visitacion, Saint Elizabeth, Saint Emydius, Saint Finn Barr, Saint John the Evangelist, Saint Kevin, Holy Angels, and Our Lady of Perpetual Help.

Some of the Catholic high schools in the San Francisco Bay Area currently have student populations that are between 20 and 25 percent Filipino, including Saint Ignatius College Prep, Archbishop Riordan, Mercy High, Bishop O'Dowd, and Sacred Heart Cathedral Prep. Catholic colleges and universities, including the University of San Francisco and Santa Clara University, have also experienced rapid growth in Filipino student enrollment. Saint Patrick's Seminary and University in Menlo Park also reported a significant number of students who are of Filipino descent training for the priesthood and enrolled in graduate theological and religious programs.[13]

Boosting Christian Faith through Filipino Evangelism

McKinley's "benevolent assimilation" policy brought many American Protestant groups to the Philippines to build churches and "save" the Filipinos. Little did these Americans know that while they were supposedly saving Filipino souls, Filipinos were bringing Protestantism back to America, precipitating benevolent Filipinization within the United States. The Filipino Protestant inflow is also a form of Filipinization because it is missionizing American Protestant teachings through Filipino culture—food, family values, and esprit de corps (further illustrated in chapters 4 and 5). Although smaller in number and distribution than their Filipino Catholic counterparts, the Filipino Protestant population in the United States is still worth examining. Filipino

Protestant agricultural workers who came to the United States began attending services and Bible studies with the various American Christian Protestant churches in Hawaii and California. As their numbers grew, they also began to establish their own Christian Protestant and Independent church congregations. Just as in the Philippines, many Filipino Catholics in the United States crossed over and joined Protestant and Independent churches.

Following the pioneering efforts of their American Methodist counterparts, who blazed a trail in Manila in response to President McKinley's 1899 call to action, Filipino Methodists started arriving in San Francisco early in the twentieth century. In 1920, with their growing numbers, they established the Filipino Wesley Methodist Church—only two decades after the beginning of the American occupation and "Christianization" of their homeland. These Filipino Protestant pilgrims gathered together regularly for fellowship and to foster a sense of belonging in a new and unfamiliar land. Later in that year, Dr. J. Stanley was appointed pastor. The congregation went on to change its name to the Filipino Fellowship Church. By the 1930s, around 100 Filipino Protestants in San Francisco were registered with the Filipino Christian Fellowship and the YMCA's Filipino Christian Endeavor.

Outside of San Francisco, Presbyterian pastor Pedro F. Royola began evangelical work among Salinas-based Filipino farmworkers in 1924. He formed the Filipino Community Church (which later became Saint Philip's Church). Trained in Manila, Reverend Royola was greatly influenced by none other than American Presbyterian Dr. James B. Rodgers. He received his formal education at the American-established Ellinwood Malate Church, the Silliman Institute, and the Union Theological Seminary. Prior to moving to California, he had ministered to Filipino plantation workers in Hawaii (Solis 2000).

In the Pacific islands between the Philippines and California, Hilario Camino Moncado, one of the early Filipino migrant laborers from the sugar plantations of Hawaii, founded the Filipino Federation of America in 1925. The charismatic Moncado eventually transformed this labor organization of U.S.-based Filipino workers into the Equifrilibricum World Religion, popularly known as the Moncadistas. The Filipino labor leader claimed to be the reincarnated Jesus Christ. Moncado was looked up to by his fellow workers and religious followers as the person who would deliver them from the economic exploitation, unfair treatment, and racial discrimination that they had been experiencing in American society. Unlike other social organizations during those times, which were notorious for their gambling, dancing, and drinking, Moncado's group claimed to promote a clean and upright lifestyle. Equifrilibricum also gained a foothold among Filipino workers in San Francisco (Mercado 1982).

Joining forces with Mexican Catholics and other Asian migrant workers, Filipino Evangelicals and Catholics were responsible for mobilizing their fellow laborers on numerous occasions. In 1928, protesting Filipino workers were driven out of the agricultural fields of Yakima Valley, Washington, and Hood River and Banks, Oregon. Of course, this was not the first time they had instigated a strike. Their frequent activism on behalf of thousands of migrant workers began to earn them the reputation of being "radicals." During that same year, several hundred miles down the long Pacific coast, another group of Filipino Christian agricultural laborers working in Southern California was also determined to organize. But this time it was for a less confrontational objective—the establishment of the first Filipino American Christian Fellowship Church of Los Angeles. However, peaceful religious worship services did not satisfy the restless Filipino faithful farmworkers, who had few recreational options in rural California. Defying racist social rules that kept Filipinos from mixing with white women, they organized socials and invited white women, to the chagrin of white society in the area. These subversive gatherings only added to existing tensions about the presence of Filipino migrant workers, who many accused of stealing low-paying jobs from white Americans. In January 1930, violent anti-Filipino riots erupted at Watsonville in Monterey County. Years later, larger American labor unions with influential Filipino leaders, like Philip Vera Cruz and Larry Itliong, took notice of their plight and together with some church leaders intervened to calm the interracial tensions.

Because of successive waves of immigration starting in the 1920s, Filipino Methodists, Presbyterians, Baptists, Adventists, Episcopalians, Mormons, and Witnesses have successfully established flourishing congregations all over the San Francisco Bay Area. Many of these Filipino religious congregations have taken over houses of worship whose membership had been predominantly European American (Caucasian). In addition to Saint James Presbyterian Church in Visitacion Valley and the San Francisco Seventh-Day Adventist Church in Pacifica, a number of other abandoned churches have been taken over by Filipino migrant faithful.

CHURCH OF JESUS CHRIST OF LATTER-DAY SAINTS

The Filipino ward of the Church of Jesus Christ of Latter-day Saints in Daly City, which also began in the 1970s, has grown to more than 350 members. Interestingly, this Mormon church has several American, non-Filipino members who were former missionaries in the Philippines. Some have Filipino spouses. Because of their language training and exposure to mission work in many parts of the Philippines, they are able to participate in Tagalog-language worship activities at the church in Daly City. Some know other Philippine dialects besides Tagalog (such as Visayan [Cebuano] and Ilocano) and thus can participate in the Bible study sessions in those languages.

JEHOVAH'S WITNESSES

The first Filipino Jehovah's Witness congregations were established in Stockton (1974) and Salinas (1975). Most of the members at these sites were Filipino farmworkers and their families. In the 1980s and 1990s, the number of Filipino Witnesses increased rapidly. Today there are twelve Filipino migrant congregations in the San Francisco Bay Area, twelve in the Los Angeles area, and four in the Washington-Oregon area, each with approximately 100 active members. These twenty-eight Filipino migrant congregations are a closely knit group and meet regularly throughout the year. The San Francisco area congregations are found in Alameda, Daly City, El Cerrito, Hayward, Milpitas, Salinas, San Francisco, San Jose, Stockton, Sunnyvale, Vallejo, and West Sacramento.[14]

SEVENTH-DAY ADVENTIST CHURCH

Organized in 1967, the San Francisco Filipino American Seventh-Day Adventist Church (SDA) is part of the sisterhood of churches of the Central California Conference of Seventh-Day Adventists. It is committed to proclaiming the gospel to its community, training and equipping its members for Christian service, and preparing believers for the Second Coming of Jesus. While the church's special focus is reaching out to individuals with Filipino backgrounds, its larger mission is to minister to people of all cultures. As a result, its active members include African Americans, Caucasian Americans, and other Asian Americans. The church offers two Bible classes in Tagalog, one in Kapampangan, and one in English every Saturday. As a testament to its popularity, the San

Francisco Filipino American SDA spawned two other Filipino congregations— the Hillside Community Church in San Bruno and the San Francisco Tabernacle Seventh-Day Adventist Church.[15]

BAPTIST-INSPIRED CHURCHES

The first worship service of the Faith Bible Church (FBC) of San Francisco was held in April 1971. At the time, the church was an informal prayer group without a meeting space of its own; it met at the Twenty-first Avenue Baptist Church until 1973, when the church was formally organized and began meeting regularly at the home of Pastor Leo Calica. In 1975, the group moved back out, but this time to Saint James Presbyterian Church, with Pastor Calica as the full-time pastor. Two years later, the FBC group finally found a permanent home when it purchased the Salvation Army chapel on Broad Street. In 1989, the FBC added a Tagalog-language service to its regular schedule. Under Pastor Calica's leadership, the FBC's membership grew, as did the breadth of its missionary activities, such as building homes for urban poor in the Philippines, food programs in Latin American orphanages, disaster assistance in South Asia, and spreading the word of God to rural communities in sub-Saharan Africa. Other Faith Bible Churches have also been established in recent years in Oakland, Vallejo, and Pittsburgh. Following in his father's footsteps, Pastor Calica's son became the pastor of the Faith Bible Church in Vallejo.[16]

UNITED METHODISTS

The Reverend Arturo Capuli is the third Filipino migrant pastor of the Saint Francis and Grace United Methodist Church in San Francisco. His two predecessors, Reverend Leonard Autajay and Reverend Juan Ancheta, were originally trained as Baptist ministers but then later became Methodists. All three men started their training in the Philippines and then did advanced theological studies in the United States. The present congregation represents a merger between the Filipino Wesley Methodist Church and Parkside Methodist Church, a predominantly Caucasian congregation whose membership had been rapidly declining. Over the years, the Caucasian members of the merged congregation diminished, and the congregation became almost entirely Filipino. Today, Saint Francis and Grace United Methodist Church is one of three United Methodist churches in the area that have a Filipino ministry. The other two are located on Geneva Avenue in San Francisco and on Southgate Avenue in Daly City. In total, there are twenty-two United Methodist churches in the San Francisco Bay Area, all with large Filipino memberships.[17]

Filipino Independent Churches in San Francisco

IGLESIA NI CRISTO

From the date of their establishment, it took the American Protestant churches more than a hundred years to cross the Pacific Ocean and establish themselves in the Philippines. By contrast, the transnational growth of the independent Iglesia ni Cristo was relatively swift; in less than five decades, it set up formal missions in the United States and other countries around the world. As early as 1967, INC migrants to Hawaii began gathering other brethren in Oahu. In 1968, the INC began its overseas work in Honolulu. Brother Eraño Manalo, son of church founder Felix Manalo and the current executive minister of the INC, traveled from Manila to Honolulu, where he spent one month formalizing the new INC outpost there. He then proceeded to San Francisco and soon thereafter announced the establishment of the first INC congregation in the continental United States (Reed 1990). Some of the largest INC congregations in the United States are found in San Francisco and in nearby Daly City. Offering worship services in both Tagalog and English, the INC has more than 1,500 members in these two locales alone. Generally, the non-Filipino members attend English-language services. However, a few at these large locales have learned Tagalog and participate in the Tagalog worship activities, such as singing and Bible studies. In December 1970, the INC purchased the historic Sixth Church of Christ Scientist building in upscale Pacific Heights. The Church of Christ Scientist had occupied the building since 1924, before declining participation rates and rising maintenance costs had forced a merger with other Scientist churches in the city, and the eventual closure and sale of the building. In the two years before the INC formally acquired the building, members of the San Francisco locale had been meeting in makeshift spaces. Today, the locale makes its spiritual home in a capacious building that is also a historical landmark in one of the most expensive neighborhoods in the city. The INC's acquisition of this building is a testament to the financial wealth that it has amassed since its inception. INC *kasamahan*-building activities are shown in table 2.1.

TABLE 2.1
Kasamahan *building at the INC*

1. Worship services: These events take place in the primary worship area and last approximately one hour. Women and men are seated on separate sides of the room. Women must wear skirts or dresses rather than pants. The service consists primarily of a Bible lesson conducted in question-and-answer format, in which the minister asks a theological question and then answers it using a passage from the Bible. A choir leads the worshipers in the singing of hymns before and during the service. Uniformed deacons and deaconesses ensure that attendees adhere to the strict order that characterizes the service, and collect monetary donations at an appointed time.

2. Grand Evangelical Missions (GEMs): A GEM is a gathering designed to introduce nonmembers to the primary tenets of the church. Each GEM is organized around a Bible lesson, which lasts for about one hour and is followed by an informal activity, such as eating, which allows for casual conversation. GEMs take place monthly, usually on the first weekend of the month. They are sponsored each month by a group within the church, such as the Tagalog choir, or the *Binhi* group (for young adults). To sponsor a GEM is to take primary responsibility for inviting newcomers and organizing the reception that follows the Bible lesson.

3. Bible expositions: Taking place once or twice a year, Bible expositions follow the format of the GEM, but after the lesson and reception there is often a program. At the INC in Daly City, attendees retire from a generous buffet to a small theater, where they are treated to a program that may include an introductory video and/or slide show about the church and musical performances by church members.

4. Bible study sessions: Prospective members are required to complete a twenty eight lesson cycle of Bible study sessions, which are offered Monday through Friday evenings, both at the church and in members' homes. Each session lasts about forty five minutes, and is organized around a particular theme, such as the expansion of this Philippines-based church to "the West," the principle of unity, or the Iglesia ni Cristo's status as the only "true church."

PHILIPPINE INDEPENDENT CHURCH

Clustered on the same street (Southgate Avenue) as the Filipinized Saint Augustine's Catholic Church, the United Methodist Church of Daly City, and the Iglesia ni Cristo's Northern California office is the Holy Child and Saint Martin Episcopal Church, which was taken over in 1993 by the Iglesia Filipina Independiente, or the Philippine Independent Church (PIC) and Filipino Episcopalians. The PIC Diocese of the United States and Canada had conducted mission work in the Chicago area from the 1960s but was not formally established until 1986. Formalized more than twenty years ago, Holy Child and Saint Martin Episcopal Church was a merger for administrative convenience between a Filipino Episcopal and PIC group from Saint Barnabas Episcopal Church, which had been closed by the diocese, and Saint Martin Episcopal Church, which needed new occupants. The Philippine Independent Church and Filipino Episcopalians have managed to occupy more than twenty abandoned Christian worship spaces all over the United States and Canada.

EL SHADDAI

Operating in Catholic church basements and meeting halls, El Shaddai, a Catholic charismatic renewal movement with approximately 10 million followers in the Philippines, has expanded its brand of spirituality to the United States. The founder and "servant leader" of El Shaddai is Mariano "Brother Mike" Velarde. In San Francisco, the followers of El Shaddai originally met in a rented hall in the basement of the towering Saint Mary of the Assumption Cathedral but then relocated to the main worship area of the Star of the Sea Church. El Shaddai USA began its first chapter in Los Angeles in July 1991 and then followed with a San Francisco chapter two years later. Since then, the number of El Shaddai chapters and cell groups has grown to fifteen in Southern California, six in Northern California, and nineteen in other states, with approximately 10,000 to 12,000 members (or "prayer partners").

Summary and Conclusion

Professor Leny Mendoza Strobel of Sonoma State University shared in an interview:

> An American Methodist missionary in the Philippines converted my grandfather at the turn of the twentieth century. Never mind that the Spanish came there first and that my grandfather's first choice was to become a Catholic priest. The white man who stood on his soapbox at the town square charmed my grandfather and seduced him to becoming one of the first Filipino Methodist pastors in the region.

Professor Strobel added that her father eventually came to the United States and, as a Methodist pastor, became a volunteer chaplain for Friends House, a Quaker retirement community in Sonoma, California.

In this chapter, I have attempted to elucidate the following findings on the transnational influences of Filipino migrant faithful to San Francisco via *kasamahan* (bonding Filipinization): First, the literature on U.S. and Philippine transnational relations has been dominated by discussion on international politics, economics, trade, and investment. Thus, I went to original sources on Filipino migrants and religion through archival research, which I supplemented with interviews of key informants. This allowed me to craft a migration story from the *kasamahan*-building narratives of Filipino parishioners, members, and pastors, as well as the voluminous church records and publications that have never before made it into scholarly studies.

Second, America's "benevolent assimilation" of the Philippines contributed to the building of the country's post–Spanish colonization *kasamahan* infrastructure, starting with the development of a grassroots-based, English-language educational system. This move raised the educational levels of Filipinos, and especially the masses, which facilitated the broad reading of and critical reflection upon the Christian Bible and other church teachings. Filipinos were receptive to these Bible activities, which had been discouraged by Spanish friars and government officials for more than 300 years. While Catholic churches sought to refurbish their tainted image among the Filipinos through newly installed American clergy, American Protestant churches and their missionaries came and spread a different brand of Christianity throughout the country, particularly to the previously marginalized masses. A group of nationalist religious leaders were even inspired by America's "breakaway" *kasamahan* groups to deviate from their own Western-dominated Filipino church hierarchies and establish their own independent churches, such as the Iglesia ni Cristo and the Aglipayan Church.

Third, this "benevolent assimilation" of the colony in turn precipitated a return of Christian *kasamahan* to the colonizer through successive waves of Filipino migrant faithful to the United States beginning in the early 1900s. Interestingly, while we do not know whether or not President McKinley's benevolent assimilation policy had any scriptural basis, the INC believes that the Filipinization of Christianity in the United States by migrant faithful from the Philippines is foretold in the Bible. According to the Moffatt translation of the Bible, which the INC often uses, God told the prophet Isaiah, "From the far east will I bring your offspring, from the far west will I gather you" (Isaiah 43:5, Moffatt edition). Indeed, the westward flow of Filipino Christians to the United States seems to bear out this biblical prophecy. Their *kasamahan*-building and *kasamahan*-enhancing networks and activities have been infused into many of San Francisco's religious spaces and replenished diminishing or lost spiritual and cultural capital.

Fourth, I found that as Filipino Roman Catholic and other Christian congregations blossomed in San Francisco and many other gateway cities in America in the 1920s, Filipinos brought to these churches new forms of worship and *kasamahan*. Many of these places of worship had been previously filled with the esprit de corps of Anglo-American migrant faithful. Asian American, African American, Caucasian American, and Latino American attendees of Filipino places of worship have learned to accept the rituals, beliefs, and nuances of Filipino Catholicism and Evangelicalism. They have learned to pray to San Lorenzo Ruiz and confess their sins to priests with Filipino accents. Non-Filipino congregants have even learned to appreciate the Filipino humor and anecdotes of their ministers and pastors. They have learned to sing English compositions from the Philippines, and in some cases, Tagalog hymns.

Fifth, in addition to the significant increases of Filipino attendance at San Francisco Bay Area churches, there has been a corresponding rise in the number of Filipino Catholic, Protestant, and Independent church leaders, ministers, administrators, and religious workers who are becoming more visible and influencing American faith communities and facilitating *kasamahan*. In addition to church members, migration has increased the number of Filipino students at San Francisco Catholic educational institutions from the elementary to the tertiary levels. Completing the cycle of transnational influence, a number of second- and third-generation Filipino migrant Methodist, Baptist, Catholic, Iglesia ni Cristo, and Presbyterian missionaries, lay workers, evangelists, ministers, and pastors are not only spreading the word of God in San Francisco and in cities with large Filipino populations. Filipinos and members of other ethnic minority groups are compensating for the reduced interest among European Americans in pursuing the priesthood. This next generation of priests, pastors, and missionaries of Filipino descent are not only all over the United States but all over the world. Many remain in touch with their roots and have gone back to the Philippines, some as short-term religious visitors and others as long-term religious workers. Many give money to build hometown churches and chapels, while some physically help build the structures themselves. This continues the cycle of transnational migration and *kasamahan* from faithful Filipinos.

Finally, I conclude that, given globalization and the Filipino diaspora of 10 million to close to 200 countries, Filipino culture, religious life, and *kasamahan* are being mainstreamed into an increasingly borderless global society, not just San Francisco and other cities in the United States. In my travels, I have seen Filipino migrant pastors, religious sisters, and parishioners in Roman Catholic churches in Madrid and Dubai, bringing forth a "resurrection" of the Christian faith in Europe and the Middle

East. This demographic phenomenon is facilitated by advances and continuing innovations in technology, transportation, communications, and education, which enable preaching and conversion across physical and spatial boundaries. Based on their migratory history, Filipino faithful will likely continue to flock and multiply, bringing with them their strong faith and traditions—to the "promised land," wherever that may be.

The next chapter goes beyond illustrations of transnational *kasa-mahan* (bonding Filipinization) through congregation formation and replenishment, new forms of worship and prayer that bring people together, and the networks and subgroups Filipino migrants cultivate, to describing how they are influencing American religion, economy, and society by faith-inspired giving to communities and economies in both the United States and the Philippines, or what I consider to be transnational *bayanihan* (bridging Filipinization).

3

Praying,
Then Delivering Miracles

With her four-year-old son in tow, Rosario C., forty-five, has
just come out of the Sunday Tagalog mass at Saint Boniface Catholic
Church in downtown San Francisco. She is walking at a fast pace toward
Lucky Money, a remittance company on Mission Street. While crossing
Market Street, I am trying my best to keep up with her. A chilly wind
pushes us to walk the three remaining city blocks at an even faster speed.
Catching our breath a block from her destination, Rosario C. looks at
me and says, "Pinagdadasal ko sila lagi sa Pilipinas pagkatapos nagpapadala ako ng pera" (I always pray for family back in the Philippines
and then I send them money). After her husband passed away a couple
of years ago, Rosario C. was forced to work two jobs (one full-time and
another part-time) to support her young son, plus two teenage children
who reside with relatives in the Philippines, in the remote province of
Pampanga. Proceeding to Lucky Money after attending the service is
part of her ritual every second or third Sunday of the month. But today
is a little bit different, since it is the beginning of June—that time of the
year when her older children, Mario and Princess, need a larger amount
of money for college tuition. Before entering the office, she grins at me
and exclaims, "Hirap talaga ng buhay!" (Life is really hard!). I hold on
to her son and wait as she joins the long line of migrant remitters, giving
her enough time to catch her breath again before getting to the counter.
Rosario C. manages a cheerful "hi" to the smiling Lucky Money cashier
and slowly hands over ten crisp hundred-dollar bills with the transaction form. On the other side of the counter, the cashier gives Rosario C.
her receipt, and in a combination of Tagalog and English, adds, "Thank
you po, see you next month ha"? Rosario C. answers, "Sigue" (So long).
After getting her receipt and exiting, Rosario C. looks up at the cloudy
skies, closes her eyes, and, with tightly clasped hands, whispers softly to
the wind, "Bahala na po kayo" (It is in your hands now, God).

Rosario C.'s routine is common among the more than 150 Filipino migrant parishioners of Saint Boniface Church, originally established in 1860 to serve the spiritual needs of the German Catholic community in San Francisco. This *dasal tapos padala* (praying then sending) ritual is further replicated on an even wider scale by many of the more than 300,000 San Francisco Bay Area Filipino migrant faithful: the Catholic, Protestant, and Independent church members who continue to maintain links to the Philippines. On the same day prayers are sent via heavenly channels, dollars are remitted through wire transfers. Both are meant to achieve the results back in the Philippines that Rosario C. has experienced by migrating to the United States—economic deliverance. In her mind, both channels work and are necessary. She is thankful to God for giving her the capacity in her new homeland to give back to the old one.

During our conversation, Rosario C. reminds me of an old Filipino saying that sums up her belief: "Nasa Dios ang awa, nasa tao ang gawa" (God sympathizes, but it is up to people to act). Accordingly, her strong faith and action have facilitated much-needed "miracles" for her family and village community in the Philippines. Besides being able to educate the children she left behind, the money she sends back pays for the monthly mortgage of a new house in Santo Tomas, Pampanga Province. Rosario C. is the first person in the Cruz clan to own a home. Not surprisingly, many of the houses surrounding hers in Santo Tomas were also funded by overseas Filipino remittances. She is hoping that when Mario and Princess join her in the United States, they can help her save for a home in the San Francisco Bay Area. Like Rosario C.'s family, many of their neighbors have been tenant farmers ever since she can remember, renting land from the same hacienda owners for generations. Breaking this economic patronage means a lot, not just to her but to the whole Cruz clan. But Rosario C., the American immigrant, must carry the burden of independence and freedom by providing the same welfare and safety nets that the old *patrons* used to give her family, their "clients." In effect, she has become the new "patroness," covering the health care costs of her aging and sickly parents. Rosario C.'s hard-earned dollars have also trickled down to her brothers, sisters, aunts, uncles, nieces, nephews, cousins, and close friends. Her money has even helped fund church and community projects in Santo Tomas, including fiestas, processions, pageants, dances, feast days, funerals, baptisms, and confirmations. It is no wonder that Rosario C. is seen as a veritable savior in two homelands.

Rosario C.'s transnational integration illustrates how her deep faith and networks through the Saint Boniface Catholic church community (*kasamahan*, or bonding Filipinization) are helping her rationalize her giving (*pagbigay*), sacrifices (*sakripisyo*), and contributions (*tulong*) to family, community, and church (*bayanihan*, or bridging Filipinization) in the Philippines. She also sends because she pities (*naawa*) her less fortunate relatives and actually feels embarrassed (*nahihiya*) and consciencitized (*nakokonsiyeusiya*) when she cannot send money. Before I examined the extent of this transnational *bayanihan* from migrant faithful like Rosario C. through a large-scale San Francisco Bay Area Religion and Remittance Survey, I scoured the literature for a conceptual grounding on works combining migration, remittances, and religion, which I discuss in the following section. Based on these texts and my analysis of the survey results, I argue that migration creates not only a transnational movement of Filipino migrant congregations and churches, that is, the *kasamahan* described in the previous chapter, but also a transnational Filipino faith-based *bayanihan* of "praying then sending," benefiting both San Francisco and the Philippines. The long-standing transnational exchange of educational and cultural information with America has given Filipinos the tools to succeed financially. The fruits of this exchange are economically savvy Filipino Catholics, Protestants, and Independent church members, like Rosario C., who have gained the financial capacity to influence not only their San Francisco communities but also their Philippine hometowns. The survey and follow-up focus group meetings that we conducted revealed that besides conducting Bible studies and praying together for relatives back home from their churches in the United States, Filipino faithful deliver on their promises to help with their family's health, retirement, and education needs, as well as community social and economic development programs and disaster-relief projects in both the San Francisco Bay Area and their hometowns and provinces in the Philippines. Knowing that all is well and secure with their families back in their hometown gives them the necessary peace of mind and security to concentrate on their integration into their new American homeland.

Diaspora, Dollars, and Spirituality

Rosario C.'s remittance story is not unique to the migration literature, but none analyze the Filipino transnational *bayanihan*. There is a plethora of research driven by academia, development agencies, and commercial entities that has studied the relative size and magnitude of outward migration and migrant remittances globally (see, among others, Athukorala 1993; Chandavarkar 1980; Keely and Tran 1989; McCormick and Wahba 2000; Puri and Ritzema 2000; Puerta 2002; Ratha 2003; Shankman 1976; Stahl and Arnold 1986; Stanton 1992). At a multilateral gathering in Manila, the Asian Development Bank, Inter-American Development Bank, and United Nations Development Program (UNDP) (2005) reported that migrant worker remittances like Rosario C.'s have overtaken Foreign Direct Investment (FDI) and Official Development Assistance (ODA) as the primary driver of growth and external development financing among many of Asia's and Latin America's sending economies. More than 175 million migrant nationals worldwide send US$127 billion worth of remittances to their home countries annually. At US$45 billion, Latin American and Caribbean remittances exceeded the combined flows of both ODA and FDI of those regions. Similarly, Asian migrant workers sent back a total of US$53 billion, which also surpassed ODA and FDI flows to the Asia-Pacific region. The lucrative profits being made from the growing remittance business have also been adequately studied (see Nilson Report 2004).

Mexico (89 percent Catholic) and the Philippines (93 percent Christian) are two of the top countries of origin for new migrants throughout the world. The spiritual and religious practices of this demographic are naturally reflected in the activities—financial and otherwise—of Mexican and Filipino migrants in their host countries. Comparatively, however, almost all of Mexico's migrant population live and work in the neighboring United States, while the 10 million overseas Filipinos are dispersed to close to 200 countries. Over 2 million Filipinos are based in the United States, translating to (even with conservative estimates) more than a million Filipino migrants filling up church pews on a weekly basis. Globally, Filipino migrants sent more than US$12 billion to the Philippines in 2004, while Mexican migrants remitted more than US$18 billion to Mexico in the same year. More than US$5 billion of Filipino migrant remittances originated from the United States, US$2 billion from California-based Filipinos alone.

A vast majority of migration studies point out the many positive and significant effects of remittances on both macro- and micro-economies of home countries. At the macroeconomic level, the monthly surges of much-needed monetary remittances to countries of origin provide the necessary liquidity to governments' deficient cash balance. That is to say, migrants sending back money subsidizes weak export earnings in gross national product (GNP). In the Philippines, the remittances from Rosario C. and the millions of other overseas Filipinos constitute a significant 13 percent of GNP and have helped the government contain its burgeoning fiscal deficits. These remittances have even strengthened the perennially weak Philippine peso in relation to the U.S. dollar.

At the microeconomic level, migrant remittances have enabled poor urban and rural families who would otherwise be living under the poverty line make the household income necessary to cover at least basic needs, and thus improve their standard of living, which may reduce the gap between higher-income and lower-income groups (Brown and Ahlburg 1999; Leinbach and John 1998; Siddiqui and Chowdhury 2003; Stark 1991). Many notable studies document examples of this dynamic worldwide.

In his observations of remittances among Indian migrants, Ballard (2005) argued that the green revolution era (post-1965), which marked a period of sustained development in India, was influenced by the remittance of capital from relatives overseas (mostly from the United Kingdom). Ballard notes that many migrants were only too willing to remit funds to purchase tractors, construct tube wells, and acquire machinery to produce higher agricultural yields. Adams (1996) carried out a study in Pakistan and found that remittances had a significant impact on productive investment. His study went a step further in revealing a significant relationship between the ownership of irrigated land and external remittances. Specifically, internal migrants (i.e., those who move within a country) were poorer than external migrants (i.e., those who move outside a country). Hence, most internal remittances were invested in lower-priced agricultural tools and implements, while external remittances were invested in the comparatively higher-priced project of buying land.

In Latin America, Orozco (2003) pointed out that remittances were used as alternative sources of funding for local Latin American businessmen and entrepreneurs. Thus, as a form of foreign savings, remittances could influence not only spending but also investment behavior. A portion of migrant remittances is generally saved or invested in education, health, or the generation of wealth. In this way, investments in the homeland by migrants also provide financial security. Remittances have also been found to positively affect asset accumulation. For instance, one study found that almost 20 percent of capital invested in microenterprises in urban Mexico came from remittances (Woodruff and Zeteno 2001). Lucas's (1987) study of South Africa's labor migration to its mining sector suggested that short-term declines in rural production due to the loss of labor are more than offset by later increases in agricultural productivity as remittances help raise farm investments. Initially, according to Lucas, remittances are apportioned toward meeting basic subsistence needs, but later they are allocated toward productive investment in the future.

Numerous studies support the notion that in the Philippines, remittances have a significant impact on families and communities (Frank 2001; Carlos 2002; King 1985; Menjivar et al. 1998). Two extensive studies conducted by Rodriguez (1996, 1998) concluded that remittances have become a major part of household incomes in the Philippines. Similarly, in their study of 1,128 Philippine households, Semyonov and Gorodzeisky (2005) found that remittances definitely make a difference in household incomes. We can therefore infer that like Rosario C., other Filipino faithful (and Mexican too) do more than just light candles or recite novenas for their friends and family back home. The money they send keeps household budgets afloat; educates siblings and children; helps rehabilitate or construct schools, chapels, and roads; assists in rental payments and the purchase of land and homes; and pays for medicines and hospitalization for aging parents and grandparents (Gonzalez 1998).

However, a number of researchers are skeptical about concluding outright that remittances have positive effects, especially without hard empirical data illustrating strong causality. For example, Tiglao (1997) argued that in some cases remittance flows can induce complacency and a lack of interest to modernize. His study of the Philippines indicates that remittances insulated an agriculture-dominated rural area from modernization. Clouding the issue further is the additional research on patterns and trends in the remittance of money that has uncovered mixed results. For instance, a study by Rozelle, Taylor, and DeBrauw (1999) of rural communities in China found that migration (internal and external) resulted in an increase in household consumption of nearly 20 percent. However, the researchers found no conclusive evidence that migration impacts productive investment. Similarly, a study by Durand and Massey (1992) of thirty-seven Mexican communities showed that although a large percentage of remittances tended to be spent on consumption in all villages (i.e. consumer goods and luxury items), the share allocated to productive investments varied greatly from village to village. This led them to state, "Rather than concluding that migration inevitably leads to dependency and a lack of development, it is more appropriate to ask why productive investment occurs in some communities and not in others" (see also Massey and Parrado 1994).

Rosario C.'s case provides a striking illustration of the intersections of migration, remittances, and religion, particularly how the transformation of *kasamahan* to *bayanihan* manifested in her thankfulness (*pasalamat*) and helpfulness (*matulungin*) is drawn from her faith. However, in my extensive searches, I found no studies—not even from the large labor-sending Christian countries like the Philippines and Mexico—correlating migrants' spiritual experiences with their financial contributions. These include contributions toward the salvation of their home countries' macroeconomic financial situation and the economic and social deliverance of households and communities. Development institutions, the World Bank, the Asian Development Bank, the Inter-American Development Bank, and UNDP, which have all shown a keen interest in remittances, have focused their research lately on enhancing the efficiency of the remittance system, reducing transactions costs, deregulating policies, and monitoring transfers that flow through informal channels for antiterrorism and security reasons.

Gathering Data on Praying and Sending

The succeeding discussion seeks to fill in the gap in the scholarly research by analyzing the remittance as *bayanihan* of Filipino migrant faithful in San Francisco. In doing so, it brings to light the otherwise invisible experience of Rosario C. and the many others who follow the same practice of praying then remitting. In order to understand clearly the transnational intersections of a Filipino migrant's faith experience and his or her remittances, I launched a large-scale, multipurpose survey. The overall research utilized a combination of quantitative and qualitative approaches. After the surveys were administered, follow-up focus group meetings were performed at community centers in Vallejo, San Jose, Oakland, Daly City, and San Francisco. The research team also conducted some in-depth interviews.

What is analyzed in this chapter is a portion of the multipurpose survey that was administered by teams of graduate students from Golden Gate

University and San Francisco State University, and undergraduate students from the University of San Francisco, among Filipino Catholic, Protestant, and Independent churchgoers. Each team had bilingual and bicultural members. They conducted the surveys before and after English and Tagalog services in San Francisco Bay Area churches. Approximately 1,700 surveys were administered using a simple random sampling. The number of responses to each survey question varied. The surveys tried to capture a broad representation of the diverse socioeconomic backgrounds of Filipinos in the San Francisco Bay Area, from recent migrants living in the less affluent South of Market and Tenderloin districts of the city of San Francisco to more settled middle- to upper-class Filipinos in the Silicon Valley.

The San Francisco Bay Area is the location of the three large, flagship Roman Catholic dioceses in California—Oakland, San Jose, and San Francisco. The vast Archdiocese of San Francisco is composed of parishes in the three counties of San Francisco, Marin (27 cities), and San Mateo (31 cities). The parishes in Alameda (14 cities) and Contra Costa Counties (23 cities) make up the Diocese of Oakland, while the parishes of Santa Clara County (15 cities) form the Diocese of San Jose. The dioceses surveyed in Oakland, San Francisco, and San Jose are also in counties of the Bay Area that have the largest Filipino populations, according to the 2000 U.S. census. As a matter of fact, according to the U.S. Catholic Bishops Conference, they are ranked fourth, fifth, and sixth in Filipino population size after the Dioceses of Los Angeles (first), Honolulu (second), and San Diego (third). To mirror the religious demographics of the migrant population, besides Filipino Catholic migrants, the research teams also surveyed Filipino migrants who were Methodists, Presbyterians, Baptists, Adventists, Episcopalians, Mormons, and Witnesses, as well as Iglesia ni Cristo and Philippine Independent Church (or Aglipayan Church) members. The approximate geographic distribution of the surveys is shown in table 3.1.

TABLE 3.1
San Francisco Bay Area Regional Coverage

AREA	TARGET RESPONDENTS
San Francisco	400
East Bay	400
South Bay	400
Peninsula	450
North Bay	50
Total	1,700

The results presented here come from the San Francisco Bay Area Religion and Remittance Survey, containing information on thirty-two demographic, psychographic, and socioeconomic variables. Demographically, there was a fifty-fifty split among the male and female respondents. A significant 87 percent of the respondents were between the productive working ages of twenty-one and sixty-four, and more than half of them were married.

Transnational Faith and Finances as Bayanihan

What follows are highlights of significant trends and patterns from the questionnaire responses of Filipino migrant faithful, reflecting distinct characteristics of their transnational *bayanihan* to prayers and action. These include the implications of minding two homes, the mechanics of making their American education work to assist two families and two economies, and the need to give back to two homes as well as their twin communities.

Two Homes, Two Hearts

According to a popular American saying, "Home is where the heart is." However, based on their prayers and actions, it seems that the heart of the Filipino migrant is often in two places: the United States homeland and the Philippine hometown. Consequently, the numerous social roles migrants play and the cultural expectations attached to them in both homes were an interesting side topic of conversation that emerged in all the focus group exchanges. A middle-aged man, working as a paralegal in Oakland, pointed out that he was "Tatay at asawa dito sa America, kuya at Tiyo naman doon sa Pilipinas" (father and spouse here in America, eldest brother and uncle in the Philippines). Of course, each of these roles carries a distinct set of social responsibilities, which can become burdensome. Other focus group participants said they were expected to be "mabuting anak" (dutiful children) by their aging parents in the Philippines and at the same time "mabuting magulang" (good parents) by their clan members in the United States.

Rosario C. says that she has no choice but to "do it," referring to her care of herself and her child, as well as her remittance of money to Pampanga. This is because she is *nanay* (mother), *anak* (child), *tiya* (aunt), *kapatid* (sibling), *apo* (grandchild), and *pinsan* (cousin), to name just a few of her home roles. On top of these family roles, there are also the religio-cultural and societal roles she plays in both homes as *ninang* (sponsor), *kumare* (old friend), *matalik na kaibigan* (best friend), *kaklase* (classmate), *kababata* (childhood friend), *katrabaho* (workplace associate), *kabarkada* (social group mate), *kamaganak* (relative), and *kababayan* (townmate). However, not being able to be physically present in both places leaves a migrant with no choice but to perform what may seem like contradictory behaviors—*gawa* (literally, "work," such as acting on a relative's cell phone text message to send money) and *bahala na* (leaving it to God's will or fate) after doing so.

Living in an ethnically diverse California community and having access to advanced information and communication technologies (e.g., TV, cell phone, and the Internet), frequent airline flights, and swift banking transactions all make it easier for Filipino migrants to mind their two homes. A recent arrival who admits missing her home in the Philippines, Melinda, thirty-one, negotiates the gap with technology: "My *lolo* and *lola* [grandpa and grandma] are just a phone call away, while my friends and cousins are just an e-mail or an IM [instant message] away." She adds that "Filipino Web sites, Facebook, and shows like TFC [The Filipino Channel] allow me to remain in touch with the latest news and gossip in Manila." She met her best friend, Joanne, twenty-nine, who has been in the United States for two years, at their Corpus Christi Church. Giggling, Joanne quipped, "And if you are really lonely and have the money . . . Philippine Airlines flies nine times a week from San Francisco to Manila." This contemporary situation is a far cry from that of earlier European migrants, who did not have these immediate and easy ways to connect to their countries of origin. Consequently, they experienced strong pressure to assimilate swiftly into the melting pot of European American culture and stay put in their new U.S. homeland. Comparatively, the current technologies of communication and travel allow twenty-first-century arrivals to adjust to a diverse American society while simultaneously remaining in close contact with the people and events in their home communities.

Like Rosario C., eight out of ten Filipino migrant faithful surveyed were Philippine-born. But pledging allegiance to the Constitution and flag of the United States apparently does not mean abandoning the Philippines. A large number (1,200, or 70.9 percent) of the remitters in the database are U.S. citizens. And since the advent of dual citizenship in

2003, a growing number of migrants (11.1 percent) have formalized their "minding of two homes" by reacquiring Philippine citizenship. Dual citizens have a political and an economic stake in both countries. They have the ability to vote in Philippine and U.S. elections and to legally own property in two places.

Thirty percent of respondents indicated that maintaining two homes gives them choices in terms of where then can spend their retirement years. With healthier lifestyles resulting in longer life spans, having two homes to choose from gives retirees or late-life migrants the option of stretching federal Social Security benefits by living in the Philippines, where their dollars go much further. The remaining 70 percent of the respondents were split as to where to retire; 35 percent said the Philippines, and 35 percent preferred the United States.

When probed about his retirement plants, Amado, one of the focus group participants, said, "Upon retirement in ten years, my wife and I would like to spend six months in the Philippines (to enjoy the holidays from Christmas through the fiestas of May) and then six months in the United States (to take advantage of the beautiful summer to fall months)." He explained that they got this idea from some of their retired family and friends who have this annual routine. It coincides neatly with the Catholic calendar of events in which Amado and his wife actively participate, particularly the May 14 feast day of the patron saint of their town, Santa Ana (the grandmother of Jesus Christ). According to Amado, "Without Santa Ana's help, we would not have been able to come to America." Hence, their celebration of this saint's feast day is a gesture of devotion that they would like to make yearly for the rest of their lives.

Another focus group participant, retiree *manang* Maggie ("older sister" Maggie—a term of respect and endearment) and her spouse, who came as late-life migrants from the Philippines, communicated the same binational aspirations but a different schedule. She said, "All of our three children and their families are now settled in the United States, so we agreed to be petitioned and become green card holders so we could spend more quality time with them." *Manang* Maggie and her husband, *Manong* Fred ("older brother" Fred) fly back to the Philippines at the beginning of the Lenten season in April to host their huge circle of family and friends at their ancestral home in Iloilo Province. They depart for San Francisco in time for the changing hues of the fall season to spend time with their children and six grandchildren.

Americanized Church, Americanized Education

The five-decade colonization and continued neocolonization of the Philippines, followed by the mass migration of Filipinos to the United States beginning in the 1960s, brought more than just clergy and congregations who performed a return colonization of American spiritual life as described in the previous chapter. This strong transnational connection also brought migrants who had been trained and educated in English and, more important, the "American way," including, to a certain degree, a Protestant work ethic. Additionally, it is worth noting that the Philippines is one of the largest English-speaking nations in the world and has a 92.6 percent literacy rate, according to UNESCO. This is surely why Filipinos have been called "brown Americans" by many of their Asian neighbors and "the least foreign among America's migrants" by some U.S. immigration authorities.

It comes as no surprise, therefore, that according to the 2000 census, Filipinos in the United States have higher education levels than Latino and other Asian migrant groups. As table 3.2 shows, their Americanized educational roots have paid off handsomely in the form of access to highly skilled positions in society. In particular, 20 percent are employed in the legal, accounting, and consulting professions, and about another 20 percent work for the high-paying health, information technology, and engineering sectors. Interestingly, remitters also included individuals who were retired, unemployed, and homemakers. Seven out of ten reported that they had one job, and two out of ten indicated that they worked two jobs. One out of every four individuals surveyed had been working in the United States for between one and five years. But more than 62 percent of the migrants covered have been praying, working, and remitting from six to twenty-five years.

Jobs requiring specialized skills lead to high income levels. The 2000 U.S. census provided empirical data to support this fact, noting that Filipinos (along with Asian Indians) have the highest median family incomes among all ethnicities in the United States due to their technical and educational preparedness. The research from the San Francisco Bay Area Religion and Remittance Survey (conducted in 2006) reinforces these census findings, since half of the respondents (or 823 out of 1,644) declared annual salaries of from $30,000 to $60,000. These earnings were five to ten times above the 2006 U.S. poverty guidelines for individuals ($6,600 a year). According to U.S. Citizenship and Immigration Services sponsor-

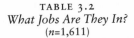

TABLE 3.2
What Jobs Are They In?
(*n*=1,611)

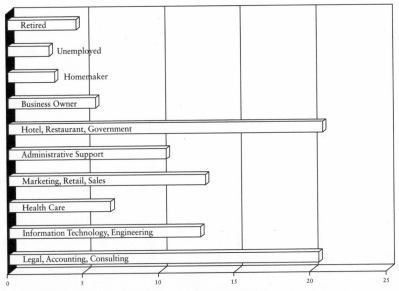

Source: *San Francisco Bay Area Religion and Remittance Survey.*

ship guidelines, these income levels essentially allowed sponsorship of between seven and sixteen family members. Nine percent of the Filipino faithful questioned were in the high-six-figure earning level.

The sizable earnings of Filipino church members makes it feasible for them to maintain twin homes, especially with a much lower cost of living in the Philippines and stronger exchange rate for the dollar to the peso ($1=45, based on 2008 rate). But for what expenses are their remittance used? While housing assistance in the form of monthly lease payments or mortgages is the most popular reason for sending money, the second is the education of the next generation back in the Philippines—some of whom may find themselves joining the diaspora in the United States or elsewhere. Housing and education are followed closely by medicine and other support for the elderly as remittance priorities.

Rosario C.'s case is a classic example of the tendencies of Filipino migrants. As soon as Mario and Princess graduate, Rosario C. expects them to follow her migration to the United States. With the San Francisco job market in mind, Rosario C. has influenced her children's choice of accounting and nursing, respectively, as their majors. Rosario C.

shared with me that she expects Mario and Princess to help her raise their younger brother, Dan, and possibly make enough money to contribute to his college fund. Like many Filipino college graduates who migrate to the United States, they will not be burdened with student loans when they start working, since their parents have fully paid their tuition. All they have to do is earn, save, and help their less fortunate kin, just as their mother did. Rosario C., who was college educated in the Philippines, did not have any difficulty finding a well-paying job in San Francisco.

Familial Giving, Societal Giving

Courses on American capitalism teach that increased savings essentially lead to a propensity to invest. Hence, it comes as no surprise that more than three-quarters of the respondents said that they were able to put aside money for themselves and others. Filipino faithful are aware that savings stored in banks yield only marginal returns and do not complement a volatile national Social Security system. So 40 percent of those studied said that they had moved their savings to higher-yielding investments such as stocks, bonds, securities, and mutual funds. Close to half of 1,673 respondents claimed that they also supplemented their federally mandated Social Security retirement funds with more stable 401k savings. They often tended to spend money on luxury items, too, such as cars and computers. A substantial majority had health (80 percent) and life (65 percent) insurance coverage, and a growing number owned homes. This home ownership rate is not only higher than that of Latinos, African Americans, and other Southeast Asian migrants nationwide, but it is also particularly notable, given that the cost of real estate in the San Francisco Bay Area is among the highest in the nation. At our focus group meetings, many who were renters or living with relatives added that they did not intend their current living situation to last for a long time, explaining that they hoped to achieve home ownership soon.

As illustrated in table 3.3, a quarter of survey respondents said they sent from $100 to $500 to the Philippines monthly, even with the high transactions fees, which can range from 12 to 17 percent, depending on the amount of money and the remittance channel used (either a bank or wire transfer agency such as Western Union). Others send money only when it is needed. "Nagpapadala lang ako kapag me-tawag" (I only send when they call), said one surveyed *kuya* (elder brother), who has been working in Silicon Valley for close to ten years. It is notable that in our

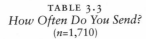

TABLE 3.3
How Often Do You Send?
(*n*=1,710)

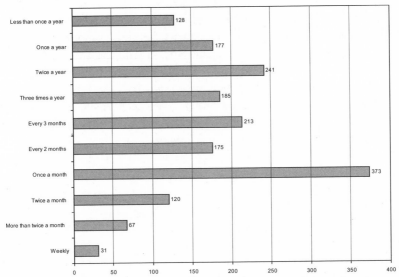

Source: *San Francisco Bay Area Religion and Remittance Survey.*

follow-up conversations, he unconsciously referred to both Milpitas (a city close to San Jose, California) and Cebu (a city in the Visayas region of the Philippines) as "home."

Survey data also revealed that 60 percent of remittances are sent to family in thirty-eight provinces outside of metropolitan Manila, while the capital city received the lion's share of 40 percent. This distribution of funds is no surprise when one considers the large population of Manila, and that many Filipinos relocate to the capital city from other areas to be closer to jobs, relatives, services, and amenities. A focus group participant living in the South of Market area in San Francisco who also calls Nasugbu, Batangas (a province south of Manila), her "home," explained this phenomenon: "It depends. I remit wherever it is needed—sometimes it is to my niece studying nursing in Manila, sometimes it is for my mother's medicine in Nasugbu." A focus group participant from Daly City added, "Sa Manila na kami nagpapadala kasi doon na lumipat ang mga magulang ko . . . walang magaling na ospital sa probinsiya namin" (We send to Manila because it is where my parents moved . . . there are no good hospitals in our province).

To the Filipino migrant faithful it seems that charity begins within their two homes. But this does not mean that they do not help philanthropies that are beyond their extended families, since they perceive their migrant roles as not only familial but also societal. When asked if they gave money to a fund or charity helping communities in the Philippines, 42 percent said they did. Not only do they help in the Philippines, but 43 percent (703 out of 1,650) of the faithful queried in the study indicated that they also give money to a fund or charity helping communities in the United States. Their generosity extends from the popular Gawad Kalinga, an organization that builds homes for the poor in the Philippines, to former President Jimmy Carter's favorite project, Habitat for Humanity. Focus group participants also said that they gave to disaster relief efforts in their home provinces and to the victims of Hurricane Katrina. Filipino nurses, doctors, and dentists spoke of having gone on medical missions to sites ranging from the northernmost parts of Luzon to the southernmost towns in Mindanao. Rosario C. noted that she makes a small, tax-deductible contribution from her salary to the United Way of the Bay Area and Catholic Relief Services. She added, "I even gave to the tsunami relief efforts in Indonesia through Catholic Charities." Filipino faithful are quick to heed calls for help from their hometown, alumni, and civic associations, but especially their churches. Thomasians USA, to which Rosario C. belongs, has helped renovate her hundred-year-old Saint Boniface Church in San Francisco but has also repaired the 250-year-old Saint Thomas the Apostle Church in her far-flung hometown of Santo Tomas. They give to charities in the Philippines even though these donations are not tax-deductible in the United States.

Besides these causes, migrants' earnings have supported spiritual and cultural practices in San Francisco while their remittances finance the continuation of religion-influenced festivities in their hometowns in the Philippines. For example, the members of the Quezonian Association of the Bay Area are not contented to simply celebrate the Pahiyas festival (seeking San Isidro's blessing for the next planting season) long distance, so they send money to help enhance the annual celebration in the streets of their hometown, Lucban. At one of the follow-up meetings with survey participants, the Reyes family of Daly City (California) and Dagupan City (Pangasinan, Philippines) noted, "We bought raffle tickets for the March 17 Saint Patrick's Day celebration in downtown San Francisco and sent $100 for the feast day of Dagupan City's patron, Saint John the Evangelist." Smiling, Jun Reyes added, "Para sa lechon . . . sa bahay" (For the roasted pig at home). We all laughed.

Summary and Conclusion

Before bidding good-bye, Rosario C. prophetically recited to me another old Filipino saying: "Ang hindi marunong lumingon sa pinanggalingan ay hindi makakarating sa paroroonan" (A person who does not know how to look back at where he or she came from will never get to his or her destination). I knew exactly what she meant. Educated in the Philippines, I also share in her migrant journey—an eldest child landing in San Francisco International Airport with just $200 in my wallet: praying to God, Jesus Christ, and Filipino icons Santo Niño and San Lorenzo Ruiz in Saint Patrick's for guidance and intercession; finding a good job; keeping two homelands; remitting dollars; giving to U.S. charities; volunteering in city hall and community-based organizations; helping send siblings to school while funding my daughter's education in one of San Francisco's Catholic high schools; and starting the chain of migration by funding the U.S. immigrant petition of my own parents and siblings.

By revealing the ways in which Filipino migrants' religion and remittances intersect, this chapter has illustrated the transformation of the transnational *kasamahan* bonds highlighted in the previous chapter (praying and sacrificing for two families and communities) to transnational *bayanihan* bridges (giving and helping two families and communities) and the influence this is having on families and communities in two homes. There are several key conclusions to be drawn from this research:

First, creating a database from the San Francisco Bay Area Religion and Remittance Survey and focus group results was the best way to credibly assess the transnational socioeconomic influences of Filipino migrant faithful, since I found the vast transnational migration and remittance literature to be filled with only business and economic studies. The migrants' faith is buried and untouched under the discussions of their economic influences to the national and subnational economies of their two homelands, as well as the financial benefits to their families and communities. There is no mention of the critical relationship of migrants' faith and giving back on this transnational *bayanihan* behavior, even though the two largest and most studied remittance and contemporary migration stories pertain to Mexico and the Philippines, both of which are more than 95 percent Christian nations.

Second, the data analysis confirmed my initial assumption that the transnational faith-and-remittance *bayanihan* experience of Filipino migrant faithful has a circular, not linear, pattern. They integrate into San Francisco society while maintaining and facilitating civic bridges that also impact their Philippine families and hometowns. They influence the economies of their American and Philippine homelands and hometowns through their churches by moving seamlessly from prayer (*dasal*) to action (*gawa*).

Third, I found that this transnational innfluence process, which helps Filipino migrants bring *bayanihan* influences to San Francisco and then back to the Philippines, is anchored in a "two homes, two hearts" mentality. They keep homeland and hometown close to their hearts because of perceived debts of gratitude (*utang na loob*) to their "old home" and "new home," to their "old family" and "new family," their "old community" and "new community," as well as to their "old church," and "new church." The traditional kinship roles that Filipino migrant faithful play in their transnational family and community situations influence their giving (*pagbigay*) and helping (pag*tulong*) behavior. Filipino migrant faithful reminded me in the interviews that they give and help because they are elder brothers (*kuya*), elder sisters (*ate*), fathers (*ama*), mothers (*ina*), uncles (*tiyo*), aunts (*tiya*), grandfathers (*lolo*), and grandmothers (*lola*) who must care for siblings (*kapatid*), children (*anak*), nieces/nephews (*pamangkin*), and grandchildren (*apo*). In short, giving back and helping his or her place of origin mentally facilitates the building of a new home in the new country. Being physically away from the Philippines is not considered an acceptable excuse for not giving. Living in another country actually creates pressure on migrants to help, since there is the perception that they are financially well off. Giving is an obligation because of the perceived debt of gratitude to those who remain in the Philippines. The stress of having to earn for two homes is outweighed by the feeling of love and care they give and receive.

Fourth, the capacity of Filipino migrant faithful to render *bayanihan* and influence socioeconomics in homeland and hometown could be partly attributed to their Americanized Philippine churches (described in the previous chapter), and partly to their Americanized Filipino education, some of which is religion-based. As American colonials and neo-colonials, Filipino migrant faithful received the training, education, and language needed to find stable and well-paying jobs in the San Francisco marketplace. Thus, this second coming of Christianity to the United States through Filipino migrants brought about transnational economic benefits. The Americanized human capital of Filipino migrant faithful has allowed them to successfully earn, save, and contribute to two economies. This twin *bayanihan* arrangement is made possible through their median family household income, which, according to the 2000 census, is higher than all ethnicities (including Caucasians) in the United States.

Finally, I discovered that praying and sending funds to two homes influences more than the immediate families of migrants in the United States and the Philippines, since Filipino migrant faithful also provide financial aid to philanthropies, disaster relief, and social welfare projects benefiting the broader societies in their two homes. By giving to causes in two places, Filipino migrant faithful in effect subsidize the social and welfare funding of local and national governments, community-based organizations, and nongovernmental organizations, as well as corporate philanthropies, through giving back to social responsibility projects. Churches in the Philippines are also big beneficiaries of the long-distance *bayanihan* of migrants through their support of capital campaigns, beautification projects, reconstruction projects, and so forth.

The next two chapters move away from the unique transnational influence approach of Filipino migrant faithful to specific examples of how they Filipinize America's cultural and civic life through their adaptive spritual practices.

4

Gathering Souls with Food

The last time I attended *misa de gallo* [early morning novena masses] was December of 1989 in the Philippines. I remember that year quite vividly. The local parish back home would wake up the neighborhood not by ringing bells but by playing Christmas carols over loudspeakers attached to the facade. That year, I was able to attend all nine mornings, and after mass I would help my uncle prepare and sell *bibingka* (rice pudding cake) outside our house, which was down the street from the church. After this dawn novena mass, I remember that people would congregate outside of the church, socializing with one another, over warm *salabat* (ginger tea), eating our *bibingka* and sharing in the festive Christmas spirit that is distinct to Filipino culture. To me, at that time in my life, the church represented a place that housed many aspects of the Filipino people; it was a place where the social, religious, spiritual, and familial desire of the people could be fulfilled. The following May, my family moved to the United States.

—Dennis M., age twenty-four

In March 1565, or 400 years prior to Dennis's migrant crossing of the Pacific Ocean, a Spanish expedition under Miguel Lopez de Legazpi landed on the island of Bohol, accompanied by Augustinian friars—the first Catholic order to reach the Philippines. The expedition was under orders from the royal court in Madrid to complete the formal colonization, civilization, and Christianization of the land and people that Ferdinand Magellan had earlier claimed for King Philip of Spain. The fleet reached the archipelago after a long voyage across the treacherous Pacific Ocean, having left Mexico the previous November. After being at sea for more than 200 days, the Spaniards badly needed to replenish their food and other basic necessities. But their first attempts to make contact with the native inhabitants from the islands were met with suspicion and hostility. The Spaniards knew that their superior military force was no guarantee of positive results given the embarrassing defeat of Legazpi's predecessor, Magellan, at the hands of Lapu-Lapu, Mactan island's chieftain. However, Legazpi's luck changed once he landed on Bohol Island, as the people there, after some hesitation, welcomed the soldiers and priests and supplied them with fresh water, fruits, vegetables, livestock, and poultry. Legazpi was moved by the Boholanos' generosity and, instead of carrying out his royal orders, agreed to execute what the Catholic friars disdained as an uncivilized ritual—a blood compact (*sandugo*) with one of Bohol's rulers, Datu Sikatuna. The two men mixed their blood in the wine that they drank while feasting to cement a treaty of friendship between the Boholanos and the Spaniards. To the Boholanos, a blood compact creates a kinship relationship symbolizing respect and equality. Six years later, this *sandugo* was abrogated when the Spaniards made their move on Maynilad (later renamed Manila) to secure full Spanish rule over the islands. Unfortunately, the Boholanos' act of hospitality and friendship did not earn Filipinos the Spaniards' respect; instead, Filipinos endured more than three centuries of tyrannical Spanish rule and forced conversion to Roman Catholicism.

The historic rituals of trust and friendship between Sikatuna and Legazpi and the modern-day gathering of parishioners outside of Dennis's church illustrate how Filipino food has been used by the past and present inhabitants of the Philippines to build kinship ties and create bridges between "strangers" and themselves. The Spaniards were hungry, and the Boholanos gave them food. But hunger is not the only reason to eat. In Dennis's case, food provided an opportunity for his neighbors to gather, strengthen their friendships, and make new friends. To the Filipino migrant faithful in San Francisco, this is the essence of *kasamahan*: the ability to adapt and accommodate "others" toward building esprit de corps. The use of the term "adaptive" in this chapter and the next one refers to the Filipino migrant's "self" (*sarili*), and the ability of the self to accommodate, accept, and reconcile "others" (*kapwa*) in new environments, whether at the family, social group, or societal levels. Multiple individuals giving up self for others creates the spirit. Filipinos' adaptive spirit allows them to minimize acculturative stressors. I believe that the impact of such stressors is less on Filipinos than on other new migrants because the Filipino migrant is already broadly exposed to Asian, Hispanic, and American cultural experiences, which are an integral part of growing up

Filipino. For instance, in particular situations, a Filipino migrant might use his or her Spanish name, Chinese or Malay face, or American English, making it possible to feel at home in the Latino and Asian neighborhoods of San Francisco or in the cities of Madrid, Singapore, or New York. Growing up, a new arrival from the Philippines is exposed to eating Spanish paella, Chinese noodles, and American hamburgers.

Thus, the culturally varied communal history of Filipino migrants helps them negotiate the sights, sounds, smells, and tastes of San Francisco's culturally diverse environment. Filipino migrants share with other Asian migrant faithful many sociological traits influenced by spirituality, for example, taking care of one's parents and grandparents; showing love, respect, loyalty, and support to family; and carrying out sacrifices for the family. They have many religious icons and practices that are similar to those of Latino migrants. Most Filipino migrants are able to communicate comfortably in English and know many aspects of American culture. According to the U.S. and San Francisco Health Department studies, many new migrants succumb to acculturative stress and end up needing mental health interventions. Some turn to substance abuse and end up in community-based programs like the one run by the Asian American Recovery Services in San Francisco. But many Filipinos, I contend, cope by using their adaptive spirit or multiculturalized esprit de corps.

After a discussion of the conceptual intersections of food and religion in migration, this chapter will expound on the ways in which Filipinos' adaptive spirit impacts the preparation and presentation of food at *kasamahan*-building events. *Kasamahan* in two case studies—the Iglesia ni Cristo Church in Daly City and Saint Patrick's Catholic Church in downtown San Francisco—will illustrate how Filipino faithful accommodate and adapt to the many practical challenges of migrant life, such as locating work, as well as the emotional pitfalls, such as homesickness and loneliness.

Intersections of Food and Religion in Migration

The intersection of food and migration has been a popular topic of study in linguistics, business, sciences, health, and social policy. Migrant cuisines and the rituals of their preparation have manifested themselves in the rhetoric, metaphors, and tropes of literary writings, debate, and oratory (Edwards, Foley, and Diani 2000; White and Kokotsaki 2004).

Poets and writers have raised mainstream society's consciousness about the migrant experience, exposing personal struggles through bittersweet stories and narratives. For example, O'Brien (2003) discusses the hidden power of food metaphors, which have the capacity to "denigrate marginalized populations" through the use of dehumanizing discourse, particularly in the immigration restriction debate of the 1900s. Award-winning poet Aimee Nezhukumatathil (2003) pays tribute to her fascinating acculturation experience, including food preparation and consumption, while growing up American with Philippine and Indian parentage. Meanwhile, a number of Filipino migrant writers glorify the sensual and nostalgic qualities of food, such as the omnipresent, fragrant rice and mouth-watering *lechon* served at home, at church social halls, or at favorite Filipino *turo-turo* stands (no-frills eateries), for *merienda* (snack), *tanghalian* (lunch), or *hapunan* (dinner), whether or not there is a special occasion like a wedding, birth, baptism, or communion (Toribio 2002).

Food has always been a concern among public policy analysts who study migrant social welfare, inequality, and justice issues. Hence, a plethora of research exists on migrant welfare and food assistance programs, especially their effects on the elderly and poor in Canada and the United States (Fix and Zimmerman 1995; Fujiwara 1998; Husbands 1999; Binstock and Jean-Baptiste 1999). In the field of economics and business, articles have emerged on the phenomenon of migrant ownership of small to medium-sized businesses (mostly in the restaurant, supermarket, and food distribution sectors), as well as the growing impact of immigration upon domestic and international business and the food industry (Smart 2004; Christian 2004; Dalla, Ellis, and Cramer 2005).

But what about the intersections of migration, religion, and food, particularly among Asian ethnic communities? Early studies examining the significance of food to faith in North America did not focus on the ethnicity or immigration status of congregational populations (see, for instance, Nieman et al. 1989). More than a decade ago, a special thematic issue of the *Journal of the American Academy of Religion* was devoted to food and religion. Topics ranged from cannibalism and Aztec rituals (Carrasco 1995) to fasting among Sufis (Hoffman 1995). The articles covered a broad geographic area, from Africa to Asia. However, the journal issue did not emphasize America's diverse migrant populations, their religions, or their foods. Similarly, in later studies of migrant groups in the United States, Sack (2000) focused only on mainstream

European American Protestant faiths and their food, while Diner (2001) concentrated on Catholic Italian and Irish as well as Jewish foodways.

Thereafter, research interests took a turn, with more migration scholars factoring in gender, ethnicity, and age as intervening variables to food and acculturation, especially among North America's new Asian, European, African, and Latin American migrants. However, physical health seems to have overshadowed spiritual well-being as a major emphasis. Nutritionists, medical researchers, and health specialists were especially interested in food and migration themes. A genre of studies has pointed out that many new migrants, in an attempt to assimilate into mainstream American culture, make significant changes in their dietary practices by trading in their traditional and indigenous foods for Western or North American ingredients and dishes. However, to cope with their acculturative stress, many others have instead opted to maintain their traditional dietary norms. A study of South Asian migrant women who had lived in Canada for less than five years identified a lack of access to indigenous food as a major stressor (Ahmad et al. 2004). Other studies argued that both approaches to dietary adjustments tend to predispose migrants to certain health risks, for example, cancer, diabetes, and cardiovascular diseases, as their diets are generally high in fat and cholesterol and low in fiber (Whittemore et al. 1996; Wei and Read 1996; Pan et al. 1999; Satia-Abouta et al. 2002; Wu, Pike, and Wan 2002; Lu and Cason 2004).

Across the Atlantic, two studies went beyond the diet and nutrition emphases of health scholars by adding faith-based practices and attitudes to migration research. In a study of British Bangladeshis, Chowdhury, Helman, and Greenhalgh (2000) argued that dietary advice by health professionals to migrant patients who see them should take into consideration religious restrictions, ethnic customs, and the varying cultural meanings of food. This point was extended further by another British study, this time of Kashmiri migrants with diabetes in Leeds, regarding their fatalistic attitude toward their deteriorating health condition (Naeem 2003). Subjects of this study were asked why they chose to "enjoy life and leave the rest to Allah" instead of improving their dysfunctional diets.

A number of anthropologists, sociologists, and social scientists studying migrant communities have highlighted the role of ethnic food in creating "social ties that bind" (Lee 1991; Mendoza and Shankar 2003). For example, Poe noted that in the early twentieth century, Catholic Italians who immigrated to the United States overcame their regional diversity by developing an amalgamation of tastes and culinary customs into what eventually became known as "Italian-American food" (2001). And in one of the first studies to focus on the relationship of food to faith among U.S. immigrants, Shankar and Balgopal similarly observed that early Indian Muslim and Sikh migrants in Northern California were able to acculturate by preserving their ethnic identities through food and religion (2001). In another study of Asian migrants, Bhugra et al. (2004) discussed acculturation and key concepts of cultural identity such as religion, attitudes toward the family, leisure activities, rites of passage, food, and language.

Owing to their scientific orientation, a majority of the food and migration studies found in the literature utilized quantitative approaches, such as correlational analyses. Although currently growing in number, few studies dealt previously with the role of food and spirituality in Asian American diasporas. The few that have covered Asian Americans concentrated mostly on Chinese and Indian migrants. Filipino migrants were the subjects of studies by Wu, Pike, and Wan (2002) but were only marginally referred to in others. Hence, there is a lack of scholarly research that intimately explores the intersections of faith, food, and migration, particularly within the Filipino *kasamahan* experience in the United States. This chapter seeks to fill this gap.

Celebrating Santacruzan in May and Adapting the Fourth of July

Filipino migrants, through their churches and other membership organizations, connect with one another through a variety of traditional Filipino *kasamahan* events. A main feature at these cultural affairs is the bountiful presentation of a unique blend of Spanish-, Chinese-, Malay-, and American-influenced Filipino fare. During the era of Spanish rule, Catholic festivals and fiestas were encouraged for religious, pacification, and colonization purposes. In modern times, these traditional Catholic festivals have blended with local Filipino beliefs, rituals, and practices, resulting in events with a distinctly Philippine flavor—Filipino folk Catholicism. Philippine fiestas are a kaleidoscope of colors, fireworks, games, eating, drinking, dancing, gambling, and beauty contests. Nearly every day of the year, there is some sort of religious festival being celebrated in a village, a town, a city, or a province in the Philippines. Given the more than 300,000 Filipinos in the San Francisco Bay Area, it should come as no surprise that there is always a gathering or celebration somewhere.

TABLE 4.1
Important Iglesia ni Cristo Gatherings

Holy Supper: The most important annual ritual. On a centrally designated Sunday in March or April, the membership of the church is invited to renew their faith through rituals that remind the brethren of Jesus Christ's sacrifices for humankind. This is the only time of the year when the church offers communion.

Anniversary *Pasalamat* (Thanksgiving): The INC was formally registered with the Philippine government on July 27, 1914. Each year the church marks this important event with a special worship service and other celebratory activities, such as choral performances.

End-of-the-year *Pasalamat*: On a designated Sunday in December locales give thanks to God for the blessings of the past year and mark the end of another fiscal cycle by collecting donations from their members.

Oath-taking ceremony: At the beginning of the calendar year, INC districts throughout the world conduct a special worship service for church officers that includes an oath-taking ceremony. En masse, they swear to uphold their official duties.

Traditional gatherings for Filipino migrant faithful, in general, happen when there is a birthday or an anniversary in the family, at church, or at one of their many Filipino associations. *Kasamahan* gatherings for baptisms, confirmations, and weddings are also common, except when the participants' religious affiliation prohibits it. Most Filipino migrant Catholic families and their churches have special gatherings during Christmas, New Year, Thanksgiving, the Fourth of July, and Easter. Other Filipino Independent churches, like the Iglesia ni Cristo, oppose celebrating Christian holidays that cannot be supported biblically by specific dates. For example, Christmas and Easter, important holidays in most Christian traditions, are not celebrated by the Iglesia ni Cristo because their dates were fixed by the Catholic Church rather than the Bible. Alternatively, the Iglesia ni Cristo's gatherings and celebrations coincide with the rhythms of the Roman calendar and important events in the church's history. Besides monthly open houses (called Grand Evangelical Missions, or GEMs), described in the case study later in this chapter, the Iglesia ni Cristo has a number of important *kasamahan*-enhancing annual gatherings described in table 4.1. These formal events are generally followed by bountiful spreads of Filipino and American food, which gives participants an opportunity to socialize informally.

In the Filipino Catholic tradition, many events provide opportunities to cook and eat special foods; some of these are feasts and festivals that have been imported by Filipino migrants to the San Francisco Bay Area. Some local Filipino Catholics celebrate the Feast of the Black Nazarene, honoring the hundred-year-old statue of the miraculous "dark-colored Christ." True to their regional loyalties, migrants from the province of Aklan have developed a local Ati-Atihan festival, which is a carnival-like celebration in honor of the infant Jesus, Aklan's patron saint. Filipino migrants from Marinduque host the Moriones festival during Lent, while those from Sariaya, Tayabas, and Lucban in Quezon Province relive the Pahiyas festival in honor of San Isidro, the patron saint of farmers. Commemorations of these religious events are not necessarily held in religious spaces such as a church; in the Philippines, many of these events occur as sprawling street festivals. Although some similarly take place in the streets of San Francisco—such as the annual Christmas Lantern (Parol) Stroll—others have been reconfigured for parks and other small areas such as hotel ballrooms, convention centers, restaurants, and bars.

San Francisco is host to several major, nonreligious Filipino American cultural events at which food from all regions of the Philipines is a significant component. The largest of these is Pistahan, a weeklong festival, which has been celebrated annually since 1994 on the grounds of Yerba Buena Gardens in front of Saint Patrick's Church. Traditionally, a parade down historic Market Street kicks off the festivities. Another major event is Fiesta Filipina, which caps the Philippine Independence Day celebration in June every year. This weekend event takes place at the Civic Center in front of San Francisco's city hall and features dancing, singing, comedy, cultural shows, and food festivals, as well as arts and crafts. And every December, the Parol Stroll—part of a larger lantern festival commemorating the star of Bethlehem which led the three kings to the manger—travels down busy Mission Street.

The presentation of Filipino cultural events at San Francisco public schools also contributes to *kasamahan*. For example, Bessie Carmichael Elementary School hosts a culture-focused Santacruzan in May. Bicolanos from San Francisco have rented boats for the fluvial Peñafrancia festival, a devotion to the miraculous image of Nuestra Señora de Peñafrancia. Not to be outdone, the Cebuanos of the Bay Area host the Sinulog, a dance ritual in honor of the miraculous image of the Santo Niño, which is reputed to be the oldest festival in the Philippines. The Catholic liturgical calendar maps out many of the Filipino religio-cultural activities. For instance, the Salubong is practiced at Easter; the Pabasa, at Lent; the Simbang Gabi novena, during Advent; and the Black Nazarene and Santo Niño festivities during the Roman Catholic Church's Ordinary Time.

Serving Both Crunchy Lechon and Roasted Turkey

These days, on dining tables in the Philippines, traditional American fare such as Boston clam chowder, French fries, baked potato, and turkey roast are relished side by side with Filipinized Spanish *paella, afritada, adobo,* and *caldereta,* as well as *siomai, pansit,* and *lumpia,* which are all derived from Chinese cuisine. On the streets of Manila, the legacy of Americanization is manifested through the presence of KFC, Pizza Hut, A&W, Dunkin Donuts, Burger King, Krispy Kreme, Seattle's Best, Bubba Gump's, and Starbucks franchises, while Hispanicization survives through Guernica's, Ilustrado, Alba's, Casa Armas, and Mario's restaurants. Chinese-influenced food flourishes through Lingnam, Chowking, Kowloon House, Peking Palace, Aberdeen Court, and Leuk Yuen.

The return of Christianity to America has accompanied a return of American dishes in Filipinized form. Philippine fast-food franchises Jollibee and Max's have brought Filipinized hamburgers and fried chicken—signature American dishes imported to the Philippines decades earlier—back to the United States for Filipino American consumers. Local franchises of Jollibee, which far surpass McDonald's in the Philippines' hamburger market, also serve "Fried Chicken Joy" and "Jolly Hotdog." Easy transnational movement has made these bicultural fast-food dishes available in both the United States and the Philippines, and at many Filipino social gatherings in both places. Many other popular Philippine-based restaurants, including Goldilocks, Aristocrat, Lingnam, and Red Ribbon, have branches all around the San Francisco Bay Area that provide catering services that are perfect for social gatherings and church events. New restaurants established by migrant families, such as Patio Filipino, Tribu Grill, Alidos, Ongpin, Kuyas, Palencia, and Polengs, are within easy reach of churches and residences. The Filipino demand for catering services has also increased the number of Filipino entrepreneurs in the market, particularly home-based ones. They can purchase ingredients for Philippine dishes from Manila Oriental, Island Pacific, Pacific Super, Ranch 99, or any Asian/ Oriental supermarket. Some of them, like UFC vinegar or Jufran banana ketchup, are even found at the "international aisles" of Lucky or Safeway. Proof of the Filipino migrants' adaptive culinary spirit is their use of halibut ends and pieces (as a substitute for *bangus* or Philippine milk fish) mixed with spinach and lemon juice (as a substitute

Figure 4.1. Jollibee, beside the Moscone Convention Center, is the place to grab an American-style hamburger with pansit palabok (rice noodles with a bright orange sauce) and buko pandan (coconut tapioca) drink during a conference break or after a church service. Photo credit: Jay Gonzalez

for *kangkong* and *sampalok*) for their fish *sinigang* when they have only mainstream supermarkets in their neighborhood.

Among the Filipino religious groups we observed, communal meals were much like those one typically finds at similar gatherings in the Philippines. Regional dishes and those made with specialty ingredients—cuts of meat, or produce, for example, not found in mainstream supermarkets—were the most prized. These meals generally began with appetizers known as *pulutan*, which include a variety of dishes such as *chicharon* (pork crackling), *dilis* (dried fish), *pusit* (squid), and *kinilaw* (raw fish marinated in vinegar). Filipino dishes are often accompanied by vinegar with *sili* (hot chili peppers) or soy sauce mixed with *kalamansi* (small lemon or lime); these sauces go with fried foods, such as chicken or fish. The appetizers we sampled at church gatherings were followed by many indigenous and Chinese-, Malay-, Indian-, American-, and/or Spanish-influenced entrées. Sometimes referred to as the Filipino national dish, *adobo* (which can be either pork or chicken) was commonly found at gatherings in the pastors' or church members' homes.

I had one of the best *tinola*, a hearty chicken soup containing green papayas, ginger, and peppercorns, for dinner at the home of a UMC member after Bible study. Pork and shrimp *sinigang* (sour soup) and beef *nilaga* (stew) were mainstays before rosary sessions or INC GEMs. Special feasts, including the monsignor's birthday or Santo Niño's feast day, would not be complete without a *lechon* (suckling pig), which is stuffed with tamarind leaves and roasted over coals until the skin is crispy and the meat is tender.

Another favorite at Filipino spiritual gatherings was *lumpia* (egg roll), prepared as either *lumpiang sariwa* (fresh spring roll) or *lumpiang shanghai* (fried spring roll). The *lumpia* filling generally consists of julienned heart of palm sautéed with pork and shrimp; the finished *lumpia* is served with garlic and soy sauce. *Kare-kare*, another all-time favorite among the religious communities we observed, consists of oxtail, ox knuckles, and tripe, stewed with vegetables in peanut sauce and served with *bagoong* (fish paste). Congregational picnics also commonly featured Filipino barbeque dishes of pork, chicken, fish, and/or prawns marinated with soy sauce, lime, and garlic. For dessert or *merienda* (snack) after Bible sessions, *halo-halo* (literally, "mix-mix"), might be served to help in the absorption of the spiritual lessons. *Halo-halo* is a sundae-like concoction of fruits and sweet vegetables, such as jackfruits, yam, corn, beans, and young coconut, served over crushed ice and milk and topped with a scoop of ice cream. Rather than the standard American ice cream flavors chocolate, vanilla, and strawberry, Filipino ice cream comes in a variety of tropical flavors such as *langka* (jackfruit), *ube* (yam), mango, and coconut. Another popular Filipino dessert is *bibingka*, a sweet rice-based cake flavored with *gata* (coconut milk) and often topped with *itlog na maalat* (salted eggs). We concluded that prayer and these desserts afterward are a perfect combination.

Filipino foods—presented at church and community events alongside popular American dishes like spaghetti with meatballs, fried chicken, and vegetable salads—represented a popular cuisine that is essentially an amalgam of several different foodways. For the migrant faithful that we met, food served as a medium for the expression and celebration of Philippine culture and a means for establishing a sense of "home" with fellow church members in the Bay Area. Many church members indicated that they look forward to spiritual and social gatherings as an excuse to eat and share Filipino food they miss; some had even become known as specialists in the preparation of certain dishes. Secret recipes are shared. Bible sessions, meditations, mass services, and other church events became instant parties once food was introduced. As mentioned earlier, ingredients used to replicate dishes from the Philippines are readily available from Filipino stores, Chinatown shops, and Asian groceries. Some are even found in mainstream San Francisco supermarkets, like Safeway or Lucky, especially where there are large Filipino populations.

Reconciliation of Multiple Cultures and Cuisines

The two San Francisco case studies in this section illustrate how *kasamahan* (bonding Filipinization) is performed in the selection, preparation, sharing, and consumption of a "culinary lingua franca," which is composed of American and Filipino cuisines and their many component foodways. These cases also describe the congregational or individual ties that are strengthened through food and feasting.

Case Study 1: Conversion through Missionary *Mechado*

In largely Filipino Daly City, the proliferation of businesses focused on the preparation and consumption of Filipino food is an indicator of the size and scope of this community. Numerous Filipino restaurants have established businesses in town, and several Filipino and Asian supermarkets also carry everything needed to create a Filipino meal, from essential ingredients to prepared foods.

In this American community in which Filipinos have become the majority, the Philippine-based Iglesia ni Cristo has also staked its claim. An unassuming building near Serramonte Mall serves as home base to the Daly City locale of the INC, where close to 1,000 brethren attend services. More than 50 percent of the brethren who belong to the Daly City locale are first-generation Filipino migrants. At GEMs—monthly events designed to introduce visitors to the church's doctrines and membership—the church welcomes newcomers with open arms and overflowing plates, balancing the serious-minded Bible lessons with more lighthearted fellowship. The INC's Daly City locale has made effective social connections over food that have facilitated the growth of its membership. Notably, while most prospective members are first- or second-generation Filipinos, some are not. Thus, food might also be seen as a medium for introducing non-Filipinos to Philippine culture—one might say that it helps to Filipinize America. The events of one particular GEM that we attended typify the way in which Filipino food functions as a social medium within the church.

On this occasion, the GEM began as usual, in the chapel, with a lesson about the INC's belief system. The lesson was taught through selected readings from the Bible and explanations by the ministers, but also through the disciplined model of behavior that is embedded in the highly structured organization of people and things in the room. Men and women sat on separate sides of the room and were guided to their places by gender-appropriate attendants. Once inside the chapel, the noise level dropped. There was no conversation but, instead, stillness and silence as we awaited the start of the lesson. Male and female choir members sat separately and quietly, moving in unison when movement was called for.

The seriousness and formality of the lesson was countered by the informality of the luncheon that followed. At the end of the lesson, the church invited its visitors down the hall to a casual buffet lunch. Churchgoers streamed out of the worship area and into the hallway. By the time they reached the social hall, where a veritable feast had been laid out, the quiet crowd had turned animated and noisy. Loud talk and laughter filled the room, where several rectangular folding tables placed end to end formed a vast buffet of restaurant-purchased and homemade foods. Large aluminum trays piled high with *pansit bihon* (Chinese noodles), *pritong manok* (fried chicken), and Filipino-style spaghetti from local restaurants crowded alongside homemade dishes in smaller, individualized containers. Filipino *pinakbet* (bitter gourd stew), Spanish-influenced *mechado* (beef stew), Malay-Indian influenced *kare-kare* (oxtail stew), and other favorite dishes from various Philippine towns and provinces spoke of both the congregation's geographic diversity and its love of food.

As we entered the social hall, our hosts sprang into action like a well-rehearsed team, staking out a table and enough metal folding chairs for each member of our group. One woman sat at the table and reserved seats with our purses and jackets, while the rest of us did battle with the crowds at the well-stocked buffet. We made our way to the food tables and scooped a little bit of rice, *pinakbet*, and *pansit* onto our plates. One of our companions urged us to try some of the other, home-cooked dishes. "This is *bopis*—it's my favorite! You've got to taste it!" she insisted, passing a serving spoon. Made with pork heart, lungs, and other innards, *bopis* is an acquired taste and is thus not commonly found at mass gatherings like this one. The rarity of this dish makes it all the more appealing, however, since its taste and smell have a singular link to the Philippines. Our attention was also directed to a paper plate laden with bits of sweetened yam. We noticed that our companion's plate was heaped in layers, with several fried sardines perched atop a generous pile of rice, noodles, and vegetables. Back at our table, we ate and talked about food: recipes, condiments, and the best local sources for Filipino ingredients, but also the memories that Filipino food conjured about "home." Speaking in Tagalog, the church members and guests reminisced about food and life and the Philippines. Here, the church's hospitality created a comfortable and inviting environment for Filipino immigrants hungry for familiar sounds, smells, and tastes. Based on the locale's rapidly growing membership, these sensory enticements seem to be effective promotional tools.

Case Study 2: *Sotanghon* for the Body and Soul

For the 90,000 Filipino Catholics in the vast Archdiocese of San Francisco, Saint Patrick's on downtown Mission Street is the closest thing to a Philippine church on American soil. It is the center of the Filipino *poblacion* in another place that has become a veritable province of the Philippines. As I discussed previously, the Catholic Church has seen a sharp decline in participation over the past few decades. However, its membership is being resuscitated by Filipinos and others from former missionary outposts—in the United States, one might say that the colonized have effectively become colonizers. Saint Patrick's exemplifies this shifting power dynamic. Formerly an Irish American parish, the church has become a place where Bay Area Filipino migrants participate in religious and social traditions transported from their motherland.

Saint Patrick's is one of the few places where Filipino Catholics can not only attend devotions particular to the Philippines, such as the Simbang Gabi, the early-morning masses celebrated during Christmas season, but also take part in the communal meals that follow. In most instances, religious ceremonies are preludes to hospitality. The meals, regardless of the occasion, reflect Filipino traditions adapted to the current social realities of many Filipino migrants in the South of Market area. Just like town fiestas in the Philippines, certain individuals or parish groups sponsor the meals. This is the traditional aspect; that is, the donors serve as the *hermano mayore* (grand sponsor) of the event. However, given the low incomes of most parishioners, the meals are usually modest; familiar dishes such as *pansit* or *lumpia* are served. These dishes are made with inexpensive ingredients that can feed many without straining the budget. In the case of the Simbang Gabi breakfasts we attended, the sponsors always made sure that there was food that would provide both physical and emotional comfort—people were served *champorado* (chocolate rice porridge), *arroz caldo* (chicken rice porridge), and *sotanghon* (glass noodle chicken soup) on various occasions, usually accompanied by American wheat bread, hot dogs, bagels and cream cheese, together with *pan de sal* (rolls). There was even *lechon* (roasted pig) on one of the mornings, which literally arrived at the very last minute—and this donated treat was a pleasant surprise for everyone.

Regardless of the fare, people were always served graciously, and the parish volunteers who helped serve always had a kind word to give. For those who came alone and would leave alone, this meal would be a source of comfort that went beyond physical satisfaction. Food was a way for the church to open its arms to its entire membership, especially the needy. Again, like the *hermano mayor*, the volunteers made sure everyone was able to partake of the meal, and the generosity of the donors ensured there was more than enough to go around. The parish took the time to acknowledge the sponsors and the donors, and the meals were greatly appreciated by the people who partook of the hospitality.

The Simbang Gabi breakfasts' aim of fostering a sense of community is quite apparent, given the communal setting and the socialization that goes on during the meal. However, it can also be read as a means of remembering not only one's identity as a Catholic but also one's identity as a Filipino. Much like the Eucharist is the most sacred element of Catholic worship—the act that affirms unity with the mystical body of Christ—these after-mass meals affirm unity with the local community of Filipinos, a secular version of communion within the context of tradition. To partake in the meal indicates an acceptance of tradition and a willingness to see it continue for years to come—to remember and to act accordingly.

But the significance of these meals reaches beyond church walls. The parishioners of Saint Patrick's are not conscious of this, but to celebrate Filipino traditions and to share them with the outside community goes beyond the mere notion of national pride. As we mentioned earlier, hospitality happens at home, and to celebrate Simbang Gabi—one of the most-loved religious traditions among Filipino Catholics—outside of the

Philippines indicates a desire to make their present surroundings home. The Filipinos of Saint Patrick's do not just want to celebrate Christmas— they want to celebrate their Christmas as they did back in their old home and share it with their new neighbors in their new home. By appropriating what was formerly borrowed space and making it a place where transplanted *kababayan* can experience a sense of continuity with what they left behind, the Filipinos of Saint Patrick's have created a haven within church walls and made the parish an informal center of cultural promotion and preservation.

From the presence of an *hermano mayor* to the festivities and the food, it is clear that Saint Patrick's has been handed off by one group of migrants to another. The former Irish American church has become one of the community centers of the Filipino *barangay* in San Francisco.

Summary and Conclusion

On July 23, 1901, close to nine decades before Dennis M. began his migrant journey, more than 500 American Protestant and Catholic schoolteachers and missionaries boarded the USS *Thomas* and left Pier 12 of San Francisco laden with ingredients and provisions not only to consume on their long voyage but also to help them prepare American meals to share in the Philippines. James Barry, one of the teachers, chronicled these food items, which included the following:

> Flour 58,700 pounds; salt pork and salt beef 8,000 pounds; hard bread 11,000 pounds; white beans 2,100 pounds; split peas 2,600 pounds; potatoes 33,100 pounds; onions 8,900 pounds; molasses and syrup 163 gallons; vinegar 300 gallons; cooking salt 3,300 pounds; assorted crackers 4,550 pounds; lima and kidney beans 1,600 pounds; corn meal 1,250 pounds; Italian pastas 1,700 pounds; butter 6,550 pounds; cheese 2,250 pounds; eggs 60,000; condensed milk 10,730 cans; fresh milk 240 gallons; frozen oysters 400 cans; frozen clams 50 gallons; pickled fish (assorted) 4,260 pounds; smoked fish 300 pounds; canned fish (assorted) 4,600 cans; fresh beef 52,000 pounds; fresh mutton 5,200 pounds; fresh pork 4,500 pounds; fresh lamb 1,300 pounds; calves' brains 200 pounds; calves' heads and feet 60 sets; veal 2,500 pounds; beef kidneys 200 pieces; calves' liver 350 pieces; sweetbreads 200 pounds; tripe 900 pounds; fresh sausages 1,200 pounds; smoked tongue 240 pieces; corned pork 700 pounds. (Ocampo 2004)

Were all these American ingredients intended to help the Thomasites promote their American Christianity? Or did these American migrants to the Philippines use these ingredients to facilitate the bonding of two cultures? The following are a number of lessons from this chapter on bonding Filipinization (*kasamahan*) and how it helps Filipinos make sense of the complexities that they face in their new homeland.

First, based on my extensive literature search, there is a lack of attention in the migration literature to the intersections of faith and food. These intersections have always been a popular topic of study in linguistics, business, sciences, health, and social policy, but not in tandem with religion or spirituality. Hence, this chapter hopes to encourage more scholarly attention into this neglected area, particularly as related to the building and rebuilding of *kasamahan* with the help of adaptive spritual practices, food, and festivals to help reconcile the many complexities of a migrant's life. It helps unleash the spirit of selflessness and civic involvement.

Second, for the churches or congregations described in this chapter, blending together Filipino and American foods is important to the propagation and reinforcement of faith-based Filipino values. Once within Filipinized churches, food helps build *kasamahan*. Congregation members, especially the young, the new, and the non-Filipino, see how these values are practiced not only in church but also at home, and at many family and community events that involve feasting.

Third, the supply of tasty Filipino food and ingredients has been impacted by Filipinized churches, which provide numerous occasions for the comunal preparation and sharing of food. Those who do not have the time to prepare a dish for church meetings can easily order and pick up entrées and desserts from American-grown Filipino restaurants that serve everything from *lechon* to *paella*. If they are craving it and need it fast, churchgoers can also opt to get their food from any of a number of Philippine franchises now in the San Francisco Bay Area. Parishioners of Saint Patrick's always have a hard time choosing between distant Jollibee and nearby Beard Papas. If they have the time and want to show off their culinary skills, they can simply get the ingredients from any one of several local Filipino or Asian supermarkets—or the ethnic food section of most mainstream grocery stores—and cook with the help of other church members.

Finally, reconciling Filipino and American cultures using food and fiestas is an important component of building church membership and, thereafter, creating *kasamahan* connections and networks. The cases of the Iglesia ni Cristo's Grand Evangelical Mission and Saint Patrick's Catholic Church's Simbang Gabi illustrate the extent to which Filipinos believe that Filipino food is a necessary social lubricant, the *grasa* (grease) that (perhaps not-so-miraculously) facilitates friendly conversation and connection, which could in turn become reasons why attendees continue going to a particular church or explore new spiritual avenues.

Thus, the small, white *puto* is actually more than just the sum of its ingredients. Served under the right circumstances, a seemingly innocuous rice cake can actually be a potent device for bonding together the complicated pieces of a Filipino migrant's life. In the San Francisco Bay Area, Filipino churches use *puto* and other Filipino foods not only to re-create familiar rituals and festivities but also to convert their new environments to their liking. So, for all its familiar qualities, food actually has hidden powers that deserve a closer look.

This chapter has shown that *kasamahan* in the form of culinary hospitality and adaptability has allowed Filipino migrant faithful to connect with American kindred spirits. Filipino Americans have infused their feasts, festivals, rituals, and food not just into America's religious spaces but also its secular spaces. The next chapter moves away from describing how Filipino migrant faithful transform their food-laced *kasamahan* into more activist *bayanihan*.

5

Converting Bowling
to Civic Involvement

Memorial Day is a cherished American holiday, made even more significant to many by the tragic events of 9/11 and the War on Terror. It is a special day for remembering war heroes and veterans but is equally popular as a day for travel and recreation with family and friends. On one recent Memorial Day, our research team visited Classic Bowl in Daly City, one of the largest bowling centers in the San Francisco Bay Area. On this day, all sixty lanes were occupied by just one group—the Iglesia ni Cristo (INC), one of the largest Filipino independent churches. Many members of the church's Daly City locale bowl together every week, and sometimes even twice a week. Brethren from throughout the Northern California district had been gathering to bowl at annual tournaments like this one since the 1970s. The event is a mix of serious athletic competition and lighthearted partying. Bowling teams donned matching shirts embroidered with the names of their church locales. Behind them, the room teemed with crowds of onlookers—spouses, children, and friends, who used the tournament as an opportunity to visit with INC members from other locales. Gathered around tables or seated on the floor, they shared homemade foods and traded the latest *balita* (news), *kwento* (stories), and *chismis* (gossip). A few months after this Memorial Day bowling event, a large group of young and old Iglesia ni Cristo members from the Daly City locale, in matching INC T-shirts, crossed the San Francisco Bay Bridge to volunteer at a cleanup event in Oakland. Oakland mayor Jerry Brown greeted and thanked the enthusiastic group at a short ceremony on Jack London Square before its members dispersed to area neighborhoods to sweep and pick up trash. The Daly City locale has provided large numbers of volunteers for similar street cleanup events when called upon by political leaders in Daly City, Livermore, Alameda, and many other San Francisco Bay Area cities.

More than an impressive display of faithful Filipino migrants' cohesion and civic involvement, however, I believe this gathering illustrates a compelling exception to the claims made by Harvard political science professor Robert Putnam (2000) in his much heralded book, *Bowling Alone: The Collapse and Revival of American Community*. Putnam's central thesis is that civic engagement and social connectedness have declined in the United States over the past several decades, a theme he expands globally in *Democracies in Flux: The Evolution of Social Capital in Contemporary Society* (2004). In this text, he and a number of colleagues argue that this dire situation is endemic in a number of Western countries. Consequently, the sustained success of democratic societies has been compromised. However, I contend that segments of the American population—in this case, Filipino migrants to the United States—are actually increasing their participation in organized *kasamahan* activities, particularly through their churches.

With this in mind, in this chapter, I provide evidence from our San Francisco area studies disputing the premise of Putnam's *Bowling Alone*—that social capital, especially the bridging variety, has declined all over the United States. Hence, I begin this chapter with the arguments behind the scholarly exchanges between Putnam, his allies and their many skeptics, and the role of Filipino faithful in San Francisco. I then build on this discussion with my own evidence to the contrary, which illustrates how the adaptive *bayanihan* spirit of Filipino migrant faithful, mediated through their San Francisco churches, allows them to balance competing social and political responsibilities in their old and new homes. Thereafter, I use two case studies to see more clearly how bridging Filipinization is cultivated at Saint Patrick's Catholic Church in San Francisco and the Iglesia ni Cristo in Daly City for the betterment of American and Philippine communities.

Social Capital and Churches

Although Putnam is not the first to "capitalize" human networks, connections, norms, and religion, his neo-Tocquevillian discussions of social capital and its significant decline in America have certainly become a centerpiece of long-standing scholarly debates. As a matter of fact, Putnam's assertion, which first appeared in a 1995 issue of the *Journal of Democ-*

racy, immediately spawned a plethora of literature across scholarly disciplines and global geographies (see Halpern 1999; Kolankiewicz 1996; Norton, Latham, and Sturgess 1997; Schuller 1997; Whiteley 1999). Special issues of leading publications, including the *Journal of International Development*, *American Behavioral Scientist*, and *American Prospect*, have scrutinized Putnam's argument, operational definition, and empirical evidence. Two edited volumes—one originating from top academics in the United States (Edwards, Foley, and Diani 2001) and the other from the United Kingdom (Baron, Field, and Schuller 2000)—illustrate the range of scholarly exchanges. Just as loyal followers of Putnam's thesis have multiplied, so have his detractors (e.g., Edwards and Foley 1997, 1998; Foley and Edwards 1999; Portes 1995, 1998; Portes and Landolt 2002; Putzell 1997). Some criticize its heavy reliance on the quantification of associational memberships. Others charge that he overemphasizes his measurements of the social connections and disconnections of a society and does not account for the independent, causal role of culture.

Putnam contends that an intensification of social networks increases the norms of reciprocity and trustworthiness that glue a society together. "Civic virtue," Putnam adds, "is most powerful when embedded in a dense network of reciprocal social relations. A society of many virtuous but isolated individuals is not necessarily rich in social capital" (2000, 19). He further notes that churches and other religious organizations have played unique roles as incubators of civic virtue in the United States (65–79). However, social capital also comes in two forms, both of which are necessary for a healthy society. On the one hand, there is *"bonding* social capital," which refers to the inward-focused connections of a social group. These connections create strong in-group loyalty that needs to be balanced by *"bridging* social capital"—the outward-looking social ties that "encompass people across diverse social cleavages" (22–23). Warner (2000) says that religious groups create their identities by segregating themselves from other groups but notes that the act of self-definition entails bridging activity. In defining their identities, religious groups develop rhetorics that match and refute those of other groups; Bramadat (2000, 59–68) calls these *fortress* and *bridging* rhetorics.

It is no secret that a primary source of America's social and cultural capital is its more than 100,000 churches, mosques, temples, synagogues, and other places of worship. Savvy politicians demonstrate the power of this capital by tapping churches and other religious organizations during elections. For those seeking office, having a charismatic preacher as a close friend can be as good as having solid party support. In doing so, they are actually participating in an old American tradition. Since the early days of nationhood, America's religious organizations have been breeding grounds of volunteerism, philanthropy, and civic behavior (Greeley 1997). They are not only places of worship but also spaces for cultivating civic engagement and for political recruitment, incorporation, co-optation, and empowerment (Verba, Schlozman, and Brady 1997). But even this enduring institution, according to Putnam, has not been spared serious decline in terms of membership and related activities. He claims that technological developments of communication, and recreation, as well as changing attitudes toward politics and the role of women, are partly to blame for this trend. Although many thought that the spiritual and patriotic fervor following the September 11 tragedy would start a sustainable renaissance of faith- and church-based volunteerism, recent controversies, such as the many allegations of sexual abuse by Catholic priests, have virtually wiped out any gains (see *Boston Globe* 2003; Gibson 2003). The aftershocks of these disturbing revelations will probably be felt for a long time, further eroding memberships, contributions, patronage, and networking within religious organizations.

In *Bowling Alone*, Putnam contends that, while the number of bowlers has increased 10 percent over the past thirty years, league bowling is down 40 percent. Given this decline in organized recreational activity, it is not surprising that far fewer Americans are affiliated with other types of organizations, namely, political, civic, and religious groups. He adds that this is particularly the case among American-born descendants of European migrants in the twentieth century. Even black churches, once launching pads of African American empowerment, have witnessed a noticeable thinning of their congregations. As a result, many faith-based spaces and networks of churches, schools, and social services have been abandoned. Memberships have also been consolidated for the sake of maintaining administrative and operational costs.

This chapter joins a number of sociological studies of American churches (particularly African American churches) that argue that not all secular and spiritual gathering places in American communities are emptying (see Lincoln and Mamiya 2003; Roozen and Nieman 2005). On the contrary, a number of them have been revitalized, are full (or even expanding), and contribute to community-organizing and American democratization efforts (Jacobsen 2001; Warren 2001). However, a number of these churches may no longer be filled with the European Americans or even African Americans who have historically constituted their memberships. Instead, migrants from places considered "new," including East and Southeast Asia, Latin America, the Caribbean, and the Middle East, have replenished these faith-based institutions and their production of social and cultural capital, particularly in America's gateway cities (Carnes and Yang 2004; Jeung 2004; Min and Kim 2002; Warner 2000; Warner and Wittner 1998; Yoo 1999). As I have elucidated in the previous chapters, many San Francisco churches have become sites for Filipinos to bond with each other while simultaneously orienting themselves toward bridges with the non-Filipino, non-Asian world. This is because the church is a habitus for the renewal, preservation, and transmission of cultural capital in the forms of community activities, traditions, rituals, family values, and work ethics.

In the preceding chapters, I described the arrival of Filipinos in large numbers after 1965, when just as many San Francisco religious institutions were on the decline. By the late 1960s, many older Catholic, Protestant, Independent, and indigenous churches in the area had experienced a significant drop in active memberships and hence financial contributions. Downtown churches started to close at an alarming rate as people left the city for a host of reasons, including commercialization, gentrification, lack of affordable housing, rising crime rates, and fire and earthquake damage. Sunday mornings became especially quiet in the downtown area, with fewer strollers and churchgoers. Lacking the money needed for basic maintenance, many churches closed permanently. Then, large numbers of Asian, Central and Eastern European, and Latino migrants arrived and initiated a "second coming" of Christianity to San Francisco. Once left for dead, many churches with new members (and money) started reviving. Itinerant congregations competed to lease space in previously empty churches.

In the previous chapters, I also indicated that the Filipino migrant revitalization of local religion is strikingly evident in the Roman Catholic churches. Filipinos have driven attendance and finances up while also adding their spiritual devotions and ethnic food, as well as religion-inspired festivals and favorite Mary, Jesus, and saint images to Catholic churches in the Bay Area. In the vast Archdiocese of San Francisco, which encompasses the counties of San Francisco, San Mateo, and Marin, Filipinos represent one out of four Catholics.

Bridging Religious Obligation and Civic Duty

In chapters 2 and 4, I showed how Filipino migrants' *kasamahan* bonding contributes significantly to San Francisco's society and culture by mixing transnational and indigenous religious practices, personalities, images, and foodways. In chapter 3, I focused on economic matters and described how transnational *bayanihan* financially impacts migrant families and communities in both the Philippines and the San Francisco. In this chapter, I provide more examples of the adaptive spirit of communal cooperation and outreach (*bayanihan*) of Filipinos toward their San Francisco Bay Area neighborhoods and communities.

The Reverend Jeremiah Resus of Saint James Presbyterian Church says that the blending of spirituality and the migrant experience at his congregation has aided in the creation of a new perspective that is oriented toward feelings of acceptance, assimilation, and the endurance of hardships. The church, he says, "is a place that changes perceptions of reality and supplies perspective to face challenges in life. As a community, Saint James provides a sense of identity for migrants. . . . Membership in the church allows the process of assimilation, movement into American life, a sense of belonging." Reverend Arturo Capuli of Grace United Methodist Church echoes this claim, stating, "The grace of God makes people productive members of society (i.e., taxpayers, and professionals with valuable services to offer) and individuals with strong moral character and which value family." Assistance is offered to new migrants in various forms. At some churches, members pick them up at the airport when they first arrive in the United States. Private basements often serve as temporary housing until new arrivals find their own places to stay. New members are often carpooled to church services while they are still familiarizing themselves with roads and public transportation routes. At these churches, bulletins boards are typically filled with important leads on job opportunities and babysitting services. These leads are particularly useful, since church members have been known to hire fellow members to work for their companies. Some churches even offer free training sessions to enable members to upgrade computer and other professional skills. Some interest-free loans are exchanged between trusting members, especially those who are related or who come from the same province or town. Used cars and trucks are frequently lent out, donated, or sold at a substantial discount.

Figure 5.1. The California hometown association office links Filipino migrants from that province to much-needed social and economic development projects.
Photo credit: Jay Gonzalez

In Reverend Resus's view, fostering a sense of community and belonging is the first step to enabling Filipino migrants to make contributions to the larger Bay Area community. To foster a strong sense of community, pride, and *kasamahan*, Saint James and many other San Francisco churches have made accommodations to popular Philippine languages and dialects, including Tagalog, Ilocano, Cebuano, Kapampangan, Bicolano, and Ilonggo. Some Tagalog hymns have even found their way into the English services, and vice versa. The pastor also says that the church provides a sense of belonging by introducing single people to each other and circulating job announcements. I have already emphasized that Filipino migrants also use their churches for hometown association meetings, dances, fiestas, graduations, parades, processions, bingo tournaments, birthday parties, anniversaries, cultural presentations, funerals, karaoke singing sessions, and so on. Such *kasamahan* gatherings become transmission points for the Filipino values described at the end of the previous chapter. Filipinized churches also teach migrants to practice these values outside of churches and church gatherings. Church mem-

Figure 5.2. *Nursing volunteers check on the health of seniors at West Bay Pilipino Multi-Services Center, a Filipino American social service organization in San Francisco. Photo credit: Jay Gonzalez*

bers are encouraged to convert the social energy they develop at church into *bayanihan* civic work outside the walls of their spiritual spaces. In response, many senior citizens and retirees, regular or occasional church-goers, or even nonmembers receive valuable companionship and camaraderie from Filipino migrant faithful. For instance, members of the San Francisco Filipino American Seventh-Day Adventist Church (Pacifica) regularly visit elderly and sick fellow members who are in hospitals, care facilities, or home alone. This focus on the elderly is notable, since the need for senior citizen care has grown over the years with the retirement of those waves of migrants who arrived prior to the 1970s, the influx of Filipino World War II veterans, and the arrival of elderly immigrants, some whom have no family support system in the United States.

Filipino migrants also reach out to non-Filipinos, nonmembers, and the San Francisco Bay Area community at large, by contributing thousands of hours of volunteer service. In our talks with members of the ten churches in our initial survey, we learned that many were involved with civic activities such as blood donation drives, tree plantings, highway and beach cleanups, and distribution of food to homeless and other needy people. Sometimes churches provided space to host these community-oriented, nonchurch outreach events.

Several Filipino churches, like the Daly City United Methodist Church and the Saint James Presbyterian Church, rented out space for preschool education. They also allowed local nonprofit organizations, such as Alcoholics Anonymous, and candidates for local office to use their space free of charge. Saint Francis and Grace United Methodist Church provided valuable meeting space for former San Francisco mayor Willie Brown during his first campaign for public office. The church effectively became a key point of contact for Brown with the neighborhood and the larger network of Bay Area Filipinos. The congregation also allows community groups in the Sunset District, including other churches that do not have buildings, to use their space.

In groups and as individuals, Filipino lesbian, gay, bisexual, and transgender people (LGBTs) contribute to organizations both inside and outside of their churches. In spite of the Vatican's disapproval of homosexuality, many have been part of the *kasamahan* and *bayanihan* developed at their San Francisco area spiritual sites. They help create bonding capital by participating in worship and other church activities. For example, at Mission Dolores Basilica, they are members of the choir, decorations committee, and fund-raising committee. There are Filipino gay Santo Niño devotees in the archdiocese. Filipino LGBTs are also visible at Most Holy Redeemer Catholic Church in the Castro District, the epicenter of LGBT pride and sprituality in the San Francisco Bay Area. The outside organizations in which Filipino Catholic gays and lesbians are actively involved include the San Francisco chapter of the Dignity Charismatic Lesbian and Gay group. They have formed the Filipino Task Force on AIDS and volunteer at the Asian Pacific Islander Wellness Center, an organization dealing with health care issues. They were also visible participants in migrant rights protests on the church's steps in 2006.

With the support of their San Francisco congregations, the missionary work of Filipino American churches has been able to expand within the United States and extend to the Philippines and many other countries. Many of these churches finance American Christian missionaries in the Philippines. They also give much-needed financial and spiritual support to the projects and programs of their home churches in the Philippines. Pastors in the Philippines regularly attest to the valuable contributions by Filipinos in America to church projects there. Examples of such projects include the restoration and beautification of old historic churches and the construction of new chapels. This generosity to home churches is not surprising; after all, that is probably where many migrants originally prayed for a smooth journey from the Philippines and success in the United States. Also, when natural calamities strike in the United States, the Philippines, or elsewhere around the globe, Filipino American churches provide relief goods and human resources to help in disaster management. For instance, Saint Francis and Grace United Methodist Church provided aid to victims of the Mount Pinatubo disaster in 1991, the September 11 bombings, and Hurricane Katrina in 2005. The church also funds clinics in Palawan and scholarships for seminary and college students in the Philippines. These charitable contributions from Saint Francis and Grace United Methodist Church represented just some of the financial support rendered by Filipinos globally. These acts of giving are part of their *utang na loob* (debt of gratitude) to their homeland. In a similar vein, some new migrants may make a *panata* (vow) to support the place where they were born, a distant source of inspirational energy.

Spirituality and Associational Memberships

Filipino migrants convert spiritual connection to community and hometown connections in San Francisco not only through their church memberships but through their multiple, overlapping organizational affiliations. For instance, I met Vic Hermoso who attends both the Catholic Church of the Epiphany and Grace United Methodist Church. He is an active member of both the Ilocano National Association and Nueva Vizcaya Organization of California, where he is the organizer of their most popular hometown fund-raising event, called "Mrs. Ilocandia," which raises thousands of dollars to help these provinces. He served as commissioner for juvenile delinquency in San Francisco's city hall. Filipino migrants breed *kasamahan* with their churches but also bring this bridging Filipinization to a multitude of clubs, associations, societies, nongovernmental organizations, community-based organizations, foundations, and nonprofit organizations. In the San Francisco Bay Area, as table 5.1 illustrates, hometown and regional associations constitute 41 percent of all Filipino organizations. San Francisco is also home to the headquarters of many Northern California and national organizations.

TABLE 5.1
Filipino Associations in the San Francisco Bay Area

TYPE	NUMBER	%
Hometown/regional	170	41
Spiritual/religious	37	9
Professional	36	9
Cultural and recreational	34	8
Filipino American social clubs	31	8
Political and civic	26	6
Senior's and elderly	22	5
Veterans	19	5
Educational/alumni	16	4
Philippine development	13	3
Lion's clubs	7	2
Total	411	100

Source: *Philippine Consulate General of San Francisco, as of January 2005.*

Filipino migrants organize around various types of geographic locations in the Philippines, from small areas such as their home cities or municipalities (e.g., Pasiguenans of Northern California and the Naga Metropolitan Society) to larger areas such as their home provinces or regions (e.g., the Aklan Association and Marinduque Association). The Philippine archipelago of 7,107 islands is clustered into three main regions—Luzon, Visayas, and Mindanao. These are then segregated administratively into 17 regions, which are divided into 81 provinces and, further, into 117 cities, 1,501 municipalities, and more than 41,000 *barangays*. Languages and dialects are also the basis for the segregation of some communities from one another; after all, the Philippines has more than 100. These numerous hometown and regional associations organize dances, language classes, beauty pageants, and neighborhood cleanups. They also organize fund-raisers for local and international causes. In doing so, they are using social and cultural capital formed in the Philippines and fostered in churches in the United States, then imparted to American society and culture.

Next in number to these vibrant hometown associations are energetic spiritual and religious organizations (9 percent of all Filipino organizations in the Bay Area, according to table 5.1), which derive from a broad array of churches in the Philippines. The most popular ones revolve around national spiritual symbols like the Santo Niño de Cebu (Christ Child), Virgin Mary, Nazareno (brown/black images of Christ), and San Lorenzo Ruiz (the first Filipino saint). There is also a natural merging of the hometown associations and spiritual organizations during the feast days of a town, as statues or images of the town's patron saint are commonly displayed on such occasions. For instance, members of hometown associations from Bicol Province are also core members and organizers of traditional fluvial events surrounding its divine patron, the Nuestra Señora de Peñafrancia. Non-Catholic spiritual groups also have their organizations in the United States, including the Filipino Full Gospel Assembly and the National Association of Filipino-American United Methodists.

The professional associations of Filipino migrants (9 percent) include organizations of nurses, engineers, architects, teachers, doctors, lawyers, executives, and public employees. Some are organized around the largest public and private institutions in America, such as the Filipino Postal Employees Association of San Francisco, Filipino American Government Employees of Northern California, and Fil-Am Communications Employees of SBC Pacific Bell. The Fil-Am Chevron Employees Association has even set up its own separate United Way fund for the Filipino community. The Philippine consulate in San Francisco has identified thirty-four Filipino cultural, sports, history, and performing, literary, and visual arts associations. They include the Fil-Am Music and Arts Society, the Mabuhay Golf Club, and the Fil-Am Basketball Association. The Filipino American Democratic Club and Filipino American Republican Club represent political interests from both ends of the spectrum. Older Filipino migrants find comfort and camaraderie in twenty-two San Francisco seniors and elderly organizations, including the Filipino Seniors Club. They can congregate and enjoy activities at the Filipino Senior Center in Oakland, for example, or the Canon Kip Senior Center in downtown San Francisco. Even before the influx of Filipino World War II veterans in the early 1990s, veterans' associations had emerged in San Francisco. Currently, forty-one area organizations represent the special interests of Filipino seniors and veterans.

Numerous alumni associations in the United States represent high schools (e.g., Morong High School Alumni Association) and universities (e.g., University of the Philippines Alumni Association) in the Philippines. Fraternity alumni groups include the Alpha Phi Omega Alumni Association of Northern California.

Robert Putnam notes that traditional American civic clubs like the Lions, Rotarians, Elks, and Jaycees have seen declining memberships. This is not the case among the Filipino migrant community in San

Francisco, where the number of Lions Clubs has increased from zero in 1965 to seven in 2005. There are also seven new Filipino American Lions Clubs outside of the Bay Area. Additionally, there are newly activated Filipino American Rotarians, Jaycees, Knights of Columbus, and Masonic circles.

The La Salle Alumni Association and Ateneo Alumni Association sponsor regular gatherings as well as special events, such as talks by distinguished fellow alumni and faculty members from their schools back home. Some Filipino American organizations specialize in channeling assistance to help address development issues back in the Philippines, such as the Coalition for Philippine Renewal and Philippine International Aid. To share informational resources and cultural capital, sister city arrangements have been established between cities in the San Francisco Bay Area and the Philippines, including Fremont and Lipa, San Francisco and Manila, Palo Alto and Palo, and Daly City and Quezon City.

Problems within the Bay Area Filipino Migrant Community

The increasing number of Filipino migrants to the San Francisco Bay Area has brought about both functional and dysfunctional results. The contributions of Filipinos to the regional economy are quite visible in the agricultural, service, technology, business, health care, political, nonprofit, and educational sectors. For instance, a large number of Filipino nurses work at health care facilities all over San Francisco; in return, these nurses receive adequate social welfare and financial safety nets. However, some within the Filipino migrant population struggle with health and substance abuse problems and have fallen through the cracks. This situation needs corrective action from San Francisco government, business, and civil society, acting either individually or in partnership. General descriptions of the most salient issues are described here.

Although dubbed "role model" Asian immigrants, some Filipino migrants have fallen by the wayside in their quest for the American dream. Many community-based health care providers, like West Bay and South of Market Mental Health, confirm that teen pregnancy rates, school dropout rates, drug and alcohol abuse, and chronic depression are increasing among San Francisco Filipino youth at an alarming rate. A San Francisco Department of Public Health (2001) report revealed that

Filipinos accounted for 34 percent of Asian and Pacific Islander AIDS cases in San Francisco. Another San Francisco study (Nemoto, Aoki, and Huang 2000) found that Filipino drug users not currently enrolled in a treatment program engage in risky behavior in terms of intravenous drug use, sex while on drugs, and sex with intravenous drug users. Among Filipino adults, heart disease is the leading cause of death, in part because they have a higher prevalence of hypertension than Caucasian adults do. Moreover, the 1998 Current Population Survey presented troubling evidence that 20 percent of Filipinos did not have health insurance. Educational programs and other interventions are desperately needed to remedy this situation and cannot be delayed.

The San Francisco Filipino immigration issue is linked to the highly explosive national debate about illegal immigration. Deportations of Filipinos are increasing. Many of the Filipino communities described earlier have also become safe havens for TNTs (Filipino illegal aliens). The draconian Patriot Act of 2001 has empowered immigration officials to pursue aggressively the estimated 11 million illegal migrants in the United States. Unfortunately, this policy punishes both the duplicitous and well-intentioned, including many who have made positive social and economic contributions to the United States for years. For instance, as commissioner for immigrant rights, I handled the case of an entire family that was deported in 2004 after the INS subjected them to expedited deportation proceedings under the 2001 law. The members of this family had lived in the United States for nineteen years, had been model citizens in the community, and had been trying to legalize their stay for ten years. Filipino migrant organizations fought and lost the battle with the federal government on behalf of this family.

Bridging Filipinization: Two Cases of Bayanihan

The following two case studies provide a more detailed look at how adaptive *kasamahan* and *bayanihan* are used to bond and bridge migrants' wishes to integrate religious obligations with their call to civic duty. The churches are Saint Patrick's Catholic Church, situated near the center of the Filipino American *barangay* in downtown San Francisco, and the Iglesia ni Cristo, a local branch of the independent Philippine-based Christian church, located in Daly City, another Filipino American *barangay* just south of San Francisco.[1]

Case Study 1: *Bayanihan* through Devotions and Allied Organizations

Saint Patrick's Church builds cultural continuity between the Philippines, where the majority is Catholic, and the United States, which has more religious diversity. It does this by creating a worship environment that is reminiscent of churches in the Philippines. In particular, Filipino ushers greet new migrants and seat them among the congregants, who are mostly Filipino also. More often than not, the celebrant is a Filipino priest. Aside from the Gothic Revival architecture, the effect upon a new Filipino migrant is that he or she is still in Manila, especially during the monthly Tagalog mass.

Icons throughout the church refer to popular devotions in the Philippines, such as those to the Mother of Perpetual Help and the Divine Mercy flanking the high altar. The Holy Infant Jesus (Santo Niño), for which Filipino Catholics have a deep affection, is enshrined close to the center of the sanctuary. Lorenzo Ruiz, the first Filipino saint, also has his own shrine. Even the Black Nazareno, an icon of Christ revered by many Filipino men at the Quiapo Church in Manila, has a place in Saint Patrick's. Additional detail about the Filipino-style worship of icons at Saint Patrick's can be found in chapter 2.

For Filipino parishioners, Saint Patrick's Church is one of the few places where they can engage in this particular form of devotion without being self-conscious. They can even pray and confess in their native tongue or through bilingual priests. Dual allegiance to both the Philippines and the United States is certainly accepted here in this church. Filipinos claim that having a safe place to practice both Filipino and American cultures definitely eases their acculturation.

The present population of Filipino migrants tends to obscure the fact that Saint Patrick's was originally one of the citadels of Irish Catholicism in the Bay Area, and that after most of the Irish left the neighborhood after the great fire, the 1906 earthquake, and World War II, the church was a forlorn space that was empty of all but priests. Filipinos have once more filled the church with life and also now have the run of the parish, from the rectory to the lay organizations. All resident priests and deacons are Filipinos who were born and trained in the Philippines. In addition, the parish frequently hosts visiting clergy from the Philippines, from fellow parish priests to ranking prelates of the Philippine Church. Even the nuns at Saint Patrick's come from a Filipino religious order, the Religious of the Virgin Mary (RVM), founded in Manila during the seventeenth century.

The Filipino presence at Saint Patrick's has led to adaptations of Philippine parish organizations and the revitalization of existing ones. For example, the Saint Patrick's chapter of the Holy Name Society, an international Catholic confraternity, has its roots in the chapter established at the parish of Guadalupe in Makati, a city in metropolitan Manila. Moreover, the Filipino migrant population has become the main influence on both the worship program and the social life of the parish. Every December for the last two decades there has been a celebration of Misa de Gallo, the last of nine early-morning masses on the days before Christmas—a ritual that is particular to the Philippines. The parish also recently reinstituted Filipino-style breakfasts after mass, and there are plans for a Filipiniana night to celebrate the feast of San Lorenzo Ruiz. Obviously, besides the feast, rituals, and prayers, the highlight of many parish organization gatherings are the Filipino food and refreshments.

The movement of adaptive spirit of *kasamahan* to the adaptive spirit of *bayanihan* at Saint Patrick's takes many forms. For instance, the parish's lay organizations provide the newly arrived migrant with an instant network of individuals who share common interests and adjustments to a new country. The church thus enables newcomers to make personal connections, as well as to experience familiar religious devotions. Indeed, personal connections play a major role at Saint Patrick's. Parishioners frequently consult the priests for advice and assistance about personal matters. Further, although Saint Patrick's does not offer many formal social programs, the church draws upon the Catholic Archdiocese of San Francisco's extensive social outreach resources, including Catholic Relief Services.

Beyond its sacred walls, Saint Patrick's opens up to newcomers its relationships with neighborhood-based organizations and small businesses in SoMa that specifically serve the Filipino population (see chapter 1). These serve as resources on health, housing, education, and employment issues. Besides providing services, these local groups and the church often play the role of advocate for Filipinos. They constitute a Social Justice Committee, which helped lobby the U.S. Congress to provide recognition to Filipino World War II veterans by granting American citizenship, health benefits, and pensions. Saint Patrick's and SoMa-based Filipino organizations have also leveraged funds from the city and county of San Francisco to assist at-risk Filipino youth and their families. The organizations involved in this effort included the South of Market Community Action Network (SOMCAN), the Filipino Education Center (FEC), the Filipino Community Center (FCC), and Seniors Action Network.

There is a symbiotic relationship between the church and these community-based organizations. Specifically, the parish helps new arrivals maintain a connection to the Philippines, while the Filipino American *barangay* organizations help them make a successful start in their new home in San Francisco. For instance, West Bay, one of the Filipino social service agencies in the area, has strong linkages to Saint Patrick's. West Bay workers, who are residents of the South of Market and the Tenderloin districts, are active members of Saint Patrick's Church, including the organization's executive past director and many of the board members. The pastor has direct communication and relationship with these individuals.

Bayanihan to Saint Patrick's Filipino migrant members is a transnational affair. After saving enough money, some Saint Patrick's members have gone back to the Philippines to become patrons (*hermano* or *hermana mayor*) of their town fiestas and lead parades; their children also are active participants of Santacruzan (Holy Cross) parades as princes and princesses. They have contributed funds to support their former elementary and high schools, as well as for the improvements to the basketball courts where they played as children. Parishioners have also made an impact back in the Philippines through their alumni, hometown, and professional associations. For instance, parishioners who are also physicians and nurses have organized medical missions to the Philippines through their San Francisco Bay Area alumni associations.

Case Study 2: Iglesia ni Cristo's Bowling to *Bayanihan*

Helping each other is an essential part of the "Iglesia ni Cristo state of mind," members say. They also call each other *kapatid*, meaning "brother" or "sister," which implies familial connections and, thus, familial obligations to one another. Indeed, the worldwide network of INC churches is like an extended family, helping and supporting its membership in a wide range of spiritual and personal matters. For example, members who migrate are required to confirm that there is a branch of the church in their destination city. If so, the church forwards information to the new church, which can then prepare to welcome its new member. In this way, the church provides centralized support for its members who are new migrants.

On every first Saturday of the month, members of the INC's Daly City locale bring friends and neighbors to church for Bible lessons, also called Grand Evangelical Missions. After hymns and prayer at a recent GEM,

Resident Minister Brother Lorenzo stood before an open Bible at the pulpit. Gripping the podium with both hands, he looked intently at the audience, then asked, "What does God command us to do, brothers and sisters?" He paused and looked at the congregation. He picked up the Bible and pointed at a passage, then said, "In 1 Corinthians 12:25, God commands his chosen people to 'be united in the same mind and the same judgment.'² God has so adjusted the body that there may be no discord . . . but that the members may have the same care for one another. Brothers and sisters, God commands us, his chosen people, to think and act together. We must be unified."

Reflecting INC's fundamentalist teachings, members attend to the biblical imperatives quoted by Brother Lorenzo as behavioral guides designed to strengthen the congregation's social cohesiveness. Their leaders teach that helping one another succeed as individuals benefits the church as a whole. Thus, a central part the church's spiritual mission is what one might call "building social capital."

The church encourages its constituents to have a sense of personal connectedness to one another that transcends distance. Church members believe that they will always find unqualified acceptance and support from brethren anywhere.

Brethren can easily detail the practical and emotional support the church provides them when they are away from home or settling someplace new. For instance, Marie, a young woman from the Daly City locale, was planning to move to Connecticut to attend medical school. Before she left, she talked about her anxiety over the transition. "The biggest reassurance I have," she said, "is the knowledge that there is an Iglesia ni Cristo congregation in my new neighborhood. It will serve as my 'home away from home.'"

The transition of migrant brethren to new locations is also facilitated by official church structures. First, members are strongly encouraged to move to a place where there is another INC locale. So when Marie considered attending Connecticut College, she also checked to see if there was a congregation nearby. The English-language *God's Message* and Tagalog-language *Pasugo*, weekly magazines published by the church, list contact information for every INC congregation throughout the world. This allows members like Marie to plan their moves with the confidence that there is a community of like-minded people at their destinations. Marie will certainly be treated like family at the Norwich, Connecticut, locale, which is not far from the college. The brethren there will be available to give her rides to and from church, enroll her in the Kadiwa singles group, and introduce her to new friends.

Mr. and Mrs. Santos are also migrant church members who moved from Manila, Philippines, to Daly City to live with their daughter. Before they moved, they informed the resident minister of their Manila locale, who forwarded their files to the Daly City resident minister. The new congregation prepared to welcome them, and in Daly City the Santoses were made part of a group of three families whose spiritual, emotional, and physical well-being was overseen by a church officer. In addition to leading prayers in the Santoses' home, the officer also ensured that their practical needs were met. He might have inquired, for example, if they were successful in locating the local Social Security office. Did they need help securing a driver's license? Were they familiar with Pacific Super, the nearby supermarket stocked with Filipino goods? If needed, the Daly City locale has classes, such as English as a Second Language (ESL) and driver's education, which are geared toward new migrants like the Santoses. The specialized assistance and social structures that the church provides are relatively consistent from place to place.

In the Philippines, the INC has a long-standing tradition of partnering with social service agencies, moving bonding to bridging Filipinization, to provide for needy members and nonmembers. There are many examples of these services such as free medical and dental care, housing for people dislocated by natural disasters, and literacy programs. In addition to these long-term programs, the church also organizes its members for onetime activities, like blood drives and the planting of trees in sites damaged by erosion. These practices are also carried over to the U.S.-based locales.

Bay Area INC church members do not just bowl regularly to cement *kasamahan* bonds of friendship among themselves and their "hometown mates." They actively bring their *bayanihan* attitude to civic projects of the Red Cross, San Francisco Food Bank, Blood Centers of the Pacific, and local governments. Over the course of a year, INC Bay Area churches do blood and food drives, free cholesterol screenings, neighborhood cleanups, and tree plantings. A single phone call by Livermore mayor Cathy Brown to the INC locale is all it took to bring in brethren volunteers who cleaned streets, landscaped public areas, and painted over graffiti, which led her to say: "If you have two thousand volunteers, it does not even compare to the number of city staff we have so you have probably done a year's work" (Iglesia ni Cristo 2000). INC volunteers did civic work that could have cost the city hundreds of personnel hours and tens of thousands of dollars. In 2002, Oakland mayor Jerry Brown made the same phone call to the INC Oakland locale and got the same results. Many San Francisco Bay Area government officials have taken notice. This includes Mayor Carol L. Klatt, who declared June 28, 2001, "Iglesia ni Cristo Day" in Daly City. The city council of Daly City has also awarded the INC with a number of community citations, including the "Most Outstanding Volunteer Group Award." According to Mayor Klatt, "The congregation's civic activities and volunteer effort occur year-round, time and again, they have come through, regardless of the odds and obstacles."[3]

Of course, Bay Area officials are also beginning to respect the *bayanihan* power of the church to call on voters during elections. Daly City has an official partnership across the Pacific with Quezon City in metropolitan Manila, which is also home to the headquarters of the Iglesia ni Cristo and several important educational, medical, and religious institutions. INC members in the United States give money to support many charitable projects in the Philippines, including housing developments and free medical and dental services for needy members and nonmembers, and relief for victims of natural calamities. Pamayanan Ng Tagumpay (Victory Town), a model INC housing development in the Philippines, provides subsidized housing to old and new church members. The extensive development, which features more than a thousand two-bedroom homes, is ironically situated near the government-run housing development, Erap City. Built during the administration of former president Joseph Estrada (nicknamed "Erap"), Erap City was initially intended as a massive, well-planned socialized housing project for the poor. However, years after its development, it is clear that the project has fallen short of this ambitious vision. Critics charge that many of the houses are poorly built or remain unfinished, and that basic services are inadequate. Moreover, the cost to buyers is higher than originally projected, rendering the homes inaccessible to many low-income families. By contrast, Pamayanan Ng Tagumpay is a model of administrative order and stability. In exchange for a nominal rental fee—and loyalty to the INC—residents live in well-constructed homes and have access to many services free of charge. The contrast between Erap City and Pamayanan Ng Tagumpay is not lost on observers, nor is its implication of the INC's power.

Naturally, past Daly City mayor Michael Guingona, a Filipino American official who sat on the Daly City–Quezon City Sister City Commission, made sure to make a courtesy call to the Iglesia ni Cristo's head-quarters when he visited the Philippines to personally thank the INC leadership for church members' support and civic contributions in the San Francisco Bay Area.[4]

The leaders of the INC also see the church as giving back to the community in unseen but fundamental ways. First, they believe that the church's moral code encourages its members to be law-abiding and hardworking, and to partake in community service activities. In other words, it fosters an industrious work ethic and good citizenship, which it believes are good for the broader Bay Area society. Second, the church says its missionary work, which spreads these values to others, is also a public service.

Summary and Conclusion

I met and observed a successful physician from Cebu City, Manny D., who came to San Francisco on a tourist visa in his midforties. After his tourist visa expired, he decided not to go back home. With little money and no legal authorization to work, Manny D. decided to earn his living "under the table," with part-time jobs in the South of Market area, and rent a room close by. He has no health insurance but is otherwise able to make ends meet. Every Sunday, he walks three blocks to Saint Patrick's Church to pray and socialize with fellow parishioners—Filipinos and non-Filipinos. At one of the breakfasts in the church basement, the Filipino pastor introduced Manny to the Filipino American executive director of one of the Filipino social service centers in the area. They saw each other regularly at church activities, including the Misa de Gallo masses and Sunday breakfasts. During one of the gatherings, the executive director invited Manny D. to help at his organization's Thursday food bank. Manny accepted and began devoting four hours a week to distributing food supplies to low-income immigrants and the homeless. He made new friends and met other Cebuanos at the center. Before the end of his weekly volunteer work at the food bank, Manny even got the chance to take home some of the leftover canned goods and groceries to augment his own meager food stock. After dropping them off at his apartment, he rushed to his part-time job.

There are many valuable lessons from Manny D.'s story and the findings from this chapter on how Filipino migrants' adaptive spirit and churches help resolve some of the complexities of migrant life, but I highlight the most salient ones here. First, contrary to Putnam's research findings, we found that Filipino religious migrants not only have brought much-needed bonding social capital (*kasamahan*) to segments of San Francisco society but also have been able to effectively leverage it into political capital (*bayanihan*). Nonetheless, just as Putnam and others have noted, not all *samahan* (organizations or associations), church-based or otherwise, encourage civic action or public protest. Some chose to channel their energies toward meditation and prayer, building spiritual capital. But the two case examples show how adaptive spirit can turn what seems like passive religious gatherings into sustained community assistance and action (*bayanihan*).

Second, as the old saying goes, "charity begins at home," so the first *bayanihan* task of Filipinized San Francisco churches is to help their new migrant members negotiate the intricacies of everyday life in America. Churches help migrants negotiate complex U.S. federal, state, and municipal bureaucracies to get a Social Security number or driver's license, to complete tax forms, and so forth. They also teach them other essentials, such as how to ride public transportation and get around the city, open a bank account, look for a job, understand American colloquialisms, and locate Filipino stores and restaurants. Churches share with migrants, especially the older ones, information on how to volunteer at museums, hospitals, city halls, zoos, parks, and other public places.

Third, while attending services and other *kasamahan*-building activities at church, migrants became involved in a host of *bayanihan* efforts benefiting local governments, civil society, businesses, and philanthropies.

Fourth, besides mainstream governmental organizations, community-based organizations, and private philanthropies, some migrant faithful, like Manny D. and church members from Saint Patrick's and the Iglesia ni Cristo, channel their civic involvement (*bayanihan*) toward (1) Filipino community centers like West Bay Pilipino Multi-Service Center (or West Bay), the South of Market Teen Center, and the Veteran's Equity Center; (2) Filipino community-based organizations like Filipino American Development Foundation and Manilatown Heritage Foundation; and (3) neighborhood action groups like the South of Market Community Action Network and United Pilipino Organizing Network (UPON). Some help other Asian Americans through community centers, community-based organizations, and nonprofit agencies targeted at that broader community.

Finally, the inclination toward *bayanihan*, which migrants probably acquired when they were still in the Philippines, comes full circle when they fly back to spearhead social development projects, church rebuilding efforts, and disaster relief back in their hometowns through their churches and their alumni, hometown, and professional associations. Such projects allow them to bridge their faith to hometown connections and actions. This bridging through adaptive spirit, practices, and values was confirmed by Manny D. and church members at Saint Patrick's and the Iglesia ni Cristo with their answers to the question: Why volunteer in the Philippines? Many replied with words like *tulong* (help or contribution), *utang na loob* (debt of gratitude), *panata* (vow), *kasunduan* (agreement), or *pangako* (promise) not just to their families, hometowns, and the Philippines but also to God.

The succeeding chapters shift the discussion from how Filipino faithful are engaging American society through adaptive beliefs and practices and organizing to the building of politicized *kasamahan* and then transforming this to activist *bayanihan* through intergenerational issues and actions.

6

Blessing Passion and Revolution

It was already past five o'clock in the evening on Monday, March 14, 2005. Inside city hall hearing room 416 was a sea of black hair and brown faces. The attendees ranged in age from ten to eighty years old. The atmosphere was tense. Number two on the evening's agenda was a resolution "strongly urging the Mayor and Board of Supervisors to support the current Filipino and Asian American immigrant communities' initiative naming the former Bessie Carmichael Elementary School site (on Sherman and Folsom) as Victoria Manalo Draves Park." Chair Diana Lau called the San Francisco Immigrant Rights Commission (IRC) meeting to order. Nine commissioners were present, and none were of Filipino descent, making the partisan crowd nervous. There was a quorum. Minutes for the February meeting were approved, and then Lau opened the floor to public comments. One by one, Filipino and non-Filipino students from the Catholic Jesuit University of San Francisco (USF)—true to their school's mission of "educating minds and hearts to change the world"— boldly but nervously took the stand. First up was sophomore Christopher Wiseman, a highly energetic politics major from upstate New York; then came junior Candice Ramirez, a feisty psychology major who grew up in San Jose; she was followed by the freshman Juree Kim, a fiery newcomer to San Francisco via Los Angeles, and many more. Some of them, like Christopher, had had no prior encounters with Filipinos. Korean American Juree knew them as fellow Asian Americans but admitted knowing little about their history and struggles. And even Candice, who was born and immersed in Philippine culture and had gone to Catholic schools filled with Filipinos since the first grade, could name no Filipino or Filipina community role model. However, they had just learned about Victoria Manalo Draves in their Philippine and Asian American studies classes. Before their testimonies, Draves was a little-known Filipina American senior enjoying her retirement in Southern California. However, the students helped ensure that more San Franciscans—and visitors to the city—would know about this Olympic champion.

This chapter explores the dynamics of this display of *kasamahan* (bonding Filipinization) by first discussing the intergenerational respect practiced in the homes and Filipinized churches I observed and then revisiting what students at the Jesuit Catholic University of San Francisco learn about community organizing, counterhegemony, the church, and Filipino migrants. Then I delve into how the students transform their classroom and library learning into concrete action. Thereafter, using an in-depth case discussion of Saint Augustine's Catholic Church in South San Francisco, I elaborate on four conditions that I believe are necessary for intergenerational *kasamahan*. In the case study, I show how these factors all come together as a passionate energy and revolutionary spirit that brings together young and old parishioners toward the confrontation of a critical immigrant rights issue at the San Francisco International Airport.

Intergenerational Respect at Filipinized Churches

For intergenerational *kasamahan* to occur, there has to be intergenerational respect. Our own personal experiences and the site observations led us to a very important Filipino value that is reinforced both at home and in church: *paggalang sa dunong ng nakakatanda* (respect for the wisdom of elders). This is a deference that is cherished by elders, resulting in mutual respect and action. There are many obstacles to overcome before generations are able to achieve such conditions. Studies of psychological stressors among young and old Filipinos confirm the predominance of a perceived generation gap between first-generation Filipino parents and their second-generation children raised in America (Espiritu 2003). A major source of conflict has to do with differing notions of the self and one's place in the new homeland. While Filipino culture depends on social hierarchy and emphasizes the shared needs of family and community, American culture values personal equality and individual rights and needs. Researchers point out that the disruption of Filipino values by American socialization often causes tension at home. For example, Filipino parents are often dismayed when their children speak to them without the proper deference, which they interpret as disrespect. Even if children speak in Tagalog, the lack of the words *po* (sir/ma'am) or *opo* (yes, sir/ma'am) after a sentence could be misinterpreted as disrespectful. But it may simply be that American social interactions between parents and children are different and such formalities are not a standard part of the socialization process outside of the home. Lisa Lowe (1996), in her analysis of Amy Tan's novel *The Joy Luck Club*, explains that the "generation gap" in the story is simply the struggle of the second-generation migrant to come to terms with the first-generation migrant's demands for respect (i.e., Asian "filial piety"), while the older generation strives to understand the younger generation's gestures of appreciation (i.e., American "beauty parlor gratitude"). Although Tan's book represents a fictional account of family dynamics in Chinese American families, the resemblance of the story to real familial relationships among Filipino Americans makes it an apt explanatory tool.

At Saint Patrick's Catholic Church, encounters between the older and younger generations of parishioners resemble those at their counterpart Catholic churches in the Philippines. Youth members participate in liturgy (as altar servers, members of the young adult choir, and in other roles), while adult members regularly perform the duties of ushers, lectors, and Eucharistic ministers. Because many adults and seniors started out in these youth roles, they have a natural connection with their young counterparts. The youth, in turn, respect their elders. The relative status of older and younger parishioners at Saint Patrick's can be seen in the interactions among the many parish organizations. Of the twenty-five different parish organizations, only four are geared toward younger parishioners. However, the presence of independent youth organizations is significant in that it addresses the question of legacy. Given the advanced age of many of the parishioners, the youth represent the future lay leaders of the parish, and their involvement in parish activities prepares them for the future assumption of leadership roles. There are special connections between the older and younger groups—the younger members of the adult organizations serve as informal mentors to the youth parishioners, and the younger members often address their elders as *ate* (older sister) or *kuya* (older brother) as if they were kin rather than merely fellow church members.

Similar generational dynamics exist among adult parishioners, with younger adults showing deference to older adults. Though most call each other either "brother" or "sister," there are times when persons are addressed as *kuya, ate, manong* (elder man), *manang* (elder woman), *tita* (auntie), *tito* (uncle), or *kababayan* (countryman/countrywoman), usually in more informal settings. This is another example of the prevalence of fictive kin relationships that are brought over from the Philippines,

Figure 6.1. A young migrant faithful helps an older member down the steps of the church after an afternoon prayer vigil. Photo credit: Jerry Berndt

much like the relationship between the youth parishioners and their mentors.

At the Iglesia ni Cristo in Daly City and San Francisco, we found that in keeping with the desire of the church to promote unity among its membership, there are several member organizations that teach teens and adults of all ages rules of respect for intergenerational harmony. The *kasamahan* group for teenagers thirteen to seventeen years old is called Binhi ("seedlings"), Kadiwa (short for Kabataang may Diwang Wagas, or "youth with pure spirit") is for unmarried people eighteen years old and up, and married couples of all ages belong to Buklod. Within the mission statement of each group is a mandate to preserve harmony in the family. For example, Binhi and Kadiwa members must swear to the following, as stated in each organization's Declaration of Principles: "I will love and respect my parents, and I shall submit to their statutes which are not against the teachings of the Iglesia ni Cristo. I will serve them and help them in ensuring the stability of our household." Similarly, Buklod members must make the following promise: "I will uphold the Christian way of managing my household. I will accord my wholehearted love to my family. I will strive to ensure that love and understanding always reign in my household."

Intergenerational Passion and Revolution in Filipino Religious Life

Intergenerational respect alone does not inspire students to testify and protest against social injustices. On the contrary, their respect for elders might even stifle their will to revolt against the long-standing wisdom justifying the hegemonic status quo. Hence, the youths' socialization in school is critical to converting respect for elderly wisdom to collaborative action. The Catholic University of San Francisco and many of the San Francisco Bay Area schools, including the University of California, Berkeley, and San Francisco State University, have earned the reputation of immersing social science and humanities students in the theory and practice of societal organizing and counterhegemonic action, including famous works by Marx (1844), Weber (1958), Freire (1970), Gramsci (1971), and Omi and Winant (1994). This is combined with their exposure to the literature on religion- and congregation-based political organizing in the United States (Dillon 2003; Jacobsen 2001; Ramsay 1998; and Wood 2002, among others). They also learn that the nature of the relationship between church and activism has always been controversial—philosophers have written about it for centuries, and policy makers have tried to avoid intruding upon matters of religion and faith. Nevertheless, the literature on liberation theology and faith-based organizing abounds in such discussions, especially in the Latin American political context (see Cleary and Steigenga 2004; Martin 1990; Smith 1991; Swatos 1995; Torres 1992). It is standard for American students of today to study the civil rights movement and the rise of African American churches, which clearly illustrate the power of congregational counterhegemonic actions against both the dominion of American society and the Catholic and Christian church hierarchies (see Lincoln and Mamiya 2003; Sales 1994; Warren 2001). But although liberation theology and religious activism are popular areas of social science research, especially among Filipino and Philippine studies scholars (Apilado 1999; Kwantes

1998; Nadeau 2002; Wiegele 2005, among others), there are few works that examine the interesting dynamics and praxis within emerging Filipino diasporic communities (e.g., Aguilar–San Juan 1994; Võ 2004), particularly with regard to their American religious experience and the building of intergenerational *kasamahan* for counterhegemonic activities (e.g., San Buenaventura 1999; Filipinas Book Team 2003).

In my own international politics classes, I have posed this question to my students: How could counterhegemonic action emerge from a hegemonic superstructure, like the powerful Catholic Church or the U.S. governmental system? I point out that it seems very possible, according to the historical evidence presented by Filipino historian Reynaldo Ileto (1979) in *Pasyon and Revolution*. Ileto's work is significant, since it illustrates how Filipino passion is transformed into revolutionary action for counterhegemonic projects within the hegemonic superstructures of both the Spanish and American churches and governments. Ileto's work echoes the counterhegemonic battles described in the vast literature on liberation theology. He makes connections between a popular Filipino religious text *Casaysayan nang Pasiong Mahal ni Jesucristong Panginoong Natin* (Account of the Sacred Passion of Our Lord Jesus Christ) or the *Pasyon*, and Filipino revolutionary movements against Spanish and American colonizers between 1840 and 1910. Although Spain imposed Catholicism upon the Philippines, Ileto argues that the Filipino people were able to create their own brand of Christianity, from which a language of anticolonialism evolved in the late nineteenth century.

A common stereotype of Filipinos that Ileto references is that of a passive, deferential, hospitable, and family-bound individual. He warns against this stereotype, taking into consideration the many instances throughout history when popular movements threatened to overturn the ruling structures—counterhegemony at its best. His study examines the possibility that folk religious traditions, which usually promote passivity, actually "have latent meanings that can be revolutionary" (10). Ileto claims that the Filipino masses' familiarity with the *Pasyon*'s revolutionary images provided them with a cultural preparedness to live out similar scenarios in response to adverse conditions under Spanish and American hegemonic rule. He analyzes the text of the *Pasyon* and emphasizes its importance as a "mirror of the collective consciousness." Its narration of Christ's suffering, death and resurrection conveys a transition from darkness to light, despair to hope, and misery to salvation.

Ileto's work is significant to our study of church, civil society, and counterhegemony because it shows how religious ideals have shaped the sociopolitical consciousness of Filipino migrant faithful, both young and old. Ileto's thoughts in *Pasyon and Revolution* go beyond the points raised by famous hegemony and counterhegemony scholars Marx (1844), Weber (1958), Freire (1970), Gramsci (1971), and Omi and Winant (1994) by asserting that indigenous Filipino thinking shaped religion and religious practice, eventually inspiring counterhegemonic behavior against two powerful colonizers.

The counterhegemonic consciousness that arose from Spanish and American Christian teachings led to the emergence of Catholic and Protestant spin-off groups. In addition to what Ileto described as "Pasyon prayer sessions," which inspired Filipinos to move from mass apathy to militant activism against Spain in 1840 and America in 1910, similar subversive actions were initiated by Filipino Catholic priests. Three junior Filipino priests, Mariano Gomez, Jose Burgos, and Jacinto Zamora, were executed by the Spanish in Manila on the recommendation of the religious orders for sharing their critical opinions about the Spanish church hierarchy with their parishioners, particularly the *indios*. This only fueled the anger and disgust of Filipino nationalists like Jose Rizal, who penned two novels exposing blatant church-state corruption and abuses; Rizal eventually left the Catholic Church and became a Freemason. But the disillusionment of Filipinos in existing church structures did not end with the departure of the Spaniards. As mentioned in previous chapters, the Philippine Independent Church (Aglipayans) and Iglesia ni Cristo were both established during the American occupation of the Philippines.

In the early twentieth century, the political domination of the U.S. government and the Catholic Church was evident in their discriminatory policies as well as the anti-Filipino sentiment that pervaded public spaces all over California. Filipino farmworkers, young and old, were confronted regularly by signs on the doors of shops and restaurants that read, "No Filipinos Allowed." Filipinos in California were also subjected to antimiscegenation laws, which prohibited Filipino migrant workers from mingling with and marrying Caucasian women. As a result, many Filipino farmworkers and service workers retired in the Philippines as bachelors. These included my paternal grandfather's brothers, Lolo Pepe and Lolo Kikoy, who came to the United States after 1910 and returned to Manila in the 1970s as seventy-year-old bachelors. In the first part

of the twentieth century, Stockton, California, had the highest number
of Filipino residents outside of the Philippines as a result of its agricultural industry. In her doctoral dissertation, Filipino American scholar
Dawn Mabalon (2003) explored the ways in which churches in Stockton
remained socially conservative at this time, siding with the more dominant forces of society rather than with the disenfranchised Filipino community. Until 1962, Stockton was part of the massive Catholic Archdiocese of San Francisco. Mabalon's study reveals the church's perception
of Filipinos. Her primary sources showed that anti-Filipino racism was
one of the factors that pushed Filipinos away from the church. In fact,
she gives undeniable evidence that the Catholic Church supported the
1935 Filipino Repatriation Act in order to reduce the local population of
Filipino migrants, who were seen as intruding upon proper, mainstream
white Catholics. She cites documents from Archbishop John J. Mitty of
San Francisco, in which he says, "I wish to emphasize my conviction,
based upon Filipino sentiment that repatriation will go far in solving
the difficult Filipino problem." Although this conviction was supposedly
based upon Filipino sentiment, "only 2082 Filipinas/os out of a population of more than 100,000 in Hawaii and the U.S. mainland volunteered
to be repatriated." In later letters in which he was pushed to articulate
the nature of the so-called Filipino problem, he drafted statements criti-
cizing Filipinos who "want white collar jobs and flashy clothes." He
believed that their difficulty stemmed from the "instability of character
of the Filipinos." He ultimately removed those statements from his final
letters to the papal representative in the United States, but the drafts that
Mabalon was able to obtain reveal Archbishop Mitty's negative bias
against Filipinos.

Mabalon's study shows how unwilling the Catholic Church in Stockton was to address problems facing the Filipino community, despite
the fact that most Filipinos were Catholic and that Stockton had such
a large Filipino population. Father McGough of Saint Mary's Church
in Stockton said, "I regret I have nothing to offer in the way of a solu-
tion for these people." Another priest at Saint Mary's stated that Filipinos are already "lost to the church." Mabalon elaborates where Filipino
American National Historical Society cofounder Fred Cordova left off
in *Filipinos: Forgotten Asian Americans*, in which he devoted a chapter to discussing the church and religion in the Filipino American community. He pointed out that although 90 percent of Filipino Americans
were thought to be Catholic, the Catholic Church did not make much of

an effort to respond to the needs of this community. Although they came from a society that had been rooted in Catholicism for more than 300 years, Filipino migrants often were denied access to church sacraments and education because of their skin color and language differences. Many Filipinos were unable to marry in the church, go to confession, attend regular Sunday masses, or have a Catholic funeral.

Another Filipino American scholar, Steffi San Buenaventura (1999, 2002), conducted extensive research on the religious experiences of Filipino communities in Hawaii and Southern California that uncovers the role that evangelical religious groups played in perpetuating the subjugation of Filipinos. She notes that migrant workers arrived in

> a plantation system that encouraged the Christianization of its labor force. Because of the Protestant origins of the sugar industry . . . the creation of ethnic missions within the Congregational and Methodist Churches was a natural step in inculcating Christian teachings and virtues to the "Asiatic" plantation workers and in instructing them in American democratic principles through the process of Americanization. To them, it was also necessary to nurture Christian religion among the converted young and old workers so as to ensure the continued civilizing effect of Christianity on their outlook and conduct . . . to prevent having a "Filipino social problem" . . . Protestant missionaries worked on the assumption that the Filipinos needed special Christian moral guidance. (158)

But the arrival of Filipino migrant faithful in California not only continued the spread of various faiths and Filipinized American spiritual spaces. New Filipino Americans were also mainstreamed into California politics via a counterhegemonic form of *kasamahan*. There was some evidence of counterhegemonic activity among the early migrants despite the hegemony of the American church and state, which I discussed earlier. The lawsuits, town hall meetings, political lobbying, and letter-writing initiatives that senior members of many Filipino fraternal and Masonic lodges (e.g., Caballeros de Dimas Alang and Legionarios del Trabajo) passed on to junior members were clear evidence of counterhegemonic thinking and action among early migrants in both small towns and big cities in California. Around the same time that liberation theology began to flourish around the world, church officials in Stockton changed their attitudes toward Filipinos. Mabalon cites instances of counterhegemonic action, in which the Franciscans, a religious order historically dedicated to serving the poor, focused its resources on the Filipino and Mexican migrant workers in the area. In fact, Father Alan McCoy, a Franciscan priest, along with labor organizers Larry Itliong and Dolores Huerta, worked to form the Agricultural Workers Organizing Committee (AWOC). The AWOC was responsible for the Delano grape strike, which was a critical event in the California labor movement. However, few are aware that this strike has roots in the Catholic Church. The AWOC would later unite young Cesar Chavez with the more senior Filipino organizer Philip Vera Cruz to create the United Farm Workers Union (UFW).

Converting Intergenerational Passion to Revolutionary Action

Students at the University of San Francisco, like Juree, Christopher, and Candice, learn about these important historical and philosophical underpinnings of community organizing and counterhegemony in the Filipino community in San Francisco through programs like the Maria Elena Yuchengco Philippine Studies Program. Students in this program are required to engage in "service learning" through community activities in San Francisco's blighted South of Market, Mission, Excelsior, and Tenderloin districts. In these neighborhoods, students mentor newly arrived Filipino youth, seniors, and their families at schools and social service organizations. They provide hundreds of volunteer hours working on real educational, environmental, employment, human rights, welfare, child abuse, substance abuse, and domestic violence issues. They have joined Filipino ethno-tours of San Francisco as well as protest marches in front of the city hall and the Philippine consulate general. Through a transnational exchange program with their sister Jesuit school in the Philippines, the Ateneo de Manila University, USF students are able to link with young and old in another homeland. Besides classroom work in Manila and exposure to the urban poor and marginalized in provincial areas, they also participate in social justice projects, such as the building of homes and schools. Students who participate in the Philippine Studies Program at USF complete the circle of Filipino migration and social justice, since many of their parents attended Ateneo and other Catholic universities in the Philippines, where they learned about social justice in the classrooms and through service learning. Essentially, the Yuchengco Philippine Studies Program has become the latest addition to San Francisco's growing list of religious institution–inspired, Filipino intergenerational community centers, an important training ground for not only *kasamahan* but also *bayanihan*. The students have formed an organization aptly called Kasamahan.

In their San Francisco classroom, Candice, Christopher, Juree, and the other USF students had learned from one of their activist Filipino Catholic professors that in the 1948 Olympic games, Victoria Manalo Draves became the first woman in history to win gold medals in both springboard and platform diving events. She had also been inducted into the International Swimming Hall of Fame and featured in *Life* magazine. Draves was born on December 31, 1924, to a Filipino, Teofilo Manalo, and an Englishwoman, Gertrude Taylor, and lived in the SoMa neighborhood where the park that would later bear her name was eventually built. She was baptized, given first communion, and confirmed and was a regular attendee of Sunday services at nearby Saint Joseph's Catholic Church. Draves's interest in diving grew in high school as she swam and dove at the Fairmont Hotel's famous indoor pool. Her diving skills were honed under Phil Patterson, a well-known coach at the time. In 1941, national diving champion Sammy Lee suggested that she train under Lyle Draves, who coached at the Athens Swim Club in Oakland, which was not too far away. Victoria and Lyle fell in love and got married. She won national championships in 1946, 1947, and 1948 and qualified for the 1948 U.S. Olympic team. However, her greatest challenge was not in sports but in facing an American society that refused to be represented on the world stage by someone named Manalo, which was not sufficiently Anglo. Draves's diving club on Nob Hill demanded that she drop her father's Filipino name and take her mother's maiden name, Taylor. At Saint Joseph's Catholic Church, Victoria prayed for America's acceptance.

None of them had ever spoken at city hall before, but the USF students, some teary-eyed and emotional, appealed to the commissioners to approve the resolution to name that park in Draves's childhood neighborhood after her. After the students spoke, their two Filipino American professors approached the podium; one was a parishioner of Saint Ignatius Church in the Richmond District and the other of Corpus Christi Church in the Excelsior District. They were acknowledged by Chair Lau, who then glanced at her colleagues and added that the two USF professors were former members of the Immigrant Rights Commission. The distinguished-looking men and women eyed the teachers and, seemingly impressed, nodded their heads in recognition. With passion and precision, the professors narrated Draves's story, underscoring her many contributions to American society. After the professors' incisive testimonies, community members—especially those who live near the park—also voiced their support. The commissioners asked numerous probing questions. Satisfied with their responses, the chair called the proceedings to order. The room became very quiet. Vera Haile, an elderly commissioner, broke the silence and loudly said, "I move for approval!" The motion was seconded, no further discussion ensued, and so the resolution was called to a vote. One by one, the commissioners voted. "Unanimously approved!" announced the chair. Pandemonium broke out as onlookers cheered the decision. A petite woman standing in the corner of the room breathed a sigh of relief, made the sign of the cross, and exclaimed: "Ay, salamat sa Dios!" (Oh, thank God!) A special thanksgiving mass was held at Saint Patrick's Catholic Church that Sunday.

Case Study: Saint Augustine's Catholic Church, South San Francisco

The following discussion demonstrates that once *paggalang sa dunong nakakatanda* (respect for elder's wisdom) has been established, there are additional key factors and conditions that enable intergenerational *kasamahan* in the form of counter-hegemonic action to grow and prosper. These include (1) compelling political issues, (2) leadership structure, (3) the socioeconomics of the congregation, and (4) parish intergenerational interest groups.

Compelling Political Issues

Based on congregational size, Saint Augustine's is the largest parish in the Archdiocese of San Francisco. As explained in chapter 1, the membership of more than 4,000 families is more than 90 percent Filipino. Because of the large number and percentage of Filipino members, Saint Augustine's functions as a social as well as a religious center. Parishioners tend to hang out after mass and greet their friends who are coming in for the next mass. The completion of each service is marked by the cheerful sound of parishioners talking and laughing and children running and playing. One can always count on the availability of snacks after mass, which encourages church members to linger and visit.

Interestingly, no Tagalog mass or Bible study is held at Saint Augustine's, unlike at many of the other Catholic and Protestant churches that have been Filipinized. There are also no strong indications of Filipinization in the external or internal features and icons of the church. However, the absence of such visible signs is more than made up for by the linguistic exchanges in Tagalog, Ilocano, Visayan, Kapampangan, Bicolano, and other Filipino dialects between and among priests, lay workers, and parishioners before and after each service. The fact that both men and women wear Filipino attire during special events such as baptisms, confirmations, weddings, and funeral services also confirms the ethnic background of the congregation. Beyond language and fashion, the displays of traditional Filipino customs (e.g., children asking for a blessing by touching the hand of their elders to their foreheads) and food during parties and gatherings are clear manifestations of the congregation's shared Philippine heritage.

Saint Augustine's caught the attention of San Francisco city officials shortly after the events of September 11, 2001, when Congress hastily passed new air transportation and homeland security legislation mandating that baggage screening for all of America's airports was to be taken over by the federal government. The new law, signed by President George W. Bush, restricted airport security screener jobs to U.S. citizens. At the time, about 90 percent of security screeners at San Francisco International Airport were Filipino, and a vast majority of them were new migrants still ineligible for U.S. citizenship. There was tremendous opposition to this mandate from the Filipino community in the Bay Area. Saint Augustine's was very involved in the struggle to protect the jobs of the more than 1,000 migrant non-U.S. citizen workers at the San Francisco airport, 900 of whom were of Filipino descent. A large number of the screeners who were affected were parishioners or relatives of parishioners. But this was not the only reason that Saint Augustine's became involved in political struggle. After an initial conversation with one of the church's pastors, Father Robert Andrey, we learned that this parish had been successfully mobilizing its congregants for political reasons since at least 1998.

In 1999, for example, parishioners used their numbers to press South San Francisco's city hall to approve the church's expansion plans. In that year, parishioners and church leaders were surprised and dismayed when the South San Francisco Planning Commission rejected a proposal to expand the church's structure and build an elementary school next door. The parish had worked with the city for more than eighteen months to come up with an acceptable project. When the proposal was rejected, members of the congregation were shocked and hurt but also adamant about not giving up. After more than a year of planning and work, they felt strongly that their voices needed to be heard. About 500 churchgoers led by Filipino community activists showed up at city hall to persuade the city council to overturn the planning commission's decision. Their mobilization proved successful, and the South San Francisco City Council ultimately approved the alternate plan.

Leadership Structure

Two different types of leadership are at work in the parish of Saint Augustine's. The first is the official leadership of the priests and nuns, which they exercise in their roles as spiritual leaders. They, in turn, foster a second type of unofficial leadership among the parishioners through their support of social or political causes. During the last five to six years, Saint Augustine's has benefited from the experiences and political values of three religious leaders: Father Eugene, the head pastor; Sister Nona, head of music ministry and education; and Father Obet, the pastor. Through interviews with each of these individuals, we learned that they brought years of political organizing experience with them to Saint Augustine's.

Father Eugene has been a priest in the Bay Area for many years. He was one of the first priests contacted by the Bay Area Organizing Committee (BAOC), which does local community organizing to empower disadvantaged groups. According to Larry Gordon, president and CEO of the BAOC, Father Eugene was contacted because he was a very talented pastor who shared the committee's progressive political vision. The BAOC began working with him even before he became the head pastor at Saint Augustine's. Father Eugene believes that his role as inspirer and motivator is critical for mobilizing the parish. He explained, "You have to be charismatic, welcoming and a little diplomatic at the same time. . . . One thing that really I learned [is] it might be very difficult from the beginning. But if you don't do anything, if you don't make that first start, you will [never] do it. I think it was difficult for me to see what's going to happen, because it was really gigantic, a really huge project. But I just found out if there's a will there's a way."

Sister Nona has her organizing roots in the Philippines. She was very involved in both the airport screener and expansion projects, which she said reminded her of the times that she was involved in political resistance in the Philippines: "It is not like there [in the Philippines], where we organize and we become very active. Here it is different. But there it takes a lot more courage to involve yourself. It is very risky." Despite the risks involved, Sister Nona enjoyed the political work in which she was involved back home. She fondly recounted her first experience in political organizing:

Well, it was already ingrained in my mind when I was young. My father was a lawyer and he was working with the poor. So I can see him. He accepted more clients with the poor. When I was a sister I had lots of experience. The first experience that I had was when our congregation went to defend the young girls from going into prostitution—giving them work so that they would not have to choose prostitution. That was my first experience. We did some marching and demonstrations. I was one of the leaders and we involved the whole town with the permission of the parish priest and somehow we were even able to involve the mayor. It involved the whole town, but it was peaceful.

According to Sister Nona, while the comparatively stable political situation here makes life easier, she misses being involved in battles against blatant social injustices. She sees social injustices here as well, but in her opinion, they tend to be more nuanced and therefore invite less resistance. As she explained,

Living here, you realize all the problems. Look at the housing conditions. There are many who are jobless. . . . Why can we not do something? At least to protect those who first came from the Philippines and other countries. They cannot anymore afford to buy a house. And for me that's not fair. Well you can say that the others were here for a long, long time. Blest are you who are here for a long, long time. But can we do something? Housing goes up and up and up and we just bow down and bow down and bow down. Even here in California, no one is saying something about the housing. And how many people here are jobless. How many have to move somewhere else just to survive. How many have no health insurance. And they cry. They are crying but no one is speaking up. We have to speak out. That's what I hate, that is what is lacking.

Sister Nona hopes to be able to teach by example. She attends organizing meetings around issues affecting the local Filipino American com-

munity and hopes that people will become aware of her and her support
of social justice issues:

> For me, it's just to continue as leaders. If they will see in us, that our pres-
> ence, our witnessing is strong, I think even if you are not saying anything.
> If they will see you that you are attending meetings. . . . "Oh, Sister Nona
> is there and Father Eugene is there, Oh they are for it." And we are also
> very lucky that our volunteers are here. It is not only the work of one, it is
> community work. The involvement is not just mine, it is everyone's.

Father Obet also established his political roots in the Philippines during the Marcos era. In contrast to the Marxist notion that religion is the
"opiate of the people," he believes that religion can be a tool for revolutionary action. He recounted the risks he undertook as a young priest
organizing parishioners against Marcos's dictatorship:

> My formative years were the martial law years. . . . We were fighting the
> martial law regime when I was a student in the seminary. Then I became a
> priest and that was when I was able to do more for the Filipinos. And then
> when I came I did not look for BAOC—it came to me. And I kind of was
> able to continue what I was doing in the Philippines. I was also involved
> with community organizing in the Philippines during the time of martial
> law. In the Philippines there was a thin line between the church and poli-
> tics. I was so active that there was a wrong report that I was suspected of
> being associated with the NPA. My rectory was raided in the middle of
> the night. When there was the People Power Revolution, when that took
> place, I wanted to make sure that was successful because if it was not, then
> I was a marked man. I was a very young priest at the time.

Father Obet's work and initiative within Saint Augustine's was critical
in the campaign to help the airport screeners. As Saint Augustine's representative to the BAOC, he helped garner an increase in the cost-of-living
accommodation for employees in San Francisco and was largely responsible for initiating the screener campaign within the parish. His political
convictions have been useful in explaining why it is important for the
church to become involved in political matters. As he explained:

> Well, I always preach about faith and justice because for me faith without
> justice is not real, not authentic. And of course we have the social teach-

ings of the church. They are a well-kept secret, but of course we try to uncover the secret. It is really hard to preach about justice especially if we talk about "to each his own" in this crisis of poverty. There is this wrong common notion that when priests talk about justice, we are going overboard because there is a separation of church and state. And you're not supposed to engage in politics. The fact is . . . that's wrong. Religion covers all aspects of our life, including politics. But what we don't do as ministers is participate in partisan politics. But politics in general is very big . . . it is a part of the social teachings of the church. The only problem is that people have this notion that you should not mix church with politics.

The religious leaders described here use their talents and experiences to help make Saint Augustine's a parish that has real political leverage in fighting for social justice. As responsible leaders, they recognize that they cannot be the only ones in charge and that the leadership should continue even after they leave Saint Augustine's. Father Eugene has been very effective at delegating leadership roles to people in the parish. The most supportive are his *kababayan* (countrymen/countrywomen). He can cite at least two dozen names when asked which parishioners help him. Filipino migrants lead the youth group, the Small Christian Communities organization, the capital campaign committee, the outreach ministry, and many more groupings within the church. Father Eugene encourages these leaders to take their own initiative and gives them the freedom to develop each project without reporting each little detail to him. They appreciate this freedom, which also gives them more accountability and ownership of these projects. The leader of the capital campaign for the expansion of the building and the school, for example, worked for months on planning the project with the city and with the other parishioners. When the project was denied by the planning commission, she was one of the most determined to fight for it.

Socioeconomics of the Congregation

Although Marx and other political theorists prioritize raising the consciousness of the working class to be the leaders of social transformation and counterhegemonic actions, Saint Augustine's provides compelling evidence that the middle class can also play an important role and can be very effective when organized.

The vast majority of the parishioners at Saint Augustine's are residents of its surrounding South San Francisco neighborhood, which is a predominantly migrant community but one that is older and more established financially than the community in San Francisco's South of Market district. Many of the people living in South San Francisco own or rent houses rather than small, urban apartments. Having migrated mostly in the 1970s and 1980s, many of these migrants now have children who are either in college or college-bound. Therefore, this community is also composed of many people with extra time to devote to church activities.

Noemi Castillo, director of the Archdiocese of San Francisco's Office of Ethnic Ministries, believes that it is sometimes more difficult to mobilize new migrants who are focused on daily survival. While it is true that they are the ones who tend to suffer from the most injustices, and can probably identify with social injustice much more easily, they are often too busy—many working two or more jobs—to become civically engaged. This is why intergenerational cohesion is necessary. Saint Augustine's, Castillo observes, has a larger number of middle-class, financially stable families than other predominantly Filipino churches in San Francisco.

Ted, a parishioner, keenly reflected upon how the stability he has been able to attain in his years here has allowed him to gain some perspective on social justice:

> I see myself as having changed from that conservative, hardworking [person], trying to make it out here in the United States. It's changed . . . now maybe we're more stable, we're no longer looking at success as a hungry beginner. We've learned to see that it's more than just grabbing for the big pie. There are less fortunate people than myself over here and in everything we do I just feel that I've been blessed and fortunate and I can't stand to just watch oppression happen in any kind of form. When there is oppression, I think there is no love and how can I say I'm a Catholic . . . how can I even say I'm a Christian if I didn't do something about it? I felt I'm being—I'm not being true to myself. . . . It took me thirty years to change the way I think. And then now, when we have attained a certain sort of stability, status in society, then your focus changes. You grow.

In addition to the insight that economic stability allows, it also offers the church needed resources: money and time. Father Eugene not only has been able to raise the money needed to expand the church and build the school but also has been able to enlist parishioners to become community organizers and leaders in their spare time. While most of the parishioners work full-time, they still have extra time to give to church projects. Father Eugene also actively engages parishioners who have retired. As soon as they complete their last day of work, Father Eugene has volunteer work planned for them at the church. And the church is so much a part of their life that they are more than willing, if not flattered, to do it.

Activists and organizers often come from the middle class because they have the luxury of time and education. But they are not so far from the working class that they cannot relate. While they have had some luck and success in gaining financial stability in this country, many of them recognize that they also hold relatively little power in society and could lose their status if economic and political conditions were to change. The majority of the families at Saint Augustine's are migrants, and their experiences as struggling newcomers in this country are relatively fresh in their memories. Moreover, many still feel that they are not completely accepted by U.S. society.

The federalization of airport security hit close to home for many parishioners. One who became very involved in the struggle to save the jobs of Filipino airport screeners said, "I think as Filipinos we saw it as a threat. We thought that Filipinos who are capable, deemed to be capable in doing their jobs, [were] yanked out of them because they're not U.S. citizens. We felt [like] airport screeners . . . and then what next? Doctors, nurses, engineers? All of these people. It was flavored with so much racism or discrimination."

Maria is an active parishioner with a relative who worked as an airport screener. Although the new legislation did not threaten her personally, it threatened her family, and she became convinced that the church needed to do something about it if possible. She recalled, "We were trying to convince the city officials that people's lives will be very much affected. It is just very unfair." She was particularly angered that the government was firing her brother because of his noncitizen status while his son risked his life in the military. "My brother cannot work in this kind of job because he was not a citizen. He was being laid off because of that citizenship thing. But you know, my brother's son is working, is in the armed forces. He is in the Air Force. It is really unfair." The way she sees it, if her nephew is putting his life on the line for the country, the least the government can do is let his father keep his job. "That is their livelihood," she stresses. Maria is keenly aware that even with his job as an airport screener, it is a struggle to live in the Bay Area. "Because, you know, here in the Bay Area, our cost of living is very high and yet the wage is not comparable to the cost of living. Rental here for a one bedroom is $1,200. And the take-home is $1,200—and that's take-home. That means one of the paychecks is already gone to rental. What about the food, the clothing, the car that you drive. Gas too is another." When Saint Augustine's became involved in the airport screener struggle, her proximity to the situation made it easy for her to see that something needed to be done. "My brother was one of them that will be laid off, and so I attended the meeting."

Parish Intergenerational Interest Groups

The first of two major parish intergenerational interest groups actually operates outside of Saint Augustine's. The Bay Area Organizing Committee is a broad-based organization composed of a mix of religious, senior, labor, youth, and civic interests. The organization's director, Larry Gordon, says that its goal is to empower diverse communities and to fight institutional injustice. The BAOC's relationship with Saint Augustine's began with the church's expansion and school construction project. Father Obet says that the BAOC wanted to help the church deepen its relationships with city government officials. The parishioners claim that it was BAOC's training that enabled them to make their case against the South San Francisco Planning Commission. It helped church delegates formulate convincing arguments to present to the city council and emphasized the importance of mobilizing a large number of people to attend the council meeting in solidarity. Ultimately, hundreds of parishioners showed up at city hall, and several delegates successfully argued for the expansion of their church and the construction of an elementary school. The church's ultimate victory was an emotional one, and some parishioners wept as they told us of their joy and relief in finally getting the city to approve their project. Although the parishioners firmly believed that denying them their right to build a bigger church and a school for their children was unjust, they were very nervous about battling the city. They felt that their success was well-deserved, but it was somewhat unexpected and therefore empowering. From this experience, Saint Augustine's relationship with the BAOC grew, and the two organizations continued to collaborate on various community issues, including advocacy for Filipino airport screeners.

The BAOC lends its organizing expertise as well as its ability to mobilize other institutions for common goals. The airport screener rally drew in hundreds of parishioners from Saint Augustine's, but also hundreds more from the other BAOC member organizations.

The second crucial parish intergenerational intrest group involved in counterhegemonic projects at Saint Augustine's is made up of Small Christian Communities—prayer groups of six to twelve parishioners. According to church members we interviewed, these communities do the most to create the conditions for counterhegemonic projects within the parish. Every last interviewee talked about the groups and how members successfully mobilized large numbers of parishioners when needed. The Small Christian Communities are active for two six-week seasons per calendar year. At the time of our interviews, the prayer groups had just completed their sixteenth season. Each season, these small groups gather once a week outside of mass, usually at one of the parishioner's homes. Together they spend an hour and a half praying, reading from the gospel, reflecting, sharing thoughts and experiences, and then coming up with ways to integrate what they have learned into their lives. The "Faith Sharing and Integration" portion of the weekly format calls for the members of each Small Christian Community to share how the reading relates to their daily lives and relationships. Afterward, in the "Response in Action" portion of the meeting, attendees decide how the given lesson might be put into action and lived out in their lives. Again, this acknowledgment that religious belief must manifest itself in action is quite different from the Marxist notion that it is an "opiate of the people," and was critical in mobilizing the parishioners toward political and social justice causes.

When we asked Boy, a member of Saint Augustine's, how he was able to help gather more than 200 parishioners to join a mobilization in support of the airport screeners, he immediately cited the Small Christian Communities. "Westborough Middle School was the venue . . . and [we] had Willie Brown come out. On the day of the rally for the screeners, Ted and I were appointed coordinators. We had to get everyone from Saint Augustine's to be at this place at this time." They made general announcements from the pulpit and in the Sunday bulletins, and made phone calls to individuals. But a crucial factor, according to Boy, was that "we ha[d] these six coordinators who were supposed to pull from the pool of the Small Christian Community facilitators and from there get the numbers." Boy adds,

The Small Christian Communities of Saint Augustine's were very, very well organized, and a very cohesive force. So even if some of [the Small Christian Communities members] admittedly did not quite understand all the issues, because we said get as many of the Small Christian Community members there and get your families and get your friends and get everybody involved. I think that's one of the reasons that we had quite a good turnout. That's where they focused. I said "grab the Small Christian Communities. Get them to start mobilizing these people."

The Small Christian Communities not only facilitate the mobilization of parishioners for political purposes but also help foster the sense of community within the church. Lisa, another parishioner who was involved in the airport screener and building expansion projects, says that the sense of *kapatiran* (brotherhood or sisterhood) is very strong at Saint Augustine's. The Small Christian Communities foster what she calls "life sharing," and she attributes the closeness of the parish to this process:

Before, you know, people just come to church. Now it's so different. People [are] putting their effort together because of the Small Christian Communities. There is more involvement now. It's not about *chismis* [gossip]. One of the rules of that Bible sharing group is everything is confidential. It has to remain in that group only. Whatever you discuss, that's it. It remains in that group . . . because of that we got a whole lot of people involved . . . with the screeners. Most of them are from the Small Christian Community.

These groups seem to create an atmosphere of trust, accountability, and closeness among parishioners, which in turn fosters a sense of responsibility for carrying out their faith through action. All the parishioners who were interviewed have a strong conviction, based on their Small Christian Community experience, that prayer and action go hand in hand. As Lisa explained, "Prayer without action doesn't do anything. Because one of the teachings of God is to pray and also to do work, you know, just like Jesus. Because he did not just make miracles, you know, in order for him to do things, he has to do some work also." The Small Christian Community readings call for believers to engage in civic action. Appropriately, the pamphlet the communities had recently used as a guide was titled "The Call to Family, Community and Participation." Its opening paragraph read as follows:

The human person is not only sacred, but social. We realize our dignity and rights in relationship with others, in community. No community is more central than the family; it needs to be supported, not undermined. It is the basic cell of society, and the state has an obligation to support the family. . . . We also have the right and responsibility to participate in and contribute to the broader communities in society. (Archdiocese of San Francisco 2003, 2)

The themes of the Small Christian Community readings are heavily oriented toward social justice and, at times, employ counterhegemonic rhetoric. The themes for a recent season allude to this: "Call to Family," "Call to Community," "Call to Participation," "Catholic Social Teaching in Action," "The Call to Family, Community and Participation," and the "Obstacle of Racism." These themes help shape the social and political consciousness of the parishioners so that the ideas of "prayer without action" and "faith without justice" are not acceptable for them.

These are just some of the conditions that allowed for the initiation of counterhegemonic projects at Saint Augustine's. Filipino values, like those mentioned in previous chapters, were mentioned in the interviews. Some parishioners believed that certain Filipino-specific values came into play when the parish decided to take a stand on the issues that affected the Filipino American community. It was this sense of *kasamanahan* and a deep sense of *pamilya* (family) that moved parishioners to rise up and protect the airport screeners—their *kababayan* (countrymen/countrywomen), whose families stood to suffer from the loss of their jobs.

Saint Augustine's exemplifies the successful activation of churchgoers in improving their living conditions, and the lives of others around them. Through their church, parishioners have seen what the power of organized people can accomplish. But there is still untapped potential and much work to do. Sister Nona and some of the parishioners touched upon some of the injustices that they continue to see every day.

Hence, just as predicted by classical scholars of power relations and contemporary Filipino American researchers, the supremacy of the U.S. state did lead to the formation of *kasamahan*-building, counterhegemonic activities through Saint Augustine's Catholic Church in South San Francisco.

Summary and Conclusion

From the actions of Christopher, Juree, and Candice, I concluded that history has a way of remembering and paying its dues to the marginalized and, at times, oppressed Filipino community of San Francisco. In an ironic and fitting turn of events, what became Victoria Manalo Draves Park in the South of Market area was ironically once a part of the notorious Columbia Square, where "Filipino booty"—valuables seized by American soldiers during the bloody Philippine-American War—had once been exhibited. During this battle, which lasted beyond its official ending date in 1902, American soldiers burned seventy-five Catholic churches and massacred thousands of Filipino civilians, including babies and children. A mixed collection of war souvenirs and spoils—crucifixes, goblets, images of the Virgin Mary, iron grills, bells, Philippine army uniforms, belts, rifles, bayonets, and boots—was publicly displayed in Columbia Square alongside a trophy cannon mounted there by famed newspaper magnate William Randolph Hearst. With loud cheers from both young and old, Victoria Manalo Draves Park was formally opened on a sunny day in October 2006. At an earlier celebration, former Philippine president Fidel V. Ramos firmly shook Draves's hand in gratitude for the honor she also bestowed on her father's homeland.

Based on our extensive archival and ethnographic research, I have attempted to provide conceptual, historical, and empirical evidence of the emergence of intergenerational *kasamahan* leading to Filipino counterhegemonic (passion and revolution) civic action within the Filipino migrant religious experience in San Francisco.

Conceptually and historically, Marx, Weber, Freire, Gramsci, and Omi and Winant provide a good philosophical framework within which to examine hegemonic and counterhegemonic action against the dominant structures of church and state. However, Ileto introduced us to a more useful, culturally adapted analytical lens by pointing out that Filipino counterhegemony against Spanish and American colonizers was inspired by the subtexts of religious teachings used to assert control over migrant groups. In this chapter, I extended Ileto's assertion, as well as data gathered by Mabalon, San Buenaventura, and Cordova, by arguing that given the proper conditions, Philippine church-inspired counterhegemony can be transferred and utilized effectively by Filipino migrants to challenge hegemonic structures in American society. Ironically, the counterhegemonic activities of Filipino migrants against American churches and state were inspired by the same teachings used by Spanish and American missionaries to the Philippines. Many of these subversive activities started within indigenous Filipino Masonic lodges, then moved into Catholic and Protestant churches.

The participant observations at San Francisco Bay Area Catholic churches allowed me to study this sociopolitical phenomenon in more depth. Following the establishment of a culture of respect for the wisdom of elders (*paggalang sa dunong ng nakakatanda*), I found the following conditions to be critical to intergenerational passionate energy and revolutionary spirit to become sucessful *kasamahan* organizing.

First, intergenerational *kasamahan* begins with compelling national or local political issues. These problems are close to the hearts of the migrant congregation and its larger ethnic community. Some church members might be directly affected, as was the case with the displacement of Filipino airport screeners at the San Francisco International Airport or, as I discuss in the next chapter, the pursuit of government benefits for Filipino World War II veterans. These two issues of national concern were also closely followed by the Filipino community in California. Members of Saint Augustine's congregation had numerous internal, but more significantly external, concerns that drew them outside the confines of their church. Additionally, socially liberal San Francisco, with its environment of tolerance, radicalism, and acceptance, is more conducive and open to counterhegemonic gestures than most cities in the United States.

Second, young and old charismatic religious and lay leaders are critical to identifying and creating the necessary *kasamahan* around these compelling issues. Such leaders must be comfortable employing the knowledge of political organizing gained in the Philippines. The leadership could be administered in an explicit, hands-on style, as was the case in Saint Augustine's. Church leaders might find themselves in front of a march protesting injustices to members of the larger community, or they could simply send signals of consent to parishioners from behind the altar during the homily in a mass.

Third, the church members' socioeconomic background is also a critical element of effective intergenerational *kasamahan* development. The current class standing (usually middle or lower class) of migrants and their region of origin in the Philippines are less important than their Filipino political socialization and willingness to combine spiritual energy and mass action to address congregational and community issues.

Finally, parish intergenerational interest groups (*kasamahan* organizations) are key determinants of successful mass action and linking with community groups. The Saint Augustine's case illustrates the significance of engaged parish intergenerational groups such as the Small Christian Communities and the Bay Area Organizing Committee. Parish intergenerational intrest groups are important for winning small battles in city hall and commission hearings, as well as big wars, such as the struggle for veterans' benefits, which is argued in front of the U.S. Congress. They are also the key to continuing struggles against chronic health and social problems, including HIV infection, drug addiction, homelessness, and lack of health insurance, among others.

Although Marx was critical of religion, he also described it as the "sigh of the oppressed creature, the heart of a heartless world and the soul of soulless conditions." Religion inspires followers to speak out against perceived moral injustices. Applying dialectics to the idea of the church as a hegemon shows that all things are in a state of perpetual change. As such, a new, more evolved Filipino American church can emerge, with endless potential for successful counterhegemonic activity directed at creating equitable conditions in this society. In the end, as Marx noted, "man makes religion," so it will be women and men who interpret religion so as to address oppression and injustices. In the next chapter, I discuss the highly controversial Filipino World War II veterans' equity issue to illustrate how *kasamahan* can escalate to *bayanihan* through intergenerational, counterhegemonic activities. In this case, the activities were spearheaded by young Filipino migrant faithful to help their oppressed elders.

7

Reconciling
Old and Young Spirits

It happened at the height of the holy Lenten season. An emotional encounter with an elderly parishioner of Saint Boniface Catholic Church who had lived through so much: serious injury as a soldier and hard labor at a prisoner-of-war camp in his early twenties, and now, in his seventies, he was coping with cancer alone and in a foreign land. His stories about his life experiences evoked religious anecdotes from the Pasyon (Passion of Christ). And yet, Idelfonso "Tatang Floro" Bagasala seemed undaunted by the many challenges he had been through. Smiling, he began his conversation with the young Filipino American audience, saying, in Tagalog, "I feel blessed to be with you tonight." The facilitator translated his humble words into English. Continuing in Taglish, the seventy-six-year-old Filipino World War II veteran proceeded to tell bittersweet life stories, which, ironically, were highlighted by his exploits not on the battlefields of Luzon but, instead, on the perilous streets of San Francisco's low-income Tenderloin and South of Market neighborhoods. He told the audience how he earned a living shoulder to shoulder with homeless people, pimps, prostitutes, street entertainers, petty thieves, gang members, as well as drug dealers and users. As a former Philippine Commonwealth Army regular, Tatang Floro explained to the attentive crowd, "We were promised U.S. citizenship by General Douglas MacArthur for fighting under his USAFFE [U.S. Armed Forces of the Far East] command." After waiting more than forty years to be naturalized at the U.S. embassy in Manila, it became clear that he could no longer count on receiving the veterans' benefits promised to him years earlier. So the aging veteran left his wife, children, and grandchildren in the Philippines to come to the United States and earn money to support them. When he arrived in San Francisco, Tatang Floro had no income, so he supplemented his welfare checks doing odd jobs along downtown Market Street. A few feet away from San Francisco's famous cable cars and trendy shops, he rented out chess tables. "After I was diagnosed with cancer at San Francisco General Hospital, I lay in the hospital begging for an interpreter," he said. The gray-haired Tatang Floro admitted that he did not understand some of the questions on the forms he was asked to sign, since he barely knew how to read English and did not know how to write. A devout Christian, Tatang Floro credits the power of prayer for what he calls his "miraculous recovery." Having no relatives in the United States, he added that his strong faith in God is what keeps him going from day to day. As Tatang tearfully implored the youth, many of whom looked at him as if he was their own *lolo* (grandfather), to take care of each other, many in the dimly lit room wept with him.

The account that Tatang Floro shared with his young audience that evening sums up the fate of many aging Filipino World War II veterans (also referred to as the *veteranos, manongs,* or elders), as well as their strong faith, which fosters the belief that with the help of the younger generation of Filipino migrants, their pleas would finally be answered in the halls of the U.S. Congress. Bound by the same religious heritage, Tatang Floro and many of the young Filipinos in the audience work and worship as a community at the former Irish and German Catholic churches of Saint Patrick's in the South of Market area and Saint Boniface in the Tenderloin. The faith community at Saint Boniface, led by former Philippine Scout J. Bunagan, had been active in the Bay Area Organizing Committee since 1993. At one of the gatherings after mass at Saint Boniface, Tatang Floro, who occasionally helps as an usher, met Gladys M., a young Filipino migrant member of the church choir and a student at the City College of San Francisco. Inspired by Tatang Floro's plight, she vowed to bring it to the attention of Filipino American student organizations at her school, as well as at San Francisco State University, the University of San Francisco, and San Jose State University. Ultimately, she did much more than speak about the predicament of Filipino veterans. Gladys also helped her peers make protest signs, which she, other students, and veterans (including Tatang Floro) carried at the grand San Francisco Veterans Day Parade in downtown San Francisco. Many students of Filipino descent and their friends from Catholic and public high schools, as well as Bay Area colleges, also participated in the parade.

For the past decade, because of the veterans' faith and Filipino youth activism, the stories of Tatang Floro and Gladys have been mainstreamed in popular dailies, including the *Los Angeles Times, San Fran-*

cisco *Chronicle, New York Times, Washington Post,* and *Seattle Times.*
Numerous films and documentaries have also addressed this topic. But
the scholarly journal writings that have emerged to enlighten the academic and policy communities focus their analyses on the legal (Sherman
1985; Georgetown University Law Center 1989; Murphy 1990), socio-
historical (Fabros 1994, 1995, n.d.; Gonzalves 1995; Nakano 2000,
2004; Posadas 1999), and gerontological (Becker, Beyene, and Canalita
2000) dimensions of this important human rights issue.

In this chapter, I examine two important human rights cases that
have reached the halls of the U.S. Congress—the Filipino World War II
veterans equity issue and the extrajudicial killings in the Philippines. I
will look at the ways in which a Filipino migrant community and its
churches have rallied around these transnational causes and developed
an intergenerational *bayanihan* network of Filipinos and non-Filipinos
in the United States, the Philippines, and the world.

Bayanihan *Case Study 1:* Veteranos, *Church, and Youth*

What brings aging Filipino veterans like Tatang Floro, the faith community, and Filipino youth like Gladys together is a complex story, which
traces its roots to America's growth as a hegemonic state in the global
political system after defeating imperial Spain. Given the allegations that
soldiers returning from America's current War on Terror in Iraq and
Afghanistan are receiving inadequate care and attention from the U.S.
Department of Defense, it is not surprising that the veterans from World
War II have not been given their due.

Making a Promise: Veterans' Rights and Benefits

The Filipino military units that would later be called the Commonwealth Army of the Philippines were started in the early 1900s at the
same time that the United States assumed formal sovereignty over its
prized colony. The Philippine Commonwealth Army was formally established through Philippine Commonwealth Act Number 1, approved by
the U.S. Congress in December 1935. As commander in chief of the U.S.
Armed Forces, President Franklin Delano Roosevelt issued the Presidential Order (6 *Federal Register* 3825) that required the Philippine Commonwealth Army to respond to the call to military service of a U.S.

president (Meixsel 1995). In addition to these recruitment initiatives, the U.S. Army established many military bases throughout the colony's various islands. These included two of the largest outside of the continental United States—heavyweights Clark Air Base and Subic Naval Base—which gave America a formidable presence in the Asia-Pacific region.

On July 26, 1941, sensing a growing threat from Japan, President Roosevelt ordered the Commonwealth Army of the Philippines—then composed of U.S. nationals—to serve under General Douglas MacArthur's U.S. Armed Forces of the Far East. At the time of the USAFFE's formation, the unit consisted of 22,532 troops; 11,972 of these were Philippine Scouts, and 10,473 were members of the Philippine Division, which consisted of 2,552 Americans and 7,921 Filipinos. All the division's enlisted men, with the exception of the Thirty-first Infantry Regiment and various military police and headquarters troops, were Philippine Scouts (Olson 2002).

Not long afterward, imperial Japan began plotting takeovers of nations along the Pacific Rim, supposedly to construct a "Greater East Asia Co-Prosperity Sphere"—a group of self-sufficient Asian nations that were free of Western powers and, of course, led by the Japanese. One of the nations targeted was the Philippines; after all, the country was America's Pacific buffer and was only a couple of hours from Tokyo by plane. Hence, Japan made plans to cut off America's ties to its Asian outpost. The Japanese military launched a surprise air raid on the U.S. Navy's fleet stationed at Pearl Harbor, Hawaii, on December 7, 1941, and a subsequent air attack the following day against key U.S. military targets in the Philippines. Having destroyed parts of Hawaii, Japanese "air attacks were conducted against Davao, Baguio and Aparri on the same day" in the Philippines, which were all places where American soldiers were stationed (Agoncillo 1990, 390). The United States and its Asian commonwealth territory had no choice but to defend themselves by entering the war against Japan.

President Roosevelt was in desperate need of men and women to serve in the U.S. military. Fighting a war on both the Asian and European fronts took its toll on the numbers of both active duty and reserve soldiers. To maintain effective air, land, and sea operations, the president and congressional leaders knew that the U.S. Army urgently needed sustained troop replenishments. Understandably, few wanted to enlist during wartime. Since the Philippines was not only an American colony but also under attack by Japan, President Roosevelt turned to Filipinos, who were then U.S. nationals, for help. The Commonwealth Government of the Philippines complied by drafting Filipino males between the ages of twenty-one and fifty.

Taking the president's cue, the U.S. Congress passed the Second War Powers Act (1942), amending the Nationality Act of 1940. This new legislation essentially liberalized "naturalization requirements for alien servicemen in the United States armed forces outside the territory of the continental United States" and eliminated barriers to naturalization (Georgetown University Law Center 1989). The drafting of regular and nontraditional Filipino combatants into the U.S. Army helped America's war effort tremendously. Nevertheless, the United States lost control of the Philippines in April 1942.

The forced departure of General MacArthur from the Philippines, the surrender of the USAFFE forces to the Japanese Imperial Army in Corregidor, and the consequent Bataan death march, in which 3,000 Americans and 10,000 Filipinos were killed, fueled the United States' resolve to continue fighting. Surviving Filipino soldiers retreated to the mountains and turned to warfare tactics they had used effectively decades earlier during the Philippine Revolution and the Philippine-American War. Welcomed by MacArthur and the USAFFE command, Filipino and American soldiers formed guerrilla and underground units that sabotaged Japanese civil and military activities, hindering Japan's full administrative control of the Philippines. Ultimately, only twelve of forty-eight provinces fell to Japan's imperial flag. From 1942 to 1946, guerrilla and underground resistance units also passed on critical intelligence to the USAFFE chain of command. In return for their loyalty and gallantry, President Roosevelt and General MacArthur reiterated their "promise of citizenship and veterans' benefit to Filipino soldiers fighting under the American flag" (Wadhwani 1999, 34). Many veterans have also recalled that U.S. government and military officials enticed them to serve by saying, "Lay your lives on the line for the American ideals . . . and we will make you Americans" (Malkin 1997, 12). As U.S. nationals, the Filipino soldiers recruited in the Philippines—Old and New Philippine Scouts, Philippine Commonwealth Army regulars, and guerrillas—would never forget these promises. But would they ever be fulfilled?

Close to 100,000 Filipino civilians lost their lives during World War II. In September 1945, Japan was convinced to surrender to the United States after U.S. Air Force planes dropped two atomic bombs on Hiroshima and Nagasaki. Japan's defeat was a proud moment for the United

States and the Philippines. A month after Japan's surrender, Congress passed the Armed Forces Voluntary Recruitment Act of 1945 authorizing the recruitment of 50,000 New Philippine Scouts. These New Philippine Scouts served under the U.S. Army from October 6, 1945, to June 30, 1947. In gratitude for their heroism in the defense of America and the Philippines, President Roosevelt in a 1945 White House policy speech reiterated his promise again that Filipino soldiers—that is, Scouts, Commonwealth Army regulars, and guerrillas—would be granted U.S. citizenship and receive the same benefits as all other U.S. veterans. Roosevelt's policy pronouncement was received by General Omar Bradley, then administrator of the U.S. Veterans Administration (VA), who began preparing his staff to process the inflow of Filipinos as American veterans. After their wartime service, the Filipino World War II veterans waited.

Breaking the Promise: Truman and the Rescission Acts

As it turned out, those Filipino veterans would have to wait for a long time. The emotional fervor of the war and America's promise died along with President Roosevelt in April 1945. Roosevelt's vice president, Harry S. Truman, ascended to the presidency to complete the unfinished business of World War II. Germany and Japan were defeated. The year 1946 ushered in three major political events that would become embedded in the national histories of both the United States and the Philippines. The first occurred on July 4, when the United States granted full independence to the Philippines after forty years of colonial rule. Having helped save the Philippines on behalf of the United States, the Filipino World War II veterans anxiously anticipated their promised benefits and pensions. However, two succeeding events in Washington, D.C., would bring the veterans only disappointment and frustration.

Democratic president Truman, assisted by a Democrat-controlled Senate and House, disregarded President Roosevelt's promise—but, even worse, the Filipino veterans' patriotism and loyalty to America—by signing and executing two rescission acts, formally breaking America's promise to them. The initial blow was the First Supplemental Surplus Appropriation Rescission Act, or Public Law 79-301, which authorized a $200 million appropriation to the Commonwealth Army of the Philippines, with the provision that those soldiers be deemed to have never been in the U.S. military. Another blow was delivered through Public Law 79-391, the Second Supplemental Surplus Appropriation Rescission

Act, enacted in May, which disenfranchised the Filipinos in the New Philippine Scouts of their U.S. military service. Those who fought in USAFFE guerrilla units were also disowned.

Therefore, only the Old Philippine Scouts, the First and Second Filipino Infantry Regiments, and others who signed up directly with the army in the United States were acknowledged as having fought for America in World War II. Ironically, before the passage of the 1946 rescission acts, VA officials considered all Filipino military service to have met the statutory requirements for U.S. World War II veteran status. But in 1945, the VA was asked by President Truman to determine how much it cost to provide veterans' benefits to the Filipino soldiers. The VA study estimated that it would cost the United States $3.2 billion to award them continuing veterans' benefits. In effect, President Truman and Congress connived to craft legislation that would deny the Filipino World War II soldiers naturalization and privileges because the VA report conceded that these benefits would be very costly. Critics therefore contend that the promises to Filipino recruits of naturalization, benefits, and pensions were also disingenuous.

Fifty Years Later: Citizenship and Welfare Benefits

Congressional justifications for cutting back on Roosevelt's promise did not put a halt to the veterans' fight for justice. Many bilateral talks between the Philippine and the U.S. governments have involved the problematic rescission acts. The veterans took a step closer toward realizing their goal of naturalization in 1990. During that year, President George H. W. Bush enacted a critical second installment to Roosevelt's promise when he signed the Immigration and Naturalization Act, or Public Law 101-649 (Pimentel 1999). After forty years of advocacy and litigation, "special provisions" on the naturalization of Filipino veterans were finally introduced by their congressional sympathizers in this comprehensive immigration reform act. Specifically, Section 405 of the law granted U.S. citizenship to Filipino veterans who served honorably in an active duty status under the command of the USAFFE, or within the Philippine Commonwealth Army, the Philippine Scouts, or recognized guerrilla units at any time during the period beginning September 1, 1939, and ending December 31, 1946. Further amendments authorized the Immigration and Naturalization Service to naturalize eligible Filipino veterans at the U.S. embassy in Manila.

This was definitely a gigantic step in the right direction for the veterans. However, there was still one large problem: although the veterans were allowed to become U.S. citizens, they still did not have the same benefits that U.S. veterans enjoyed. All in all, veterans who had been naturalized found themselves in a situation that was far different than they originally expected. That is, before immigrating, many viewed the United States as the land of opportunity and open doors. However, those same migrants often find later on that those impressions are not quite accurate. Since President George H. W. Bush signed the 1990 Immigration Act, about 28,000 veterans have moved to the United States from the Philippines and been naturalized. Most of them have settled in various parts of California, but many have also found homes in Hawaii, Nebraska, New Jersey, Illinois, Florida, Texas, and New York. Many of these veterans were not able to bring their families with them because they simply could not afford the travel costs. Far from home and separated from their families, these men often suffer from depression, poverty, and loneliness. Having no family to turn to, many veterans bond together, creating a community among themselves. With little money, they often live under impoverished conditions. Some veterans have told of spending "their first months homeless and destitute, in a chilly storage room basement" (Lat 1997, 6). Others gathered in "groups of four or more and crowded into cheap, single-room apartments" (6). Their living conditions are often unsanitary, overcrowded, and unsafe. Nevertheless, many veterans choose to contend with such conditions as they wait for the government to fulfill its promise to them.

Most of the veterans are in their seventies and eighties and too old to work, but they have discovered sources of money to help them survive. For example, they have learned that the government provides welfare. However, this was not the more generous veterans' welfare that would enable them to support their families; instead, the naturalized veterans were eligible only for the same lower welfare payments as nonveterans. Veterans also obtain money from organizations and individuals who support their struggle.

For these late-life migrants, there was no doubt about it—life was hard in expensive San Francisco. Not having enough money to live on their own, many veterans banded together, sharing expenses and small living spaces. But some who did not do this instead ended up on the streets, homeless and penniless. One residential building that housed many of the veterans at rates they could afford was the Delta Hotel. This former hotel had been converted into tiny apartments to accommodate the high demand for living space, primarily from the Filipino veterans. The areas in which they settled, SoMa and the Tenderloin, are known as neighborhoods where homelessness, drug problems, gang encounters, vehicle break-ins, petty thefts, street harassment, prostitution, sex shops, and violence abound; these are all particularly frightening to lonely, aging men who have very little money and speak limited English. Obviously, jobs are extremely hard to find in these areas, but some have managed to find employment as custodians, janitors, security guards, kitchen helpers, and doormen in various San Francisco businesses—essentially low-paying, undesirable jobs. To supplement their Social Security income, some of them also provide paid child care or work as companions to the elderly for other migrant families in the area (Aranda 1999).

Displaced and impoverished, a group of veterans and their family members experienced further devastation when the residential Delta Hotel burned down on August 11, 1997. The four-alarm fire "destroyed the five-story hotel and left many people either dead or homeless." The Red Cross came to the aid of the veterans; to some, the "Red Cross cots and the gray blankets brought back memories of the war." The veterans were provided with temporary shelter in a gymnasium. One veteran wryly remarked, "This is like the Army again." A woman—one of the few veterans' wives—tried to put the loss in perspective, adding, "We only lost our means of shelter. We lost everything when we moved here" (Tsong 1998, 25).

Help from Church and Community

At the informal Filipino *barangay* that formed in the South of Market and Tenderloin areas, Saint Patrick's and Saint Boniface churches, Filipino social service agencies, and the Veterans Equity Center provide assistance to the veterans as well as the larger community. The veterans also have access to numerous Philippine-oriented services and establishments in the area. They also join other Filipino seniors in the daily subsidized lunches and ballroom dancing sessions that are funded by the city and county of San Francisco at the South of Market Recreation Center.

Many Filipino veterans show that their sense of duty to God is just as steadfast today as was their sense of duty to the U.S. government decades ago. Their strong relationships to spiritual spaces have sustained their faith in their fight for equitable treatment. Located in the heart of the South of Market, Saint Patrick's Catholic Church on Mission Street is one of the spiritual centers of gravity for the veterans. At the 7:30 A.M. Sunday mass, many Filipino veterans work as ushers and greet the early morning congregants, who also are mostly Filipino. More often than not, the celebrant is a Filipino priest who weaves Philippine humor and anecdotes into his homily. Previous chapters have already described the Filipino characteristics of spiritual life at Saint Patrick's in detail. This church is also where Filipino youth, like Gladys, and veterans, like Tatang Floro, are able to share information about incidents of social injustice and plan responsive action.

In Saint Patrick's, as in other area Filipino American churches, veterans and youth add their petitions to the community's prayers to icons of popular devotions in the Philippines; many of these, including the Mother of Perpetual Help, the Divine Mercy of the Holy Infant Jesus, the Santo Niño of Cebu, San Lorenzo Ruiz (first Filipino saint), and the Black Nazareno of Quiapo, Manila, are present at Saint Patrick's. According to Monsignor Fred Bitanga, the church pastor, the veterans are not just regular Sunday churchgoers and ushers. They also actively volunteer during mass and church functions as greeters, Eucharist ministers, collectors, banner bearers, lectors, cleanup crew members, and food servers. Monsignor Bitanga adds that they have also provided financial and material support to the church and its causes, even with their meager incomes. The Filipino veterans are also active members of the church's many lay organizations. Saint Patrick's consistently assists with activities directed at veterans, including fund-raisers, Christmas parties and dinners, the purchase of gifts, and referrals to social and support services. After the Delta Hotel fire, Monsignor Bitanga and some of his altar boys and girls were highly visible, moving people and belongings from temporary Red Cross shelters to available rooms in the South of Market and Tenderloin areas. Since the monsignor's retirement, his successor, Father Dura, continues the tradition of attending to the special needs of the veterans in the congregation.

All the Filipino American churches that we surveyed in the San Francisco Bay Area have faithful Filipino veterans and youth among their congregations who participate actively in masses, Bible studies, and church organizations and functions and who perform community outreach, donate funds, and receive counseling and support. The veterans who are not able to travel to religious spaces pray in their homes and are visited regularly by ministers, pastors, and church members, who also bring them food and other necessities. Besides offering prayers, church leaders and their congregations have appealed to their local and congressional representatives to act on the veterans' issue. They have joined other Filipino American community-based organizations in protests in front of city hall. Church members have raised funds to help fly veterans to Washington, D.C., to meet with congressional staff and testify in hearings. Appropriately, on these trips, they have been hosted by Filipino Methodist, Catholic, Iglesia ni Cristo, and Jehovah's Witness families.

Veterans and Youth Action

During the most heated battles with the U.S. Congress, the aging Filipino World War II veterans staged numerous demonstrations and garnered plenty of public support from private individuals and public officials in San Francisco, especially the youth in high school and college. Veterans like Tatang Floro and youth like Gladys know that local officials are powerless to change the veterans' situation, since theirs is a federal government issue, but this has not stopped San Francisco politicians from declaring their support of the veterans in official terms. For instance, on May 27, 1999, heavy lobbying from Filipino veterans and students convinced the San Francisco Human Rights Commission (HRC) to pass a resolution acknowledging and supporting the battle against the "unjust and inequitable treatment" of Filipino veterans who fought under the American flag in World War II. After all, San Francisco government units, like the Department of Health, will essentially have to care for the veterans, whether or not they get their benefits from Congress and the federal agencies concerned. With Filipino community and church lobbying, the mayor's office and board of supervisors have agreed to budget for social programs that help to fill in the veterans' "equity gap." These include accommodations such as meals, a food bank, and skills enhancement programs to improve their employability. While these programs are helpful, they are ultimately unsatisfying to the veterans and their supporters, as they constitute welfare rather than the well-deserved benefits and pensions they seek. Table 7.1 summarizes what the Filipino veterans have received from the U.S. Congress.

In Washington, besides engaging in meditations, prayers, and candlelight vigils, Filipino veterans and members of Student Action for Veterans Equity (SAVE) have risked their health and lives by participating in hunger strikes, chaining themselves to the White House fence, and staging fake deaths (or die-ins). But this has only gotten them the minor legislative installments mentioned earlier. Nevertheless, they have earned a

TABLE 7.1
Congressional Action for Filipino Veterans Benefits

YEAR	LAW	DESCRIPTION
1948	Public Law 80-865	Authorized the construction of the Veterans Memorial Hospital in Manila.
1963	Public Law 88-40	Allowed the Veterans Memorial Hospital in Manila to care for non-service-connected conditions of Filipino and U.S. veterans.
1973	Public Law 93-82	Authorized U.S. assistance to help the Philippine government provide medical care to Filipino veterans.
1981	Public Law 97-72	Reauthorized U.S. assistance to help the Philippine government provide medical care to Filipino veterans.
1990	Public Law 101-649	Made certain Filipino veterans who served during World War II eligible to apply for naturalization to U.S. citizenship.
1999	Public Law 106-169	Allowed receipt of 75% of federal Social Security Income (SSI) rate for certain Filipino veterans who permanently reside in the Philippines and were present in the United States in 1999. Eligible veterans who were California residents receive an additional cash benefit as a result of AB 1978.
2000	Public Law 106-377	Allowed Commonwealth Army (USAFFE) veterans and veterans of the recognized guerrilla forces already receiving disability compensation the full statutory rate while in the United States and treatment at VA medical facilities for service-connected disabilities, if they are permanent legal residents. (50 cents:$1.00 rate for veterans in the Philippines)
2000	Public Law 106-419	Provided full burial benefits to survivors of Commonwealth Army veterans and veterans of the recognized guerrilla forces if they are permanent residents of the United States and meet other entitling conditions.
2003	Public Law 108-170	Provided hospital care, nursing home care, and outpatient medical services regardless of disability to Commonwealth Army veterans, veterans of the recognized guerrilla forces, and New Philippine Scouts in the same manner and subject to the same terms and conditions as apply to U.S. veterans, subject to enrollment prioritization and resource availability.
2003	Public Law 108-183	Provides for full-dollar disability compensation and DIC to members of New Philippine Scouts receiving such if the veteran resides in the United States, burial in the national cemetery, and maintenance of the Veterans Affairs Regional Office in Manila until December 31, 2009.

Source: U.S. Congress

good amount of publicity, so much that many more people are acknowledging their struggle and joining them in their fight. As mentioned at the beginning of this chapter, Filipino American youth have joined the Filipino churches and other Filipino community-based organizations in their support of the veterans. As the next generation of activists, listeners, and leaders, this group of youth has proven its commitment and usefulness in demonstrations, marches, parades, and protests for the veterans' cause. SAVE members come from the San Francisco Bay Area's colleges and universities, including the Jesuit Catholic University of San Francisco, University of California–Berkeley, City College of San Francisco, California State University–East Bay, Stanford University, and San Francisco State University. They have been politicized by information gathered from the Internet, newspapers, their peers, documentaries, Filipino American nonprofit organizations, and their teachers.

At the 2001 San Francisco Veterans Day parade, a smiling Tatang Floro waved from a bright red rented trolley designed to look like a traditional San Francisco cable car, while Gladys, who became a SAVE volunteer, handed over a protest poster to Glen Andag, a student from the University of San Francisco. According to Andag, the veterans issue changed his view of the society around him and inspired him to look deeper into his faith and social justice. In a paper for a Philippine studies course about politics, Andag wrote this impassioned reflection on his experience engaging in civic action on the veterans' behalf:

On Sunday November 11, 2001, Veterans Day was celebrated, as it is every year on the same day. It is a time for Americans to pay tribute to those who fought in America's battles for justice. But it is somewhat dementedly amusing when some of the people who fought for justice are being treated unjustly. During this year's Veterans Day Parade, members of the Filipino American youth marched in the parade alongside our veterans. To everyone else in the parade, it was just like any other procession down a major street. But to us, it was taking a stand against an injustice that has been overlooked, ignored and denied for 55 years-too long. We started at 2nd and Market streets to join the parade. Instead of smiling and waving to the crowds that came to watch, we screamed and proclaimed our struggle; the veterans are our fathers, uncles, grandfathers and friends—their struggle is now our struggle. We screamed to let our voices be heard and we chanted "They fought, they died, you promised, you lied!" "U.S. Government, do what's right. End this 50 year old fight!"

Speaking for myself, I can say that I admire these soldiers for what they have done and what they have been through for the past fifty-five years. I look to these men as soldiers leading a revolution toward equality and progression. Since this country has progressed with its values and accepting of diversity, I feel that the veterans had made a contribution, because if not for them, then possibly the 1990 Naturalization Law may have not been nullified until decades after, and the Immigration Act of 1965 that allowed more migrants to enter the United States may have been passed during a later year as well. I am not alone in my opinions; many of my peers marched alongside the veterans and me during our demonstrations. A promise is a promise, and the U.S. government should understand that it is so hard to break a promise and then stick by their decision to break it. Many of us agree that there has to be a reason other than a huge portion of the budget diminishing to break the promise of 1942. There has to be some other motives of doing so.

But it did not end as a term paper. Andag was so inspired that he wrote the veterans' story into the annual student production of "Barrio: Philippine Cultural Night," which was watched and applauded by hundreds of students, faculty, parents, and guests. After Andag graduated, the fight for the Filipino World War II veterans was carried on by subsequent migrant youth leaders, including Mark Sagado from Seattle, Diane Romualdez from Los Angeles, Juner Valencia from Oakland, and Aethel Cruz from San Jose. They have sustained the fight for Filipino World War II veterans' equity through intergenerational *bayanihan* in Filipino youth-supported organizations, including the South of Market Community Action Network, SAVE, Filipino Community Support (FOCUS-Bay Area), and the Filipino Community Center (FCC-San Francisco).

The Results of Intergenerational Bayanihan

The activation of intergenerational, church, and community-based *bayanihan* has produced significant results. In 1999, President Bill Clinton signed Public Law 106-169, which expanded income-based Social Security disability benefits to certain World War II veterans, including Filipino veterans of World War II who served in the organized military forces of the Philippines. It gave them the opportunity to return to the Philippines to receive a portion of their Social Security income there. In October

2000, a non-welfare-based veterans' benefit law was passed (Public Law 106-377). In it, Congress authorized the VA to provide full-dollar-rate compensation payments to veterans of the Commonwealth Army or recognized guerrilla forces residing in the United States if they were either U.S. citizens or lawfully admitted permanent resident aliens. Public Law 106-377 also requested the VA to provide care at its clinics for any non-service-related conditions of those same veterans. These Filipino veterans benefit provisions were supplemented by Public Law 106-419, which authorized the payment of burial benefits on behalf of veterans in these groups. Only the New Philippine Scouts remained ineligible for burial allowances. Table 7.2 describes the differences in VA benefits among the various Filipino veterans of World War II.

In 2003, Congress passed Public Law 108-170 (Veterans Health Care, Capital Asset, and Business Improvement Act of 2003) and Public Law 108-183 (Veterans Benefits Act of 2003). Signed into law by President George W. Bush in December 2003, this legislation expanded compensation and burial benefit payments to the full-dollar rate for New Philippine Scouts residing in the United States if they were either U.S. citizens or lawfully admitted permanent resident aliens. It also increased Dependency and Indemnity Compensation benefits to the full-dollar rate for survivors of veterans who served in the New Philippine Scouts, Philippine Commonwealth Army, or recognized guerrilla forces if the survivor resided in the United States and was either a U.S. citizen or a legally admitted resident alien. As a result of this legislation, Filipino veterans can now receive care in VA hospitals, clinics, and nursing homes. However, these benefits are still not on a par with those of other veterans of America's wars. What is still missing? Of the numerous benefits and pensions that require corrective legislation, the most pressing are the death pension and non-service-connected disability pension, since most of the veterans are currently in their late seventies. For this reason, the *veteranos* and youth continue to testify in congressional committees. In 2007, following statements from surviving veterans and their lobby groups, senators heard from Jenah Mari Paloy Yangwas, a SAVE member and granddaughter of a Filipino World War II veteran. Meanwhile, at related hearings in the U.S. House of Representatives, attendees heard an impassioned speech by another SAVE advocate, Jaymee Faith Sagisi, who is also the granddaughter of a World War II guerrilla fighter. The intergenerational faith of the veterans and their young advocates fuels their continuing *bayanihan* activities.

TABLE 7.2

VA Benefits for Filipino Veterans Legally Residing in the United States

Benefit	Old Philippine Scouts	First and Second Infantry	Commonwealth Army	Recognized Guerrillas	New Philippine Scouts
Health care for service-connected disabilities	Yes	Yes	Yes*	Yes*	Yes*
Health care for non-service-connected disabilities	Yes	Yes	Yes*		
PL 106-377	Yes*				
PL 106-377	Yes				
PL 108-170					
Outpatient care for service-connected disabilities	Yes	Yes	Yes*	Yes*	Yes*
Outpatient care for non-service-connected disabilities	Yes	Yes	Yes*		
PL 106-377	Yes*				
PL 106-377	Yes				
PL 108-170					
Service-connected disability compensation**	Yes	Yes	Yes	Yes	Yes
Non-service-connected disability	Yes	Yes	No	No	No
Dependency and Indemnity Compensation (DIC)**	Yes	Yes	Yes		
Full rate					
PL 108-183	Yes				
Full rate					
PL 108-183	Yes				
Full rate					
PL 108-183					
Death pension	Yes	Yes	No	No	No
Burial allowance	Yes	Yes	Yes		
PL 106-419	Yes	Yes			
PL 108-183					

*Subject to enrollment prioritization and resource availability.
**Service-connected disability compensation and DIC full-dollar rates are given to veterans and survivors who are residing in the United States. Half-dollar rates are given to eligible veterans and survivors residing in the Philippines.
Source: U.S. Department of Veteran Affairs (VA)

Bayanihan *Case Study 2: Protestant Churches and Extrajudicial Killings in the Philippines*

Decades after World War II, America is still at war. Its most current battle, the global War on Terror, has critical human rights consequences for citizens, particularly pastors and lay workers in its former colony. For this reason, Filipino American migrant faithful and their churches, through *bayanihan* activism, take advantage of their influence inside their relatively safe American homeland by voicing their concern, protesting, and seeking action from their U.S. political representatives against abuses and atrocities in the Philippines. The case illustrates the leadership and grassroots efforts of mainstream Protestant groups, particularly the United Methodist Church, in weaving together expansive interfaith, intergenerational networks, which are the foundation of effective transnational *bayanihan*.

Militarization, Human Rights in the Philippines and
America's War on Terror

During the days of the Philippine-American War, U.S. authorities militarized civil law enforcement in the Philippines with their creation of the Philippine Constabulary (PC). The PC was designed as a special paramilitary unit for quelling and infiltrating pro-independence Filipino civilian and military groups that were planning to destabilize the political administration of the Philippines. PC officers were given sweeping military and civilian powers to arrest, detain, interrogate, and, in certain directives, to kill. They patrolled the highways, guarded government buildings and facilities, and performed regular police and military functions in urban and rural areas. The PC was based inside the infamous Camp Crame, a military encampment in the heart of metropolitan Manila. Granted nationwide jurisdiction, Philippine Constabulary officers were drafted from the elite Philippine Military Academy and commanded soldiers trained in both police and military operations.

Under martial law, the Philippine Constabulary essentially became a critical "fourth branch of service" in the Armed Forces of the Philippines (AFP), besides the army, navy, and air force. President Ferdinand Marcos used the PC as his elite Gestapo-like unit to arrest opposing politicians, activist students and professors, labor leaders, as well as

Figure 7.1. Aging but energetic Filipino American World War II veterans and their youth supporters continue to keep faith by protesting at the San Francisco Veterans Day parade. Photo credit: San Francisco Veterans Equity Center

outspoken journalists and religious workers, keeping them indefinitely detained in dreaded Camp Crame without bail or a trial. To remain in power, Marcos used the AFP, the PC, and the Integrated National Police for counterinsurgency operations not only against the Moro uprising in Mindanao and the Communist Party of the Philippines (CPP)–New People's Army (NPA) but also to silence any group that would threaten his rule. The draconian accomplishments of his elite police units were rewarded with promotions and choice government positions after their retirement. Many loyal officers were sent to elite U.S. military training schools, such as Fort Bragg in North Carolina, to learn the latest in counterinsurgency and low-intensity conflict techniques. These training programs were funded with generous annual military assistance disbursements from the U.S. Congress. At their U.S. advanced training courses, Philippine military officers learned the latest in inhumane methods of interrogation and intimidation. Oppositionists who could not be silenced were either jailed, tortured, or killed (also known as "salvaged") by police and soldiers. American economic and military aid to the Philippines was at an all-time high during the Marcos regime. As long as Marcos kept America satisfied by promising to quell the growth of communism, allowing U.S. military installations to operate freely, and protecting U.S. business interests in the Philippines, the flow of U.S. aid was guaranteed to continue.

In the end, the Marcos regime's tally of 3,257 extrajudicial killings, 35,000 tortured, and 70,000 incarcerated without trial exceeded the 2,115 extrajudicial deaths under General Pinochet in Chile. Under his repressive regime, the numbers of CPP-NPA and Moro National Liberation Front (MNLF) armed regulars increased, and so did their civilian sympathizers. Marcos's eventual ouster in 1986 and the ratification of a new Philippine constitution in 1987, complete with human rights provisions, were heralded by the international community. In 1991, the infamous Philippine Constabulary was merged with the police to form the Philippine National Police. However, reports of military and police abuses and extrajudicial killings committed by the military and police continued under the post-Marcos presidencies of Corazon Aquino, Fidel Ramos, and Joseph Estrada and would reach another all-time high under President Gloria Macapagal Arroyo, with more than 800 extrajudicial deaths by the end of 2007.

Figure 7.2. An ecumenical group of pastors leads an interfaith prayer session for victims of extrajudicial killings in the Philippines.
Photo credit: Pacific School of Religion

With the closure of U.S. military installations in the Philippines in 1991 came a sharp decline in U.S. military assistance. But under the U.S.-sponsored global War on Terror, the Arroyo administration saw an opportunity to ask Washington for increases in American military aid. The Philippine government successfully lobbied to have the Abu Sayyaf and Jema'ah Islamiyah, both separatist Philippine Muslim groups, and the Communist Party of the Philippines/New People's Army (NPA), included in the U.S. Designated Foreign Terrorist Organizations List. Arroyo has gained more favor in Washington by supporting President Bush's Iraq War with Philippine troops. By doing so, U.S. taxpayers' dollars have effectively contributed to the funding of Philippine military and police counterinsurgency operations. These maneuvers were aimed not just at terrorist organizations but also at their supposed suspects and sympathizers, which included civil rights lawyers, politicians, trade unionists, youth organizers, farmers, students, journalists, indigenous peoples, religious workers, and clergy who oppose the Arroyo administration. They are accused of being "NPA or communists," "NPA or communist sympathizers," "destabilizers," or "terrorists." Counterinsurgency operations used to intimidate and eliminate these suspects are summary executions, massacres, forced evacuations, and other types of extrajudicial violations.

Filipino Protestants and the Dire Consequences of Faith-Based Social Action

Some of the most active civil society groups that have consistently been fighting for the rights of peasant farmers, urban slum dwellers, exploited factory workers, and the oppressed groups, from the Marcos dictatorship to the Arroyo regime (1970s to present), are the Philippine Protestant and Independent churches and their congregations. Through the influential and highly respected National Council of Churches in the Philippines (NCCP), which is the largest coalition of non–Roman Catholic churches in the Philippines, they not only bring prayer and faith to the downtrodden but also act as their voice and hope. The NCCP is composed of the Apostolic Catholic Church (ACC), Convention of Philippine Baptist Churches (CPBC), Episcopal Church in the Philippines (ECP), Iglesia Evangelica Metodista En Las Islas Filipinas (IEMELIF), Iglesia Filipina Independiente (IFI), Iglesia Unida Ekyumenical (UNIDA), Lutheran Church in the Philippines (LCP), Salvation Army (SA), United

Methodist Church (UMC), and United Church of Christ in the Philippines (UCCP).

Pastor Arturo Capuli, of Saint James and Grace United Methodist Church in San Francisco, emphasized why people of faith are targeted by the Philippine military and police. "They are leaders, for one thing," Capuli said. "They awaken people. They enlighten people. They encourage people to stand up for their rights." Hence, it is not surprising that the military included persons of faith in their video titled *Knowing the Enemy* and manual for "neutralization," making specific mention of the United Church of Christ in the Philippines, Iglesia Filipina Independiente, the Association of Major Religious Superiors in the Philippines (AMRSP), the Catholic Bishops Conference of the Philippines (CBCP), and the National Council of Churches in the Philippines (NCCP).

As a result, pastors, church leaders, and lay workers of the United Methodist Church in the Philippines, the United Church of Christ in the Philippines and the Philippine Independent Church are among those named as "enemies of the state" and have been summarily killed. One significant case involves the murder of Pastor Andy Pawican, a licentiate pastor of the UCCP. Pastor Pawican was a social activist in his community and is fondly remembered as a great listener by his church members in Barangay Fatima, Pantabangan, in Nueva Ecija, northeast of Manila. Witnesses interviewed by a UCCP fact-finding team claimed that Pastor Pawican was shot to death by soldiers from the Philippine army's 48th Intelligence Battalion, Delta Company. Another notable case involves UMC pastor Isaias Santa Rosa from Legaspi City, South Bicol District, south of Manila. A freelance writer, he was also a project consultant for nongovernmental organizations and the executive director of Farmers' Assistance for Rural Management Education and Rehabilitation. A fact-finding mission organized by the UMC received testimonies from family members that Pastor Sta. Rosa was abducted and murdered in Barangay Malobago, Daraga, Albay, allegedly by soldiers from the Ninth Military Intelligence Battalion of the Philippine army's Ninth Infantry Division, from Camp Weene Martillana, in Pili, Camarines Sur.

On the morning of October 3, 2006, Supreme Bishop Alberto Ramento of the IFI, a staunch peace and human rights advocate known as the "Bishop of the Poor Peasants and Workers," was stabbed to death inside the rectory of his church in Tarlac province. Bishop Ramento was the former chair of the powerful ecumenical National Council of Churches in the Philippines. He was also a strong supporter of a group of farmworkers who filed a complaint against the family of former Philippine president Corazon Cojuangco Aquino, the owner of Hacienda Luisita, one of the largest agricultural areas in the Philippines owned by a single family. The United Luisita Workers Union had staged a strike that was violently suppressed by the police and military in November 2004, resulting in the death of seven striking farmworkers on the picket line. Churches were intimidated by the situation and refused to minister to the workers. Bishop Ramento was one of the few who continued to meet with the workers. The late church leader was even quoted in an IFI bulletin as saying, "I know they are going to kill me next, but never will I abandon my duty to God and my ministry to the people."

By the end of 2006, the martyrdom of Pastor Pawican, Pastor Sta. Rosa, and Bishop Ramento had raised the number of church leaders slain to twenty-five. This total includes ten clergy, six lay workers of church-based programs, seven members of the UCCP, and two members of the UMC. All were slain heeding the call of their faith and working for poor and oppressed communities. They were killed as part of a larger global plan to eliminate members and supporters of the CPP-NPA, a Philippine terrorist group in the United States as specified on the Designated Foreign Terrorist Organizations List. In effect, U.S. military assistance to the Philippines' own "war on terror" contributed to these extrajudicial deaths.

Interfaith, Intergenerational Bayanihan Bridging Two Homelands

Together with many civil society groups, church leaders and church members from the Philippines did more than just pray for the extrajudicial killings to stop. They appealed for investigations and other actions from local and national politicians, including President Gloria Macapagal Arroyo. Protestant churches also banded together to appeal to the international community, including their "mother" churches in the United States. In May 2006, distraught attendees of the General Assembly of the UCCP—the church that has been the hardest hit in terms of the number of victims—called for a human rights and peace summit. At the resulting summit, hosted by the UCCP in cooperation with the NCCP, the UMC, IFI, the Ecumenical Bishops' Forum (EBF), and the Benedictines for Peace, the ecumenical and intergenerational participants called for a thorough independent investigation by the United Nations high commissioner for human rights to determine the truth about these extrajudicial deaths and to hold accountable those responsible.

By phone and the Internet, these pleas for help were heard by Filipino American Protestants, who helped convey them to their U.S. church
leaders. The accounts of the murders were made even more compelling
by the fact that many first-generation Filipino American UMC migrants
personally knew the victims and their families, since they had worshiped
together in their hometown UMC churches. In June 2006, a disturbed
intergenerational gathering of pastors and laypersons at the annual UMC
California-Nevada Conference overwhelmingly accepted, approved, and
supported Resolution 58, titled "The Philippines: Disappearances, Extrajudicial Killings, and Human Rights Violations." Through this resolution,
the American UMC members expressed solidarity with the UMC in the
Philippines, the UCCP, the NCCP, and the many other church and secular voices in a common cry for justice and peace. Church leaders in the
Philippines—both clergy and laity—and peace and human rights advocates, including journalists, had been subjected to harassment and summary executions. Clearly, something needed to be done. The secretary of
the California-Nevada Annual Conference sent copies of Resolution 58
to political leaders in the Philippines and the United States.

Moved to act, former NCCP social worker Wilson DeOcera, pastor of
the Daly City United Methodist Church and chair of the Filipino Caucus
at the California-Nevada Annual Conference, helped raise awareness of
these egregious human rights violations and rally support by cospon-
soring an unprecedented interfaith and intergenerational worship service
(Pagsambang Bayan, or People's Worship) to mourn the death of peace
and justice in the Philippines. Besides UMC members, the Daly City
church's worship area was filled with members and supporters of the
Institute for Leadership Development and Study of Pacific Asian North
American Religion (PANA Institute) and Pacific Asian American Ministries of the United Church of Christ. Youth from the Filipino Community Support (FOCUS-Bay Area), Filipino Community Center (FCC-San
Francisco), Bayan USA, League of Filipino Students, families from the
Liwanag Cultural Center in Daly City, and students from area schools
and universities were also present. The e-mail invitation to the service
also reached many non-Filipino faith communities—African American
and Latino Evangelical church members were just some of those drawn
to the event. Some came from as far away as New York. They joined a
very solemn ecumenical candlelight vigil and procession that were covered by the Filipino American and national media in the United States. At
the service, the interfaith, intergenerational gathering of clergy and lay-

persons sadly reflected on the unsolved murders over the past five years of hundreds working for social justice in the Philippines. It was the first time that pastors of Filipino descent from the Iglesia Filipina Independiente, the UMC, UCC, Baptist, Episcopal, and other Filipino Evangelical congregations had come together as one in the San Francisco Bay Area.

After their invocations, the church leaders strongly condemned the murder of Bishop Ramento and the other wanton killings and urged their respective religious congregations to write formal protest letters to the Philippine ambassador to the United States, the U.S. State Department, and their U.S. congressional representatives. After the Daly City service, Filipino American leaders and members of the Episcopal Church asked their newly installed presiding bishop, the Most Reverend Katharine Jefferts Schori, to immediately write a letter to Philippine ambassador Willie Gaa expressing "deep concern among U.S. denominations over the deplorable number of extrajudicial killings."

From Kasamahan Prayers to Bayanihan Action

This grassroots, interfaith, and intergenerational *kasamahan* contributed to the following consequential *bayanihan* actions: Bayan USA, League of Filipino Students (LFS), BABAE Women's Group, and other progressive intergenerational groups, many based in U.S. universities and colleges, launched massive marches in New York, Washington, D.C., San Francisco, and Los Angeles calling for an end to "U.S. imperialism in the Philippines," which they view as fueling the extrajudicial atrocities. They also protested in front of the Philippine embassy in Washington, D.C., and Philippine consulates in Los Angeles and San Francisco.

To emphasize the seriousness of this issue to the UMC church—not just in the United States but globally—Bishop Beverly J. Shamana, the head of the global United Methodist Church and chair of the UMC's General Board of Church of Society, joined the seventeen-member Cal-Nevada United Methodist Philippine Fact-Finding Team/Solidarity and Pastoral Visit mandated by Resolution 58. The February 2007 mission included sizable representation from concerned UMC pastors and lay members from the San Francisco Bay Area, especially those representing large Filipino migrant congregations.

In February 2007, the United Nations' special rapporteur Philip Allston conducted an independent investigation and produced a comprehensive list of recommendations. His most important recommendation was to ask the Philippine president Gloria Macapagal Arroyo, as commander in chief of the armed forces, to eliminate extrajudicial executions from the country's "war on terror" counterinsurgency operations. The UN report also requested that the Philippine government direct all military officers to cease from making public statements linking political or other groups to those engaged in armed insurgencies. Any such connections were to remain confidential and known only to the civilian authorities.

Publicity on the ecumenical gathering in Daly City moved U.S. senator Barbara Boxer and California congressman Tom Lantos to call for separate congressional meetings and consultations. Senator Boxer chaired a special session of the Senate Foreign Relations Committee, which heard testimony from U.S. State Department officers and representatives of civil organizations from the Philippines and the United States, including the general secretary of the United Church of Christ in the Philippines, representatives of Amnesty International, and the U.S. Institute of Peace. A copy of the NCCP report was circulated. One of those who shared his views at the congressional meeting was Chris D., a second-generation Filipino American who, along with his family, attended the Geneva United Methodist Church. He was a student at San Francisco State University and had learned about these human rights violations from his professors and fellow Filipino American students at a League of Filipino Students teach-in. He had also attended the Pagsambang Bayan at Daly City UMC. Chris admonished political and military leaders in both his homelands for tolerating and even encouraging the extrajudicial slayings, especially of Evangelical pastors. The many fervent testimonies such as that of Chris D. and the well-attended candlelit vigils convinced U.S. congressional leaders to make the partial release of the 2008 U.S. military aid to the Philippines conditional upon the Arroyo administration's adherence to human rights and international laws.

In response to the pleas of their constituents, including Filipino faithful and their fellow Protestant church members, forty-nine Democratic and Republican members of the U.S. House of Representatives sent an urgent compliance reminder to President Gloria Macapagal Arroyo in August 2007. The bipartisan letter stated, "Since the extrajudicial killings in the Philippines continue unabated, and given the fact that there are many unanswered questions about the role of the Philippine government and military in these deaths, we respectfully request your strong and immediate leadership in investigating and prosecuting those individuals and/or groups, including those in the AFP [Armed Forces of the Philippines] and PNP [Philippine National Police], responsible for these killings, and in eliminating the underlying causes of the violence."

In November 2007, the World Council of Churches (WCC) also sent a fact-finding delegation, headed by WCC general secretary Reverend Samuel Kobiaa. The mission included Sophia Adinyira, a justice of the Supreme Court of Ghana and a member of the (Anglican) Church of the Province of West Africa; Reverend Sandy Yule, the national secretary for Christian Unity of the Uniting Church in Australia; and WCC program executive for Asia, Mathews George Chunakara.

Extrajudicial killings declined in 2007, which suggests that the multigenerational *bayanihan* pressure applied to the Philippine government was effective. But the most important lesson of this experience may be that the United States needs to rethink and reexamine the wide-ranging human rights and moral side effects of its military and economic aid to countries enforcing America's global War on Terror.

Summary and Conclusion

While listening to Tatang Floro in Berkeley on that chilly spring evening, I could not help but remember my own Lolo Tony, the brother of my paternal grandmother. He was one of the young men enticed by General Douglas MacArthur to sign up for the U.S. Armed Forces of the Far East in exchange for full citizenship, benefits, and pensions. Before leaving the Philippines for the United States in 1988, I went to my hometown of Biñan, Laguna, to say good-bye to him. I cried when he gave me a beautiful black Santo Niño that he had carved from a water buffalo (*kalabaw*) horn and told me to always pray for him. I became emotional because Lolo Tony suffered from chronic pain in his arms and back ever since he was wounded in a Japanese grenade attack on his USAFFE unit and had to be operated on without anesthesia to remove the shrapnel. This parting gift must have caused him a lot of additional pain to carve. Before I exited the door of his home, he smiled at me and started reciting America's "Pledge of Allegiance." I laughed, but in a serious tone he reminded me that we have always been "brown Americans" and that he had been pledging allegiance to the United States since before July 4, 1946, when the Philippines was still part of the Union. Lolo Tony finally arrived in the United States in 1991 as a U.S. war veteran and was treated at the Veterans Medical Center in San Diego, California. After subsisting on Social Security income, Lolo Tony passed away quietly not too long ago without ever receiving the other benefits and pensions he was promised and rightly deserved for defending his two homelands. Like him, I am an American citizen and no stranger to long-drawn-out causes. My daughter, his great-granddaughter, also carries the spirit of the cause, as do many surviving veterans and youth, who will continue fighting until a corrective law is enacted by the U.S. Congress.

There is no doubt that migrant faithful like Lolo Tony, Tatang Floro, and the 250,000 other Filipinos who heeded the call of President Roosevelt and General MacArthur in their youth deserve their long-overdue veterans' benefits as a basic human right. After all, they and their spouses are old and dying. Similarly, U.S. military assistance to Philippine security forces as part of America's global War on Terror needs to be stopped, or at minimum, its annual disbursement by the U.S. Congress should be continuously linked to improved human rights conditions to avoid any more civilian casualties.

The victories achieved by the Filipino faith communities so far in San Francisco and Washington, D.C., are the results of converting their congregational invocations to spirit-filled action. Sustained intergenerational and interfaith cohesion has been critical. Hence, based on the lessons from the discussion in this chapter, the large *kasamahan* network initiated by Filipino migrant faithful like Gladys, Glen, Tatang Floro, Pastor DeOcera, Chris, and other student leaders around this issue should be reinforced with the following intergenerational, interfaith *bayanihan* efforts.

First, *bayanihan* should include more than just Filipino stakeholders and networks. I believe there needs to be a continued "Americanization" of the veterans' equity and extrajudicial concerns, from all generations of American society. The veterans did not fight solely to defend California and Nevada, but the entire Union. There need to be more congressional leaders who are willing to take more political risks. After all, the Filipino veterans risked their lives and showed that they were willing to die for America. UCC pastor Pawican, UMC pastor Sta. Rosa, IFI bishop Ramento, and 800 others were not killed just to eliminate terrorism in the Philippines but also to quell terrorist threats to America. All of Congress, as well as all San Francisco Bay Area cities, the state of California, and the nation should be concerned about these human rights issues.

Veterans from all of America's wars should be concerned with this veteran's issue. Human rights activists from all over the world should press for action on these extrajudicial killings.

Second, there is a need for more "Pan-Asian Americanization" of the Filipino veterans' equity and extrajudicial killings issues and related *bayanihan* actions. PANA's leadership, through the Reverend Debbie Lee, is critical to the effectiveness of Pan-Asian *bayanihan*. Filipinos are the second-largest Asian migrant population in the United States, but they have not been as effective as other Asian Americans in terms of securing elected and appointed political offices, particularly at the national level of governance. Hence, they need to emphasize to their Asian American brothers and sisters that the veterans' equity and extrajudicial killings are not just a Filipino issue but also an American and Asian American concern. The precedents set by the Filipino veterans should be used as bases for introducing or amending legislation for other Southeast Asian American veterans (e.g., Hmong and Laotians), who are experiencing similar injustices. They also fought for America's wars in Asia. Moreover, many extrajudicial abuses and killings occur in the name of the War on Terror all over Asia. Asian American youth at universities and colleges should be concerned.

Third, there is a necessity for further "Catholicization" and "Christianization" of the Filipino migrant veterans' equity and extrajudicial killings issues and the *bayanihan* activities associated with them, since the Catholic, Evangelical, and Independent churches are some of the largest lobbies in the city of San Francisco, the state of California, and Washington, D.C. Leaders of the Archdiocese of San Francisco, Diocese of San Jose, and Diocese of Oakland have acknowledged that they rely heavily on the financial and social capital of Filipino parishioners of all ages. Prayers have been said for the Filipino World War II veterans and the victims of the extrajudicial killings during church services. However, isn't it time that more Catholic, Protestant, Independent, and other Christian church leaders listened to these prayers for help and joined the *bayanihan* efforts? Pastors Bayani Rico of Holy Child and Saint Martin Episcopal Church (Daly City), Pastor Wilson De Ocera of the United Methodist Church of Daly City, Pastor Arturo Capuli, and many UMC Bay Area churches have already publicly voiced their concerns. But what about the other Evangelical and Independent churches? Those pastors and congregants should follow the lead of the youth who have moved from *kasamahan* to *bayanihan* to help fight for their elders' rights.

Fourth, the veterans' equity and extrajudicial killings should also be pitched in *bayanihan* initiatives as side effects from American hegemony and empire building. How can the richest and most powerful hegemon in the international system not render human dignity and human rights to the young men and women whom it recruits to fight its wars? And what about Filipino clergy and civilians who are killed indirectly by the U.S. taxpayers' support that Congress allocates annually to America's coalition armies? These are just some of the reasons why the San Francisco Human Rights Commission passed a resolution in support of Filipino World War II veterans. The San Francisco Immigrant Rights Commission, Board of Supervisors, and Commission on the Aging should pass similar resolutions. Other cities all over the United States should also express their dismay over this human rights issue by passing resolutions in support of the veterans.

Finally, there needs to be continued faith, rhetoric, and action (*bayanihan*), especially from Bay Area Catholic, Evangelical, and public schools and universities. They should join the students from University of San Francisco, San Francisco State University, and San Jose State University in their passionate expressions of *bayanihan*. Valuable intellectual and political capital comes from these groups, which represent the next generation of leaders and voters. The flow of inspired protests and marches, letters, faxes, phone calls, and e-mails that come from Filipino American youth must continue until these two critical human rights issues are addressed.

8

Conclusion

Embracing New Bonds and Bridges

From the outside, the church—a neoclassical, red brick building with a steep roof—looked no different from the many Lutheran churches that sprouted south of San Francisco during the early decades of the twentieth century. This particular one was an American Lutheran Church that was established in 1925. Inside, a young, second-generation migrant with German and Norwegian roots, the Reverend Henry N. Brodersen, was loudly proclaiming passages from the Bible to an attentive flock, mostly faithful of German, Irish, Italian, and English descent who had moved from the Midwest and the East. Some had resettled in Pacifica as early as the 1850s, after the frenzy of the California gold rush had died down, to work in limestone and granite quarries. The opening of the Ocean Shore Railway in 1906 increased access to the area and attracted more settlers. In 1910, when the young Pastor Brodersen first began leading prayer meetings, there was no church building. Thus, the congregation had every reason to be proud of the eventual construction of its new facility. From then on, this beacon of faith helped attract worshipers from the beach to the hills. But after World War II, attendance dipped as European American members moved, passed away, or joined other Protestant congregations, especially the two new and dynamic Lutheran churches not too far away. Finances at the church ran dry. At one point, fewer than five families were regularly attending services. Badly in need of maintenance and repairs, the church building was eventually sold. In 1967, the building reopened its doors to the community, but this time as an enthusiastic Filipino American Seventh-Day Adventist Church, and an integral part of the sisterhood of churches of the Central California Conference of Seventh-Day Adventists. When we visited the church, it was bustling with *kasamahan* activity. Before lunch, we heard Bible discussions in English, Tagalog, and Kapampangan. More than 150 church members attended, coming from a broad representation of the more than eighty provinces that constitute the Philippines, ranging from Pampanga in the north to Cebu in the south. But we also met some African American and European American members at the Bible study and at the hearty Filipino and American lunch spread that followed.

On October 16, 2007, at San Francisco's city hall, I was hoping and praying that a majority of my fellow commissioners (ten of the twelve were not Filipino) would be convinced to approve a draft resolution condemning a remark made by Susan, a character played by actress Terri Hatcher, on the popular television show *Desperate Housewives*, which denigrated Philippine-educated doctors practicing in the United States. The derogatory slur was made on the season premiere, which was watched by millions of Americans, including Filipino Americans. Because the show is also exported internationally, there was an outcry from the broader Filipino diaspora, which is spread out over approximately 100 countries. In just a week, more than 100,000 individuals had signed an online petition calling for an apology from Disney-ABC, the show's producer. Prodded by Philippine president Gloria Macapagal Arroyo, the Philippine embassy in Washington, D.C., even sent a diplomatic protest note to the U.S. State Department. But back in San Francisco, would viewers care about nine seconds of TV dialogue? As the public comments poured in, I realized that the answer to my question was a resounding yes. Present at the commissioners' meeting were longtime, first-generation Filipino migrant activists, including Terry B., Lillian G., Rudy A., Maria M., and Rodel R., who came from Protestant, Independent, and Catholic church backgrounds. Terry B., Lillian, G., Rudy A., and Maria M. are not only advocates but active voters, like many Filipinos who are U.S. citizens. Some, who have dual citizenships like me, also try to influence electoral contests in the Philippines. City College of San Francisco trustee Rodel R. is the highest-ranking elected Filipino American politician in San Francisco. Lillian G. is the executive director of Filipinos for Affirmative Action. Rudy A. is executive director of West Bay Pilipino Multi-services Center. Benny G., a sixty-four-year-old Filipino Catholic migrant and veteran of the 1986 Philippine People Power revolution, was also present. He had arrived just a month earlier from Manila and was a new parishioner at Saint Thomas the Apostle Catholic Church. True to the Filipino tradition of including religion in secular matters, he began his statement from a biblical standpoint:

And God said as He wrote on the stone tablet on Mount Sinai, "Thou shalt not bear false witness against thy neighbor." God then highlighted the greatest importance of inviolately upholding and preserving the fragility of another person's dignity, honor and character by including this moral mandate as one of the ten among a zillion commandments He could have emphasized to His people. Juxtaposed against this Divine Light therefore, the spurious diatribe "some med school in the Philippines" cannot and should not be dismissed as a "brief reference" but rather unmasked as the scandalous innuendo it really was and still is.

But these old-time Filipino migrant faithful–cum–political activists were not alone. Their emotional pleas were echoed and reinforced by the next generation of Filipino American student leaders from the Catholic University of San Francisco—Aethel C., Kyle J., and Valerie F. The room at city hall was filled to capacity with young and old supporters of various ethnic backgrounds. Aethel, Kyle, and Valerie's Latino, African American, and Caucasian classmates were also there to cheer them on. Like Glen A. and Gladys, who marched for aging Filipino World War II veterans, and Jenah and Candice R., who testified in Congress and at San Francisco's city hall, the young migrant faithful in attendance on this day were products of San Francisco Bay Area churches and Christian and Catholic schools and universities. They gave impassioned speeches asking the commissioners to approve the resolution. As I listened intently to each of them, I started to relax and leaned back in my chair, knowing that everything was going to be just fine. Convinced, all twelve commissioners signed off on a strongly worded letter I prepared asking the mayor and the board of supervisors to join the San Francisco Immigrant Rights Commission and the Filipino American community in condemning Disney-ABC, and urging the network giant to support public educational campaigns to prevent unfortunate incidents like this from ever happening again. *Bayanihan* prevailed! Reflecting on the passage of this resolution, and the earlier one naming Victoria Manalo Draves Park, I realized that San Francisco society had indeed embraced Filipinization, in the form of both bonds and bridges.

These two narratives illustrate clearly the dynamics of Filipino migrant *kasamahan* and *bayanihan* and the ways in which they both integrate and influence religion and politics in the San Francisco Bay Area. Filipinos in the United States have come full circle in this book—from Jose Rizal, the Filipino hero who descended in San Francisco on his way to inspiring revolutionary fervor in the Philippines, to the community mobilization leading to the reclamation of Victoria Manalo Draves Park, to the fight for human rights for Filipino World War II veterans and victims of extrajudicial killings in the Philippines. These San Francisco stories epitomize how Filipino migrant faithful integrate as new Americans and global citizens and are able to influence societies via their spiritual spaces, personas, objects, and practices.

Because of their strong, faith-centered, civic-oriented religious life, I sought to relate the story of Filipino migration to the United States through the lens of several churches in the San Francisco Bay Area. From the grounding of their new California spiritual homes, Filipino migrants clearly have been able to integrate into segments of the religious, social, and political experiences of their San Francisco communities as well as impact their Philippine families and hometowns in three ways: (1) transnational influence, (2) adaptive spirit, and (3) intergenerational cohesion. I would like to share some concluding thoughts:

In chapter 1, I laid out the two main threads that weave together the narratives and experiences in this book. These intertwined strands of Filipino migrant influences are elicited by and through their religious spaces—bonding Filipinization, or *kasamahan* (community organizing), and bridging Filipinization, or *bayanihan* (community action). Understanding the *kasamahan* and *bayanihan* stories of Filipino migrants and their San Francisco churches is critical to solving America's long-standing immigration debacle, since they show how the competing assumptions of two of America's most pervasive migration paradigms—melting pot via assimilation and rainbow society through multiculturalism—might be reconciled. Filipino migrant faithful in San Francisco have shown that it is possible to align with the rest of American society without having to disengage themselves from their Philippine cultural heritage. Perhaps U.S. immigration regulations could be changed to reflect this more conciliatory approach (a Filipino "middle way") brokered by migrant spiritual spaces.

In chapters 2 and 3, I elaborated on how Filipino migrant faithful utilized a dynamic, nonlinear process of transnational influence and integration using *kasamahan* and *bayanihan* to claim their share of San Francisco society, while maintaining a stake in their Philippine hometowns. Their hearts beat for two homes, so they replenish community organizing and civic involvement in both places. When Filipino Catholic, Protestant, and Independent church members go to church, they begin the continuous back-and-forth flow of "Filipinization" and "Americanization" from San Francisco and the Philippines through strong *kasamahan* bonds organized around Filipino spiritual personas, objects, symbols, values, and practices. Although some of their *kasamahan*-building remains "passive," in the form of activities like Tagalog Bible study or Santo Niño devotions, many other spiritual alliances move easily from prayers to actions, creating *bayanihan* domestically and internationally. Like me, many Filipino migrants have heeded the calls of their Filipino pastors and families to give back, both to our homeland and to our local community. The most obvious manifestations of this transnational influence and community action are the massive amounts of *padala* (remittances) and *balikbayan* boxes (care packages) flowing from San Francisco to various hometowns across the Philippines. Filipino migrant faithful deliver the "miracles" that forever change families and communities back home. But they also support charities and make donations to San Francisco Bay Area nonprofit agencies, community-based organizations, and philanthropic foundations, acknowledging their connection to their new homeland. With the contributions from these two chapters, I hope that the literature on faith and the Filipino American transnational experience will be enriched.

In chapters 4 and 5, I illustrated how the adaptive spirits of Filipino migrant faithful through their churches allow them to transcend the acculturative stress caused by the complexities of migrant life in liberal, multicultural San Francisco. Evidently, the food they eat and festivals they practice are an adaptive mix of American, Malay, Chinese, and Spanish influences. But Filipino Catholics, Protestants, and Independent church members do not just eat Kentucky Fried chicken and Tribu's *fresh lumpia* and then play a few frames at Classic Bowl (forming *kasamahan*). Their spiritual socialization also moves them to perform thousands of hours of volunteer work (*bayanihan*) for local cities and community-based organizations both in their new homeland and in their old hometowns. This community service (*lingkod*) is sometimes performed to help commemorate the feast day of a hometown in the Philippines or Thanksgiving Day in the United States. Either way, both state and civil society profit.

In chapters 6 and 7, I analyzed how Filipino migrant faithful were able to engage government and society through intergenerational *kasamahan* and *bayanihan*. Besides using Filipino counterhegemonic attitudes (passion and revolution) and behavioral respect for elders (*paggalang sa nakakatanda*) to explain the cohesion between young and old members at Filipino religious sites in San Francisco, I contended that, for intergenerational *kasamahan* to be effective, the following preconditions are needed: (1) compelling political issues, (2) charismatic leadership, (3) a congregation that is predominantly middle class, and (4) active parish intergenerational interest groups. Intergenerational *kasamahan* and passion among young and old Catholic, Independent, and Protestant Filipino migrant faithful have been transformed successfully into revolutionary actions to effectively tackle two human rights issues linked to American ascension as a global power: intergenerational *bayanihan* for veterans' benefits for Filipino World War II USAFFE soldiers, and interfaith *bayanihan* to condemn extrajudicial killings in the Philippines.

I am predicting that San Francisco will continue to witness more experiences of transnational influence, adaptive spirit, and intergenerational cohesion as the next generation of Filipino migrant faithful follow in the footsteps of their parents and grandparents. This creates a win-win situation for both homelands, echoed, fittingly, in Victoria Manalo Draves's name, which alludes to "victory" in both English and Tagalog. With Filipino American role models like her inspiring the ongoing creation of new *kasamahan* and *bayanihan*, how could communities in the United States and the Philippines possibly lose?

Notes

1. *Kasamahan* is a Tagalog word, which literally translates as "togetherness." *Bayanihan* refers to a coming together out of national pride. In the Filipino American context, the former is commonly used to refer to community organization, whereas the latter describes community action.

2. Back in the Philippines, I had already done civic duty as an anti–Marcos activist while attending Santa Ana Catholic Church and studying at La Salle, a Christian Brothers' elementary school, high school, and university.

3. Adapted from Putnam (2000) and expounded on in chapter 5.

4. These include Bonus 2000; Choy 2003; Espiritu 2003; Ignacio 2005; Manalansan 2003; and Parreñas 2001, 2005.

5. For instance, Brother Mariano "Mike" Z. Velarde, the charismatic shepherd of El Shaddai, a Catholic spin-off group, has risen to become one of Asia's most powerful leaders, not just spiritually but also politically. Every politician running for public office, whether at the municipal or national government level, tries to woo the endorsement of Brother Mike. Electoral candidates know that the millions of El Shaddai votes could make or break their prized political objective. In the 2004 presidential elections, regular El Shaddai attendee Gloria Macapagal Arroyo secured not only the group's blessings but its vote against a very popular actor—the then incumbent, President Estrada. Church leaders have also actively participated in the drafting of the 1987 Philippine Constitution, the fundamental law of the land. They have sponsored pro-church provisions, including Article II, Section 12, which bans abortion, and Article XV, Section 2, banning divorce. Almost every Philippine political phenomenon is given a religious explanation. For example, the People Power Revolution of 1986 is also referred to in the Philippines as the "Miracle at EDSA," since not a single drop of blood was shed during this military-civilian showdown on EDSA, a main thoroughfare in Manila. Highly influential Cardinal Jaime Sin, the controversial archbishop of Manila, played a pivotal role in calling for Christian Filipinos to the streets, precipitating the ouster of long-time dictator Ferdinand Marcos.

6. Philippine Comission on Filipinos Overseas.

7. From original letter displayed at the Philippine National Historical Institute, Manila.

CHAPTER 2

1. "People Power" refers to the popular uprising and mass mobilizations in Manila that persuaded Ferdinand Marcos to end his dictatorship and step down from his position as president of the Philippines.

2. This was part of the privilege speech to the U.S. Senate by Senator Albert Beveridge, January 9, 1900, regarding America's trade position on the Philippines.

3. The first Protestant missionaries to the Philippines came from Spain during their occupation of the country, including Dominican priest turned Protestant missionary Manrique Alonso Lallave (see Apilado 1999; Kwantes 1998).

4. There was no Mormon missionary activity in the Philippines until the end of World War II, when Maxine Grimm, wife of a U.S. Army colonel, serving the American Red Cross in the Philippines, introduced the gospel to Aniceta Pabilona Fajardo, the first Filipino to join the Church of Jesus Christ of Latter-day Saints in the islands. Sister Fajardo was baptized in 1945.

5. Doctrinally, Seventh-Day Adventists are heirs of the interfaith Millerite movement of the 1840s. Although the name "Seventh-Day Adventist" was chosen in 1860, the denomination was not officially organized until May 21, 1863, when the movement included some 125 churches and 3,500 members.

6. Serious schisms would later reduce PIC membership significantly.

7. E. B. Lenane, "Survey Catholic Filipino Club, 1421 Sutter Street, San Francisco, California," March 25, 1935, Archives of the Archdiocese of San Francisco.

8. Based on interviews with Noemi Castillo, director, Office of Ethnic Ministries, Archdiocese of San Francisco, May and June 2001.

9. Simbang Gabi is a series of early-morning masses celebrated on each of the nine days leading up to Christmas. Flores de Mayo (Flowers of May) is a monthlong celebration devoted to the Virgin Mary. It culminates in the Santacruzan (Festival of the Holy Cross), a colorful procession that is part historical tradition and part beauty pageant. The Salubong consists of a procession that takes place on Easter morning, depicting the risen Christ's meeting with Mary.

10. Archdiocese of San Francisco Official Directory, various years; Catholic Directory of the Philippines, various years.

11. Supplemented with interviews from Sister Avelina Macalam and Sister Gloria Burganoy, RVM, May and June 2001.

12. Memo, September 30, 1963, from Monsignor Foudy to Most Reverend Joseph T. McGucken, STD, regarding "Minority Group Students in Catholic Elementary Schools, City of San Francisco."

13. Based on interviews with Noemi Castillo, director, Office of Ethnic Ministries, Archdiocese of San Francisco, May and June 2001.

14. From interviews with Brother Ismael Laguardia, San Francisco Filipino Jehovah's Witness, March 2001.

15. From interviews with the Reverend Gerry Ebora, pastor, Filipino American Seventh-Day Adventist Church, March 2001.

16. From interviews with Reverend Leo Calica, pastor, Faith Bible Church of San Francisco, March 2001.

17. From interviews with Reverend Arturo Capuli, pastor, Saint Francis and Grace United Methodist Church, San Francisco, March 2001.

CHAPTER 5

1. All personal names in both cases are pseudonyms.

2. Specifically, the apostle Paul said, "I appeal to you, brethren, by the name of our Lord Jesus Christ, that all of you agree and that there be no dissentions among you, but that you be united in the same mind and the same judgment" (1 Corinthians 1:10, RSV).

3. Mayor's message, June 28, 2001.

4. Similarly, San Francisco is the sister city of Manila, with a joint commission that has Filipino Catholic parishioner representation.

References

Adams, R. 1996. Remittances, Income Distribution and Rural Asset Accumulation. FCND discussion papers 17. International Food Policy Research Institute. http://www.ifpri.org/divs/fcnd/dp/papers/dp17.pdf.

Agoncillo, T. 1990. *History of the Filipino People*. Quezon City: Garotech.

Aguilar-San Juan, K. ed. 1994. *The State of Asian America: Activism and Resistance in the 1990s*. Boston: South End Press.

Ahmad, F., Shik, A., Vanza, R., Cheung, A., George, U., and Stewart, D. 2004. Voices of South Asian women: Immigration and mental health. *Women and Health* 40 (4): 113–123.

Almario, C. R., ed. 1993. *Evangelization in Asia: Proceedings of the Asian Congress on Evangelization*. Quezon City: Claretian.

Apilado, M. C. 1999. *Revolutionary Spirituality: A Study of the Protestant Role in the American Colonial Rule of the Philippines, 1898-1928*. Quezon City: New Day.

Aranda, C. 1999. Benefits for Filipino veterans. *Philippine News*, September 15.

Archdiocese of San Francisco 2003. *Small Christian Community*. San Francisco: Roman Catholic Archdiocese of San Francisco.

Asian Development Bank. 2004. *Enhancing the Efficiency of Overseas Filipino Workers' Remittances*. Manila: Asian Development Bank.

Asian Development Bank, Inter-American Development Bank, and United Nations Development Program. 2005. Proceedings of the Joint Conference on Remittances. Manila, Philippines, September 12–13. CD-ROM.

Athukorala, P. 1993. Improving the contribution of migrant remittances to development: The experience of labour-exporting countries. *International Migration* 31 (1): 103–121.

Ballard, R. 2005. Migration, remittances, economic growth and poverty reduction: Reflections on some South Asian developments. In T. Siddiqui, ed. *Migration and Development: Pro-Poor Policy Choices*, 417–463. Dhaka: University Press.

Banlaoi, R. 2002. The role of Philippine-American relations in the global campaign against terrorism: Implications for regional security. *Contemporary Southeast Asia* 24 (2): 24–36.

Baron, S., Field, J., and Schuller, T., eds. 2000. *Social Capital: Critical Perspectives*. Oxford: Oxford University Press.

Baviera, A., and Yu-Jose, L. 1998. *Philippine External Relations: A Centennial Vista*. Manila: Foreign Service Institute.

Becker, G., Beyene, Y., and Canalita, L. 2000. Immigrating for status in late life: Effects of globalization on Filipino American veterans. *Journal of Aging Studies* 14 (3): 273–290.

Bello, W. 1983. Springboards for intervention, instruments for nuclear war. *Southeast Asia Chronicle* 89:45–71.

Bhugra, D., Bhui, K., Mallett, R., Desai, M., Singh, J., and Leff, J. 2004. Cultural identity and its measurement: A questionnaire for Asians. *International Review of Psychiatry* 11 (2): 244–261.

Binstock, R., and Jean-Baptiste, R. 1999. Elderly immigrants and the saga of welfare reform. *Journal of Immigrant Health* 1 (1): 31–56.

Bonus, R. 2000. *Locating Filipino Americans: Ethnicity and the Cultural Politics of Space*. Philadelphia: Temple University Press.

Borah, E. 1995. Filipinos in Unamuno's California expedition of 1587. *Amerasia Journal* 21 (3): 78–90.

Boston Globe. 2003. *Betrayal: The Crisis in the Catholic Church*. New York: Little, Brown.

Bourdieu, P. 1986. The forms of capital. In J. Richardson, ed., *Handbook of Theory and Research for the Sociology of Education*. New York: Greenwood Press.

Brah, A., and Coombes, A. E. eds. 2000. *Hybridity and Its Discontents: Politics, Science, Culture*. London: Routledge.

Bramadat. P. 2000. *The Church on the World's Turf: An Evangelical Christian Group at a Secular University*. Oxford: Oxford University Press.

Brands, H. W. 1992. *Bound to Empire: The United States and the Philippines*. New York: Oxford University Press.

Brook, J., Carlsson, C., and Peters, N. J., eds. 1998. *Reclaiming San Francisco: History, Politics, and Culture*. San Francisco: City Lights Books.

Brown, R., and Ahlburg, D. 1999. Remittances in the South Pacific. *International Journal of Social Economics* 26 (1/2/3): 325–344.

Burns, J. M. 2001. *San Francisco: A History of the Archdiocese of San Francisco*. Vol. 1, *1776–1884, From Mission to Golden Frontier*. Vol. 2, *1885–1945, Glory, Ruin, and Resurrection*. Strasbourg, France: Girold Gresswiller.

Burns, J. M., Skerrett E., and White, J. M., eds. 2000. *Keeping Faith: European and Asian Catholic Immigrants*. New York: Orbis.

Cabotaje, M. 1999. Equity denied: Historical and legal analyses in support of the extension of U.S. veterans' benefits to Filipino World War II veterans. *Asian Law Journal* 6: 139–154.

California Department of Industrial Relations. 1930. *Facts about Filipino Immigration into California*. San Francisco: Department of Industrial Relations.

Canlas, M.C. 2002. *SOMA Pilipinas Studies 2000*. San Francisco: Arkipelago.

Carlos, M. 2002. On the determinants of international migration in the Philippines. *International Migration Review* 36 (1): 81–102.

Carnes, T., and Yang, F., eds. 2004. *Asian American Religions: The Making and Remaking of Borders and Boundaries*. New York: New York University Press.

Carrasco, D. 1995. Cosmic jaws: We eat the gods and the gods eat us. *Journal of the American Academy of Religion* 63 (3): 429–444.

Castillo, N. M. 2001. *Ethnic Diversity in Parishes: Archdiocese of San Francisco*. San Francisco: Archdiocese of San Francisco.

Chandavarkar, A. G. 1980. Use of migrants' remittances in labor-exporting countries. *Finance and Development* 17 (3): 36–39.

Chao, J. 1999. Filipino veterans fight for fairness. *San Francisco Examiner*, December 19.

Chowdhury, A., Helman, C., and Greenhalgh, T. 2000. Food beliefs and practices among British Bangladeshis with diabetes: Implications for health education. *Anthropology and Medicine* 7 (2): 209–223.

Choy, C. 2003. *Empire of Care: Nursing and Migration in Filipino American History*. Durham, NC: Duke University Press.

Christian, F. 2004. The influence of immigration and international tourism on the demand for imported food products. *Acta Agriculturae Scandinavica* 1 (1): 21–36.

Cleary, E., and Steigenga, T. 2004. *Resurgent Voices in Latin America: Indigenous Peoples, Political Mobilization, and Religious Change*. New Brunswick, NJ: Rutgers University Press.

Coleman, J. 1988. Social capital in the creation of human capital. *American Journal of Sociology* 94 (S1): 85–120.

———. 1990. *Foundations of Social Theory*. Cambridge, MA: Harvard University Press.

Constantino, L. R. 1989. *Recalling the Philippine-American War*. Quezon City: Education Forum.

Constantino, R. 1998. *The Philippines: A Past Revisited*. Manila: Renato Constantino.

Cordova, F. 1983. *Filipinos: Forgotten Asian Americans*. Dubuque, IA: Kendall/ Hunt.

Dalla, R., Ellis, A., and Cramer, S. 2005. Immigration and rural America. *Community, Work and Family* 8 (2): 163–179.

Dasgupta, P., and Serageldin, I., eds. 2000. *Social Capital: A Multifaceted Perspective*. Washington, DC: World Bank.

Delmendo, S. 1998. The star entangled banner: Commemorating 100 years of Philippine independence and Philippine-American relations. *Journal of Asian American Studies* 1 (3): 211–214.

Dillon, M., ed. 2003. *Handbook of the Sociology of Religion*. Cambridge: Cambridge University Press.

Diner, H. 2001. *Hungering for America: Italian, Irish, and Jewish Foodways in the Age of Migration*. Cambridge, MA: Harvard University Press.

Doran, C. F. 1971. *The Politics of Assimilation: Hegemony and Its Aftermath*. Baltimore: Johns Hopkins University Press.

Durand, J., and Massey, D. 1992. Mexican migration to the United States: A critical review. *Latin American Research Review* 27 (2): 340–357.

Edwards, B., and Foley, M. 1997. Social capital and the political economy of our discontent. *American Behavioral Scientist* 40 (5): 669–678.

———. 1998. Civil society and social capital beyond Putnam. *American Behavioral Scientist* 42 (1): 124–139.

Edwards, B., Foley, M., and Diani, M., eds. 2001. *Beyond Tocqueville: Civil Society and the Social Capital Debate in Comparative Perspective*. Hanover, NH: University Press of New England.

Edwards, L., Occhipinti, S., and Ryan, S. 2000. Food and immigration: The indigestion trope contests the sophistication narrative. *Journal of Intercultural Studies* 21 (3): 297–312.

Espiritu, Y. L. 2003. *Home Bound: Filipino American Lives across Cultures*. Berkeley: University of California Press.

Estrella, C. 2004. "Manilatown" will rise again: 2 blocks of Kearny designated to honor Filipino immigrants. *San Francisco Chronicle*, July 28.

Fabros, A. 1994. *The Filipino American Newspaper Collection: Extracts from 1906–1953*. San Francisco: Filipino American Experiences Research Project.

———. 1995. *The Filipino Americans' Fight for Civil Rights: 1898–1965*. San Francisco: Filipino American Experiences Research Project.

———. N.d. California's Filipino Infantry: A Short History of the 1st and 2nd Filipino Infantry Regiments of the U.S. Army in World War II. The California State Military Museum, http://www.militarymuseum.org/Filipino.html.

Fast, J., and Richardson, J. 1982. *Roots of Dependency: Political and Economic Revolution in 19th Century Philippines*. Quezon City: Foundation for Nationalistic Studies.

Femia, J. V. 1981. *Gramsci's Political Thought: Hegemony, Consciousness, and the Revolutionary Process*. Oxford: Clarendon Press.

Filipinas Book Team. 2003. *Filipinos in America: A Journey of Faith*. San Francisco: Filipinas Publishing.

Fix, M., and Zimmerman, W. 1995. When should immigrants receive public benefits? *Migration World Magazine* 23 (5): 14–33.

Foley, M., and Edwards, B. 1999. Is it time to disinvest in social capital? *Journal of Public Policy* 19:669–678.

Frank, R. 2001. Checks in the mail: For a Philippine town, monthly allowances pave a road to riches. *Wall Street Journal*, May 22.

Freire, P. 1970. *Pedagogy of the Oppressed*. New York: Seabury Press.

Fujiwara, L. 1998. The impact of welfare reform on Asian immigrant communities. *Social Justice* 25 (1): 82–102.

Georgetown University Law Center. 1989. Naturalization of Filipino veterans. *Georgetown Immigration Law Journal* 3 (2): 281–286.

Gibson, D. 2003. *The Coming Catholic Church: How the Faithful Are Shaping a New American Catholicism*. San Francisco: HarperCollins.

Golay, F. H. 1998. *Face of Empire: US-Philippine Relations 1898–1946*. Madison: University of Wisconsin Press.

Gonzalez, J. L. 1998. *Philippine Labour Migration*. Singapore. Institute of Southeast Asian Studies.

Gonzalves, T. 1995. "We hold a neatly folded hope": Filipino veterans of World War II on citizenship and political obligation. *Amerasia Journal* 21 (3): 154–173.

Gramsci, A. 1971. *Selections from the Prison Notebooks*. New York: International Publishers.

Greeley, A. 1997. The other civic America: Religion and social capital. *American Prospect* 32:68–73.

Halpern, D. 1999. *Social Capital, Exclusion and the Quality of Life*. London: Institute for Public Policy Research.

Hiraldo, C. 2003. *Segregated Miscegenation: On the Treatment of Racial Hybridity in the U.S. and Latin American Literary Traditions*. London: Routledge.

Hoffman, V. 1995. Eating and fasting for God in Sufi tradition. *Journal of the American Academy of Religion* 63 (3): 465–489.

Husbands, W. 1999. Born in Canada . . . or not: Immigration status and food bank assistance in the Greater Toronto Area. *Journal of International Migration and Integration* 44:57–70.

Iglesia ni Cristo. 2000. *An Introduction to the Iglesia ni Cristo: The History and Christian Fellowship*. Daly City, CA: Iglesia ni Cristo Northern California. Video.

Ignacio, E. N. 2005. *Building Diaspora: Filipino Cultural Community Formation on the Internet*. New Brunswick, NJ: Rutgers University Press.

Ileto, R. 1979. *Pasyon and Revolution: Popular Movements in the Philippines, 1840–1910*. Manila: Ateneo de Manila University Press.

Jacobsen, D. A. 2001. *Doing Justice: Congregations and Community Organizing*. Minneapolis, MN: Fortress Press.

Jeung, R. 2004. *Faithful Generations: Race and New Asian American Churches*. New Brunswick, NJ: Rutgers University Press.

Karnow, S. 1989. *In Our Image: America's Empire in the Philippines*. New York: Random House.

Keely, C., and Tran, B. 1989. Remittances from labor migration: Evaluations, performances and implications. *International Migration Review* 23:500–525.

Kim, R. 1999. Center offers aid, sense of community to Filipino vets. *San Francisco Examiner*, November 12.

King, A. 1985. Social and economic benefits and costs. *Philippine Labor Review* 9:43–50.

Kolankiewicz, E. 1996. Social capital and social change. *British Journal of Sociology* 473:427–441.

Kwantes, A. C., ed. 1998. *A Century of Bible Christians in the Philippines.* Manila: OMF Literature.

Laclau, E., and Mouffe, C. 1992. *Hegemony and Socialist Strategy: Towards a Radical Democratic Politics.* London: Verso.

Lat, E. 1997. Aging Filipinos who fought for U.S. live lonely lives waiting for promises to be kept. *San Francisco Examiner*, May 25.

Lee, J. F., ed. 1991. *Asian American Experiences in the United States: Oral Histories of First to Fourth Generation Americans from China, the Philippines, Japan, India, the Pacific Islands, Vietnam, and Cambodia.* Jefferson, NC: McFarland.

Leinbach, T., and John, W. 1998. Remittances and circulation behavior in the livelihood process: Transmigrant families in South Sumatra, Indonesia. *Economic Geography* 74 (1): 4519–4534.

Lenane, E. B. 1935. Survey of the Catholic Filipino Club, 1421 Sutter Street, San Francisco California, March 25.

Lincoln, C., and Mamiya, L. 2003. *The Black Church in the African American Experience.* Durham, NC: Duke University Press.

Lomas, J. 1998. Social capital and health: Implications for public health and epidemiology. *Social Science and Medicine* 479:1181–1188.

Lowe, L. 1996. *Immigrant Acts: On Asian American Cultural Politics.* Durham, NC: Duke University Press.

Lu, N., and Cason, K. 2004. Dietary pattern change and acculturation of Chinese Americans in Pennsylvania. *Journal of the American Dietetic Association* 104 (5): 771–792.

Lucas, Robert E. B. 1987. Emigration to South Africa's mines. *American Economic Review* 77:313–330.

Lyon, J., and Wilson, K. 1987. *Marcos and Beyond.* Sydney, Australia: Kangaroo Press.

Mabalon, D. 2003. Lost to the Church, But Saved by Jesus Christ. Life in Little Manila: Filipinas/os in Stockton, 1917–1972. Ph.D. diss., Stanford University.

Maggay, M. 1989. *Communicating Cross-Culturally: Towards a New Context for Missions in the Philippines.* Quezon City: New Day.

Malkin, M. 1997. FDR's forgotten promise to Filipino war veterans. *Seattle Times*, April 22.

Manalansan, M. 2003. *Global Divas: Filipino Gay Men in the Diaspora.* Durham, NC: Duke University Press.

Martin, D. 1990. *Tongues of Fire: The Explosion of Protestantism in Latin America*. Oxford: Basil Blackwell.

Marx, K. 1844. Economic and philosophical manuscripts of 1844. Unpublished manuscript. February.

Massey, D., and Parrado, E. 1994. Migradollars: The remittances and savings of Mexican migrants to the United States. *Population Research and Policy Review* 13:3–30.

McCormick, B., and Wahba, J. 2000. Overseas employment and remittances to a dual economy. *Economic Journal* 110 (463): 509–534.

McKay, S. 2006. *Satanic Mills or Silicon Islands: The Politics of High-Tech Production in the Philippines*. Ithaca, NY: Cornell University Press.

Meixsel, R. 1995. Major General George Grunert, WPO-3, and the Philippine Army. *Journal of Military History* 59 (2): 303–324.

Mendoza, L., and Shankar, S., eds. 2003. *Crossing into America: The New Literature of Immigration*. New York: New Press.

Menjivar, C., Da Vanzo, J., Greenwell, L., and Burciaga Valdez, R. 1998. Remittance behavior among Salvadoran and Filipino immigrants in Los Angeles. *International Migration Review* 32 (1): 97–126.

Mercado, L. N. 1982. *Christ in the Philippines*. Manila: Divine Word University.

Miller, S. 1982. *Benevolent Assimilation: The American Conquest of the Philippines, 1899–1903*. New Haven, CT: Yale University Press.

Min, P. Y., and Kim, J. H., eds. 2002. *Religions in Asian America: Building Faith Communities*. Walnut Creek, CA: AltaMira Press.

Murphy, D. 1990. Immigration law: Citizenship courts lack authority to grant citizenship to Filipino war veterans under the expired Nationality Act of 1940. *Suffolk Transnational Law Journal* 13 (2): 841–854.

Nadeau, K. 2002. *Liberation Theology in the Philippines: Faith in a Revolution*. Westport, CT: Praeger.

Naeem, A. 2003. The role of culture and religion in the management of diabetes: A study of Kashmiri men in Leeds. *Journal of the Royal Society for the Promotion of Health* 123 (2): 110–126.

Nakano, S. 2000. Nation, nationalism and citizenship in the Filipino World War II Veterans equity movement, 1945–1999. *Hitotsubashi Journal of Social Studies* 32:33–53.

———. 2004. The Filipino World War II Veterans Equity Movement and the Filipino American Community. Paper presented at the Seventh International Philippine Studies Conference, International Institute of Asian Studies, Leiden, Netherlands, June 16–19.

Nemoto, T., Aoki, B., and Huang, K. 2000. HIV risk behaviors among Asian drug users in San Francisco. *AIDS Education Prevention* 12 (2): 22–34.

Nezhukumatathil, A. 2003. *Miracle Fruit*. Dorset, VT: Tupelo Press.

Nieman, D., Underwood, B., Sherman, K., Arabatzis, K., Barbosa, J., Johnson, M., and Shultz, T. 1989. Dietary status of Seventh-Day Adventist vegetarian and non-vegetarian elderly women. *Journal of the American Dietetic Association* 89 (12): 1663–1678.

Nilson Report. 2004. Latin America Remittance Study: The Remittance Marketplace. Washington, DC: Inter-American Development Bank.

Nolte, C. 1995. 400th Anniversary of Spanish shipwreck, rough first landing in Bay Area. *San Francisco Chronicle*, November 14.

Norris, P. 1996. Does television erode social capital? A reply to Putnam. *PS: Political Science and Politics* 29:474–480.

Norton, A., Latham, M., and Sturgess, G., eds. 1997. *Social Capital: The Individual, Civil Society and the State*. Sydney: Centre for Independent Studies.

O'Brien, G. 2003. Indigestible food, conquering hordes, and waste materials: Metaphors of immigrants and the early immigration restriction debate in the United States. *Metaphor and Symbol* 18 (1): 33–48.

Ocampo, A. 2004. What the Thomasites ate. *Philippine Daily Inquirer*, June 18.

Olson, J. ed. 2002. *The Philippine Scouts*. Daly City, CA: Philippine Scouts Heritage Society.

Omi, M., and Winant, H. 1994. *Racial Formation in the United States: From the 1960s to the 1980s*. New York: Routledge.

Orozco, M. 2003. Remittances, the rural sector and policy options in Latin America. Inter American Dialogue (Research Series). http://www.migrationinformation.org/feature/display.cfm?ID=128.

Palloni, A., Massey, D., Ceballos, M., Espinosa, K., and Spittel, M. 2001. Social capital and international migration: A test using information on family networks. *American Journal of Sociology* 106 (5): 1262–1298.

Pan, Y., Dixon, Z., Himburg, S., and Huffman, F. 1999. Asian students change their eating patterns after living in the United States. *Journal of the American Dietetic Association* 99 (1): 54–72.

Parreñas, R. 2001. *Servants of Globalization: Women, Migration, and Domestic Work*. Stanford, CA: Stanford University Press.

———. 2005. *Children of Global Migration: Transnational Families and Gendered Woes*. Stanford, CA: Stanford University Press.

Paxton, P. 1999. Is social capital declining in the United States? A multiple indicator assessment. *American Journal of Sociology* 105 (1): 88–127.

Pido, A. J. 1985. *The Pilipinos in America: Macro/micro Dimensions of Immigration and Integration*. New York: Center for Migration Studies.

Pimentel, B. 1999. Filipino WWII veterans seeking funds to build a place to receive help. *San Francisco Chronicle*, January 2.

Poe, T. 2001. The labour and leisure of food production as a mode of ethnic identity building among Italians in Chicago, 1890–1940. *Rethinking History* 5 (1): 131–149.

Pomeroy, W. J. 1970. *American Neo-Colonialism: Its Emergence in the Philippines and Asia.* New York: International Publishers.

Portes, A. 1995. *The Economic Sociology of Immigration.* New York: Russell Sage.

———. 1998. Social capital: Its origins and applications in modern sociology. *Annual Review of Sociology* 24:1–24.

Portes, A., and Landolt, P. 2002. The downside of social capital. *American Prospect.* http://www.prospect.org/cs/articles?articleId=4943.

Posadas, B. M. 1999. *The Filipino Americans.* Westport, CT: Greenwood Press.

Puerta, R. A. 2002. Remittances and development: USAID/Honduras consultancy report. Washington, DC: U.S. Agency for International Development.

Puri, S., and Ritzema, T. 2000. Migrant worker remittances, micro finance and the informal economy: Prospects and issues. Working paper. Geneva: International Labor Office.

Putnam, R. 1995. Bowling alone: America's declining social capital. *Journal of Democracy* 6:65–78.

———. 1996. The strange disappearance of civic America. *American Prospect* 24:34–48.

———. 2000. *Bowling Alone: The Collapse and Revival of American Community.* New York: Simon and Schuster.

———, ed. 2004. *Democracies in Flux: The Evolution of Social Capital in Contemporary Society.* New York: Oxford University Press.

Putzell, J. 1997. Accounting for the dark side of social capital: Reading Robert Putnam on democracy. *Journal of International Development* 97:939–949.

Ramsay, M. 1998. Redeeming the city: Exploring the relationship between church and metropolis. *Urban Affairs Review* 335:595–609.

Ratha, D. 2003. Workers' remittances: An important and stable source of external development finance. In *Global Development Finance.* Washington, DC: World Bank.

Recio, D. 2000. *The Filipino Experience: Through One Man's Eyes.* San Francisco: Recio Press.

Reed, R. 1990. Migration as mission: The expansion of the Iglesia ni Cristo outside the Philippines. In R. Reed, ed., *Patterns of Migration in Southeast Asia,* 78–94. Berkeley: Center for South and Southeast Asian Studies/International and Area Studies, University of California, Berkeley.

Reyes, B. J. 2004. San Francisco's Pilipino community. In M. Orendorff, ed., *Asia in the San Francisco Bay Area: A Cultural Travel Guide,* 43–56. Emeryville, CA: Avalon.

Rodriguez, E. R. 1996. International migrants' remittances in the Philippines. *Canadian Journal of Economics* 29:4276.

———. 1998. International migration and income distribution in the Philippines. *Economic Development and Cultural Change* 46:329–350.

Roozen, D., and Nieman, J., eds. 2005. *Church, Identity, and Change: Theology and Denominational Structures in Unsettled Times.* Grand Rapids, MI: Eerdmans.

Rozelle, S., Taylor, E. and DeBrauw, A. 1999. Migration, remittances, and agricultural productivity in China. *American Economic Review* 89:37–56.

Sack, D. 2000. *Whitebread Protestants: Food and Religion in American Culture.* New York: Palgrave.

Sales, W. 1994. *From Civil Rights to Black Liberation: Malcolm X and the Organization of Afro-America Unity.* Cambridge: South End Press.

San Buenaventura, S. 1999. Filipino folk spirituality and immigration: From mutual aid to religion. In D. K. Yoo, ed., *New Spiritual Homes.* Honolulu: University of Hawaii Press.

———. 2002. Filipino religion at home and abroad: Historical roots and immigrant transformations. In P. G. Min and J. H. Kim, eds., *Religions in Asian America,* 52–86. New York: AltaMira Press.

San Francisco Department of Public Health. 2001. *Quarterly AIDS Surveillance Report, June 30, 2001.* San Francisco: Department of Public Health.

San Juan, E. 1998. *From Exile to Diaspora: Versions of the Filipino Experience in the United States.* Boulder, CO: Westview Press.

Sassen, S. 1998. *Globalization and Its Discontents.* New York: New Press.

Satia-Abouta, J., Patterson, R. E., Kristal, A. R., Teh, C., and Tu, S. P. 2002. Psychological predictors of diet and acculturation in Chinese American and Chinese Canadian women. *Ethnicity and Health* 7 (1): 21–40.

Schirmer, D. B., and Shalom, S. R., eds. 1987. *The Philippines Reader: A History of Colonialism, Neocolonialism, and Dictatorship, and Resistance.* Quezon City: Ken Incorporated

Schuller, T. 1997. Building social capital: Steps towards a learning society. *Scottish Affairs* 19:77–91.

Semyonov, S., and Gorodzeisky, A. 2005. Labor migration, remittances and household income: A comparison between Filipino and Filipina overseas workers. *International Migration Review* 39 (1): 4524–4538.

Shalom, S. R. 1981. *The United States and the Philippines: A Study of Neocolonialism.* Philadelphia: Institute for the Study of Human Issues.

Shankar, L., and Balgopal, P. 2001. South Asian immigrants before 1950: The formation of ethnic, symbolic and group identity. *Amerasia Journal* 27 (1): 55–76.

Shankman, P. 1976. *Migration and Underdevelopment: The Case of Western Samoa.* Boulder, CO: Westview Press.

Shaw, A. V., and Francia, L. H. 2003. *Vestiges of War: The Philippine-American War and the Aftermath of an Imperial Dream 1899–1999.* New York: New York University Press.

Sherman, D. 1985. Naturalization of Filipino war veterans. *San Diego Law Review* 22 (5): 1171–1192.

Siddiqui, T., and Chowdhury, A. 2003. Migrant worker remittances and microfinance in Bangladesh. Working paper. Refugee and Migratory Movements Research Unit.

Smart, J. 2004. Ethnic entrepreneurship, transmigration, and social integration: An ethnographic study of Chinese restaurant owners in rural western Canada. *Urban Anthropology and Studies of Cultural Systems and World Economic Development* 32 (3–4): 311–333.

Smith, C. 1991. *The Emergence of Liberation Theology: Radical Religion and Social Movement Theory.* Chicago: University of Chicago Press.

Sobredo, J. 1998. From Manila Bay to Daly City: Filipinos in San Francisco. In J. Brook, C. Carlsson, and N. Peters, eds., *Reclaiming San Francisco History, Politics, Culture,* 273–286. San Francisco: City Lights Books.

Solis, M. M. 2000. *A Brief History of St. Philip's Church, Salinas, California.* Salinas: St. Philip's Church and SRMNK.

Stahl, C., and Arnold, F. 1986. Overseas workers' remittances and Asian development. *International Migration Review* 20:899–925.

Stanton, R. 1992. Migrant remittances and development. *International Migration* 30:267–287.

Stark, O. 1991. Migration in LDCs: Risk, remittances, and the family. *Finance and Development* 28:39–41.

Swatos, W. 1995. *Religion and Democracy in Latin America.* Edison, NJ: Transaction.

Takaki, R. 1987. *Strangers from a Different Shore: A History of Asian Americans.* New York: Penguin.

———. 1995. *In the Heart of Filipino America: Immigrants from the Pacific Isles.* New York: Chelsea House Press.

Tan, A. 1989. *The Joy Luck Club.* New York: Putnam.

Taylor, J. E., and Wyatt, T. J. 1996. The shadow value of migrant remittances, income and inequality in a household-farm economy. *Journal of Development Studies* 32 (6): 164–179.

Teachman, J., Paasch, K., and Carver, K. 1997. Social capital and the generation of human capital. *Social Forces* 75 (4): 1343–1359.

Tiglao, R. 1997. What tiger? Problems affecting the Philippine economy. *Far Eastern Economic Review* 160 (43): 921–943.

Toribio, H., eds. 2002. *Seven Card Stud with Seven Manangs Wild: An Anthology of Filipino-American Writings.* San Francisco: East Bay Filipino American National Historical Society.

Torres, C. A. 1992. *The Church, Society, and Hegemony: A Critical Sociology of Religion in Latin America.* London: Praeger.

Tsong, N. 1998. Filipino WWII vets seek U.S. benefits. *San Francisco Examiner,* July 23.

Tucker, R. C., ed. 1978. *The Marx-Engels Reader.* New York: Norton.

Tuggy, A. L. 1978. Iglesia Ni Cristo: An angel and his church. In D. J. Hesselgrave, ed., *Dynamic Religious Movements*, 85–101. Grand Rapids, MI: Baker Book House.

U.S. Bureau of the Census. *U.S. Census 2000*. Washington, DC: U.S. Bureau of the Census.

U.S. Department of Veterans Affairs. Veterans benefits. http://wwww.va.gov/opa/fact/vafacts.html

U.S. Public Law 301. 79th Cong., February 18, 1946. *First Supplemental Surplus Appropriation Rescission Act.*

U.S. Public Law 391. 79th Cong., May 17, 1946. *Second Supplemental Surplus Appropriation Rescission Act.*

U.S. Public Law 865. 80th Cong., 1948. *Act Approving Funds for the Construction of a Veterans Hospital in Manila.*

U.S. Public Law 40. 88th Cong., June 13, 1963. *Grant-in-Aid to the Republic of the Philippines for the Hospitalization of Certain Veterans.*

U.S. Public Law 82. 93rd Cong., August 2, 1973. *Veterans Health Care Expansion Act of 1973.*

U.S. Public Law 72. 97th Cong., November 3, 1981. *Veterans' Health Care, Training, and Small Business Loan Act of 1981.*

U.S. Public Law 649. 101st Cong., November 29, 1990. *Immigration Act of 1990.*

U.S. Public Law 169. 106th Cong., December 14, 1999. *Foster Care Independence Act of 1999.*

U.S. Public Law 377. 106th Cong., October 27, 2000. *An Act Making Appropriations for the Departments of Veterans Affairs and Housing and Urban Development, and for Sundry Independent Agencies, Boards, Commissions, Corporations, and Offices for the Fiscal Year Ending September 30, 2001, and for Other Purposes.*

U.S. Public Law 419. 106th Cong., November 1, 2000. *Veterans Health Care Improvement Act of 2000.*

U.S. Public Law 170. 108th Cong., December 6, 2003. *Veterans Health Care, Capital Asset, and Business Improvement Act of 2003.*

U.S. Public Law 183. 108th Cong., December 16, 2003. *Veterans Benefit Act of 2003.*

Uslaner, E. 1999. Morality plays: Social capital and moral behaviour in Anglo-American democracies. In Van Deth, J., Maraffi, M., Newton K, and Whiteley, P., eds., *Social Capital and European Democracy*, 213–239. London: Routledge.

Vallangca, R. V. 1977. *Pinoy: The First Wave 1898–1941*. San Francisco: Strawberry Hill Press.

Verba, S., Schlozman, K. L., and Brady, H. E. 1997. The big tilt: Participatory inequality in America. *American Prospect* 32:74–80.

Võ, L. T. 2004. *Mobilizing an Asian American Community*. Philadelphia: Temple University Press.

Wadhwani, A. 1999. Seniors play waiting games. *San Francisco Examiner*, October 3.

Wallovits, S. E. 1966. *The Filipinos in California*. Los Angeles: University of Southern California Press.

Warner, S. 2000. Religion and new post-1965 immigrants: Some principles drawn from field research. *American Studies* 41 (2/3): 267–286.

Warner, S., and Wittner, J., eds. 1998. *Gatherings in the Diaspora: Religious Communities and the New Immigration*. Philadelphia: Temple University Press.

Warren, M. 2001. *Dry Bones Rattling: Community Building to Revitalize American Democracy*. Princeton, NJ: Princeton University Press.

Weber, M. 1958. *The Protestant Ethic and the Spirit of Capitalism*. New York: Scribner's.

Wei, Y., and Read, M. 1996. Dietary pattern changes of Asian immigrants. *Nutrition Research* 16 (8): 1277–1290.

Wells, J. 2000. Filipino veterans of WWII angry about net benefits. *San Francisco Chronicle*, March 24.

White, H., and Kokotsaki, K. 2004. Indian food in the UK: Personal values and changing patterns of consumption. *International Journal of Consumer Studies* 28 (3): 284–300.

Whiteley, P. 1999. *Social capital and European democracy*. London: Routledge.

Whittemore, A., Kolonel, L., Wu, A., John, E., Gallagher, R., Howe, G., Burch, J. D., Hankin, J., Dreon, D., West, D., Teh, C., and Paffenbarger, R. 1996. Prostate cancer in relation to diet, physical activity, and body size in blacks, whites, and Asians in the United States and Canada. *Journal of the National Cancer Institute* 87 (9): 652–669.

Wiegele, K. 2005. *Investing in Miracles: El Shaddai and the Transformation of Popular Catholicism in the Philippines*. Honolulu: University of Hawaii Press.

Williams, D. R. 1926. *The United States and the Philippines*. New York: Doubleday, Page.

Wood, R. L. 2002. *Faith in Action: Religion, Race, and Democratic Organizing in America*. Chicago: University of Chicago Press.

Woodruff, C., and Zeteno, R. 2001. Remittances and microenterprises in Mexico. Working paper. Graduate School of International Relations and Pacific Studies, University of California, San Diego.

Woolcock, M. 1998. Social capital and economic development: Toward a theoretical synthesis and policy framework. *Theory and Society* 27:151–208.

Wu, A. H., Pike, M.C., and Wan, P. 2002. Adolescent and adult soy intake and the risk of breast cancer in Asian-Americans. *Journal of Nutrition* 132 (3): 578–601.

Yang, F. 2000. The growing literature of Asian American religions: A review of the field, with special attention to three new books. *Journal of Asian American Studies* 3 (2): 251–256.

Yoo, D. Ed. 1999. *New Spiritual Homes*. Honolulu: University of Hawaii Press.

Zhou, M., and Bankston, C. 1998. *Growing Up American: How Vietnamese Children Adapt to Life in the United States*. New York: Russell Sage.

Index

1906 earthquake, 114

abstinence, 16
Abu Sayyaf, 168
acceptance, 105
accountability, 144
acculturation, 10, 19, 85, 114
acculturative stress, 35, 83–84
activism, 165
activists, 4, 180
adaptive spirit, 2, 10, 12–13, 83, 101, 105, 122, 181
adult organizations, 125
Advent, 89
advocacy, 155
advocates, 4
affordable housing, 104
Afghanistan, 151
African American, 1, 3, 5, 26, 61, 76, 86, 103–4, 127, 171, 179–80
Aglipay, Gregorio, 44
Aglipayan Church, 44, 60. *See also* Philippine Independent Church; Iglesia Filipina Independiente
Agricultural Workers Organizing Committee (AWOC), 132
Aklan Association, 110
Alameda, 26, 70, 100
Alaskan canneries, 22
Alcoholics Anonymous, 108
All Saints' Day, 16
All Souls Church, 30
All Souls' Day, 16

Allah, 86
Allston, Philip, 172
Alpha Phi Omega Alumni Association, 111
alumni associations, 111, 116
American: Adventists, 38; Anglicans, 38; Bible Society, 44; Catholic, 43, 46, 97; Christian, 6, 98, 129; citizens, 7; clergy, 33; colonization, 35, 74, 82; consumers, 7; culture, 6; democracy, 10; economic aid, 166; English, 84; Episcopalians, 38; faith, 35; fare, 90; hamburger, 84; liberal democracy, 7; Lutheran Church, 178; Methodists, 38, 53, 59; Mormons, 38; Navy, 22; neo-colonization, 74; Northern Baptist church, 39; political rhetoric, 36; public, 14; Protestant, 38–39, 43, 46, 60, 97; social history, 5; society, 7, 9, 12, 14; studies, 11; taxpayers, 7; volunteers, 7; voters, 7; Witnesses, 38; workforce, 8
American Behavioral Scientist, 102
American Idol show, 8
American Prospect, 102
Americanization, 36, 90, 131, 175, 182
Americanized church, 74, 80; education, 74, 80
AmeriCorps, 10
Amnesty International, 173
Andag, Glen, 161–62

Andrey, Robert, 135
Anglo-Saxon, 35
annexation, 22
Aparri, 152
APL song, 8
Apostolic Catholic Church (ACC),
    168
Aquino, Corazon, 167, 170
Arab American, 3
Archdiocese of San Francisco, 25, 31,
    70, 95, 104, 115, 130, 134, 140,
    145, 176, 186n10
Aristocrat, 90
Arkipelago Bookstore, 27
Armed Forces of the Philippines
    (AFP), 165–66, 174
Armed Forces Voluntary Recruitment
    Act, 154
Arroyo, Gloria Macapagal, 167–68,
    170, 173, 179, 185n5
Ash Wednesday, 16
Asia, 15, 176
Asian American Recovery Services, 84
Asian American, 1–2, 5–6, 61, 86, 87,
    123, 176; studies, 10
Asian Development Bank, 66, 69
Asian Indian American, 9
Asian Pacific Islander Wellness Center,
    108
Asian, 14; Christian, 20; culture, 6,
    83; migrants, 104; studies, 10; su-
    permarket, 90, 93
Asian, 26, 29
Asia-Pacific region, 152
Asiatowns, 14
assimilation, 5–6, 11, 105, 181;
    theory, 5–6
assistance, 105
Association of Major Religious Supe-
    riors in the Philippines, 169
Ateneo Alumni association, 112
Ateneo de Manila University, 132

Augustinians, 41, 82
Aztec rituals, 84

BABAE Women's Group, 172
Baguio, 152
balikbayan box (care packages), 182
balita (news), 100
Banal na Pagaaral (Holy Study), 50
Bankston, Carl, 5–6
baptism (*binyag*), 19
barangay (village), 7, 19, 24, 27, 110,
    113, 116, 157
barrio fiesta, 31
Barrio: Philippine Cultural Night, 162
Barry, James, 97
Bataan death march, 153
Batangas, 77
Bay Area Organizing Committee
    (BAOC), 136, 138, 142–43, 148,
    150
bayan (community), 15
Bayan USA, 171–172
bayanihan (community action), 2,
    9–10, 12, 14, 19, 65, 69, 71,
    79–81, 101, 105, 107–8, 113, 116,
    118–19, 121–22, 133, 151, 162–
    63, 172, 174–77, 180, 182,185n5.
    See also bridging Filipinization
Bayanihan Center, 25, 27
beauty parlor gratitude, 125
Bebot song, 8
Bell, Franklin, 22, 40
Benedictine Sisters, 42
Benedictines, 41
Benedictines for Peace, 170
benevolent assimilation, 22, 52, 60
Benevolent Missionaries Association,
    46
Bessie Carmichael Elementary School,
    27, 89
Beveridge, Albert, 36, 186n2
Bible: discussions, 178; exposition, 58;

reading, 94, 117; study, 9, 16, 32,
   58, 134
Bicolano, 33, 106, 135
bicultural fast-food, 90
Bindelstiff Studios, 25
Binhi (young adults), 58, 126
Bishop of the Poor Peasants and
   Workers, 169
bisita Iglesia (church visit), 16
Bitanga, Fred, 3, 158
Black Saturday, 16
blessing *(bendisyon)*, 19
Blood Centers of the Pacific, 118
Board of Supervisors, San Francisco,
   123, 177
Bohol, 82–83
Boholano, 33
bonding Filipinization, 9, 12, 14, 34, 98,
   118, 124, 181. *See also kasamahan*
bonding social capital, 102, 121
bonds, 2, 9, 14
Bonus, Rick, 5–6
bowling, 100
Bowling Alone, 13, 100, 103
Boxer, Barbara, 173
Bradley, Omar, 154
bridges, 2, 6, 9, 14
bridging activity, 102
bridging Filipinization, 9, 12, 14, 101,
   118, 181. See also *bayanihan*
bridging social capital, 102
Broad Street, 4
Brodersen, Henry, 178
Brown, Cathy, 118
Brown, Jerry, 100, 119
Brown, Willie, 3, 108, 143
Bukas Loob sa Diyos (Open in Spirit
   to God), 50
Buklod, 126–27
Bunagan, J., 150
Burgos, Jose, 129
burial *(libing)*, 19

Burlingame, 31
Burnett, Peter, 1, 3
Burton, Rodgers, 39
Bush, George H. W., 155–56
Bush, George W., 135, 163, 168

Cabaleros de Dimas Alang, 49, 131
Calica, Leo, 56
California State University, East Bay,
   161
California, 9, 20, 23, 156; crops, 22;
   gold rush, 22, 178; Golden State,
   26; Northern, 23; schools, 8
California-Nevada Conference, 171
"The Call to Family, Community and
   Participation," 144
Cal-Nevada United Methodist Philip-
   pine Fact-Finding Team/Solidarity
   and Pastoral Visit, 172
Camp Crame, 165–66
cannibalism, 84
Canon Kip Senior Center, 111
Capuchins, 41
Capuli, Arturo, 56, 105, 169
Carter, Jimmy, 78
*Casaysayan nang Pasiong Mahal ni Je-
   sucristong Panginoong Natin*, 128
Castillo, Noemi, 140, 186n8, 187n13
Castro District, 108
Catholic, 11, 15, 17–18; calendar, 17;
   masses 15; priests, 16, 18
Catholic Bishops Conference of the
   Philippines (CBCP), 169
Catholic Charities, 78
Catholic Church, 41–44, 49, 104,
   128–30, 146
Catholic Church of the Epiphany, 109
Catholic Filipino Club, 48–49, 186n7
Catholic Italian, 86
Catholic Relief Services, 78, 115
Catholicization, 176
Cavite Province, 1

Cebu, 77, 120, 179
Cebuano, 33, 106
Central California Conference of Seventh-Day Adventists, 55, 178
charismatic, 15, 18
Chavez, Cesar, 132
Chile, 167
China 20
Chinatown, 14
Chinese, 26, 84; cuisine, 90; migration, 14; noodles, 84
Chinese American, 3, 14, 20, 125
chismis (gossip), 100, 144
Christian: liturgical calendar, 16; church, 44; pastors, 18
Christianity, 12
Christianization, 22, 37, 46, 53, 82, 131, 176
Christmas, 16, 73, 82, 88, 115, 158, 186n9
Christmas Lantern Stroll, 89
Church of Christ Scientist, 57
Church of Jesus Christ of Latter-Day Saints, 55
citizenship, 153, 160, 174; *See also* U.S. citizenship
City and County of San Francisco, 3
City College of San Francisco, 150, 161
city hall, 3
City of refuge, 24
civic: action, 13, 144; behavior, 103; clubs, 111; connections, 14; contribution, 10; duty, 113; engagement, 6, 10, 32, 103; involvement, 10, 101, 121 181; virtue, 102
civil liberties, 3
civil rights movement, 127
civilization, 82
Clark Air Base, 152
Classic Bowl, 100, 182
Clinton, Bill, 162
Coalition for Philippine Renewal, 112

collaborative action, 127
Colma, 31
Columbia Square, 146
commercialization, 104
Commission on the Aging, San Francisco, 177
Commonwealth Army of the Philippines, 153, 154. *See also* Philippine Commonwealth Army
Commonwealth Government of the Philippines, 153
Communist Party of the Philippines (CPP), 166, 168, 170
Community Chest, 48
community: organizing, 13, 138, 181; survey, 32
compelling political issue, 134–36, 183
confirmation (*kumpil*), 19
Confradia de San Jose, 46
Congregational Church, 131
Congregationalists, 39
Congregations of San Jose, 42
Connecticut College, 117
Contra Costa, 26, 70
Convention of Philippine Baptist Churches (CPBC), 168
Cordova, Fred, 130, 146
Corpus Christi Church, 30, 72, 133
Council of Priests, 51
counterhegemony, 13–14, 127–29, 131, 139, 145–48
counterinsurgency, 166, 168, 173
Couples for Christ, 9, 50
Cruz, Aethel, 162
cultural capital, 9, 104, 110
Current Population Survey, 112

Daly City, 25, 26, 28, 50, 57, 69, 78, 93, 100, 112–13, 118, 126, 171–72
Daly City United Methodist Church, 58, 108, 171, 173, 176

Daly City-Quezon City Sister City Commission, 119
Dancing with the Stars show, 8
dasal (prayer), 19, 63–64, 80
Davao, 152
De Los Reyes, Isabelo, 44
Declaration of Principles, 126
Delta Hotel, 156–58
Democracies in Flux, 101
democratization, 103
DeOcera, Wilson, 171, 175
Dependency and Indemnity Compensation benefits, 163
deportation, 112
Desperate Housewives, 179
development institutions, 69
devotion, 89, 104, 114–15
Dewey, George, 22, 41
diaspora, 10–11, 20, 75
diasporic community, 128
Dignity Charismatic Lesbian Gay group, 108
Diocese of Oakland, 50, 70, 176
Diocese of San Jose, 70, 176
Diocese of Seattle, 48
disaster management, 109
Disciples of Christ, 39–40
Disney-ABC, 179–180
Divine Mercy, 50, 114, 158
Dominicans, 41–42
dot-com, 24
Draves, Lyle, 133
Draves, Victoria Manalo, 123, 133, 146, 183
dual allegiance, 114
dual citizenship, 23, 72–73, 179
Dura, Father, 158

Easter, 88
Easter Salubong, 50, 89
Eastern European, 104
economic exploitation, 53

ecumenical, 170
Ecumenical Bishops' Forum (EBF), 170
Ed De La Cruz Building, 27
El Shaddai, 11, 15, 18, 50, 59, 185n5
empowerment, 103
English as a Second Language (ESL), 118
English proficiency, 26
Episcopal Church, Philippines, 168
Episcopal Church, USA, 172
Episcopals, 39
Erap City, 119
Espiritu, Yen Le, 5–6
esprit de corps, 52, 83
Estrada, Joseph, 119, 167, 185n5
ethnic bonds, 6; ties, 9; media, 9
ethnographic, 10–11, 146
Eugene, Father, 136, 139–41
European American, 5, 72, 86, 104, 178–79
Evangelical Christians, 37
Evangelical Church, 46
Evangelicals, 18
Excelsoir District, 3, 132–33
export earnings, 67
extrajudicial killings, 151, 165–77, 181, 183

Fairmont Hotel, 133
Faith Bible Church, 29, 56, 187n16
familial giving, 76
family dynamics, 125; gatherings, 6
farmworkers, 54
fasting, 16
Fathers of the Divine Word, 42
Feast of the Black Nazarene, 88–89. *See also* Nazareno of Quiapo
festival: Ati-Atihan, 89; Moriones, 89; Pahiyas, 78, 89; Parol Stroll, 89; Peñafrancia, 89; Santo Niño, 89; Sinulog, 89

fiesta, 73, 87
Fiesta Filipina, 89
filial piety, 125
Filipinization, 7–8, 10, 20, 26, 34–35, 48, 135, 180–81
Filipino: Adventists, 2, 70; Aglipayans, 2; activists, 25; airport screeners, 135, 138, 141–45, 147; associations, 110; bachelor, 25; Baptists, 2, 54, 61, 70; businesses, 30; Catholics, 16, 19–20, 33, 49, 52, 61, 64, 70, 96, 129, 133, 159, 181; Catholic church, 12, 16; Catholic gay and lesbians, 108; celebrations and devotions, 17; Catholicism, 30; Christian, 6, 10, 37, 54; community, 26; community meeting, 15; congregations, 30; cultural and recreational associations, 111; diaspora, 11; doctors, 8; eateries, 27; Episcopalians, 2, 54, 58, 70; faithful, 14; families, 27; fast-food, 26; flock, 33; global diaspora, 20; health care professionals, 24; heroes, 27; immigrants, 15; independent church, 11, 12, 16, 88; Independents, 16, 19–20, 61, 64, 181; issues, 33; Methodist, 2, 39, 54, 61, 70, 159; migrants, 11, 13, 26; migrant workers, 23; Mormons, 2, 54–55, 70; Muslim, 15, 19; nurses, 8, 24; population, 15, 26–27; Presbyterians, 54, 61, 70; principals, 27; products, 15; professional, 24, 27; Protestant church, 11, 12, 16; Protestants, 16, 19–20, 52, 61, 64, 181; queer community, 34; residents, 28; restaurants, 90; seamen, 21; social service agency, 27; sojourners, 35; spiritualities, 34; team, 11; traits: 19, 69; TRIP team, 28–29, 31; veterans benefits, 160;

Witnesses, 2, 54–55, 70, 159
Filipino American, 2–3, 6–7, 20, 34, 35, 179–80; churches, 9; consumers, 7; community, 9; groups, 9; migrants, 14; newspapers and magazines, 8–9; studies, 11; taxpayers, 7; vote, 20; youth, 14
Filipino American Christian Fellowship Church, Los Angeles, 54
Filipino American Democratic Club, 111
Filipino American Development Foundation, 121
Filipino American National Historical Society, 130
Filipino American Republican Club, 111
Filipino American Seventh-Day Adventist Church, 178
The Filipino Channel (TFC), 8, 72
Filipino Christian Fellowship, 53
Filipino Community Center (FCC), 162, 171
Filipino Community Church, 53
Filipino Community Support (FOCUS), 162
Filipino Cultural Center, 25
Filipino Education Center (FEC), 27, 115
Filipino food: *adobo* (soy dish), 91; *afritada Filipina*, 90; *almusal* (breakfast), 32; *arroz caldo* (chicken rice porridge), 96; *bibingka* (rice pudding cake), 82, 92; *caldereta Filipina*, 90; *champorado* (chocolate rice porridge), 96; *halo-halo* (mixed fruit and shaved ice dessert), 92; *handaan* (food feast), 33; *hapunan* (dinner), 32, 85; ingredients, 90–92; *itlog na maalat* (salted eggs), 92; *kare-kare* (oxtail and vegetables in peanut sauce

stew), 92, 94; *lechon* (roasted pig),
79, 85, 90, 92, 96, 98; *lumpia* (egg
roll), 92, 96, 182; *mechado* (beef
stew), 93–94; *merienda* (snack),
32, 85; *nilaga* (stew), 15, 92; *paella Filipina*, 90, 98; *pansit bihon*
(Chinese noodles), 94; *pinakbet*
(bitter gourd stew), 94; *pritong
manok* (fried chicken), 94; *pulutan*
(appetizers), 91; *puto* (rice cake),
99; *sinigang* (sour soup dish), 92;
sotanghon (glass noodle chicken
soup), 96; *tanghalian* (lunch), 32,
85; *tinola* (chicken soup and green
papaya dish), 92
Filipino kinship roles: *ama* (father),
80; *anak* (child), 71; *apo* (grandchild), 72, 80; *ate* (elder sister), 80,
125; *ina* (mother), 80; *kababata*
(childhood friend), 72; *kababayan*
(countryman/countrywoman), 8,
72, 97, 125, 139, 145; *kabarkada*
(social group mate), 72; *kaklase*
(classmate), 72; *kamaganak* (relative), 72; *kapatid* (sibling), 18, 72,
80, 116; *kumare* (old friend),
72; *kuya* (elder brother), 76, 80,
125; *lola* (grandmother), 80; *lolo*
(grandfather), 80, 150; manang
(elder woman), 73, 125; manong
(elder man), 73, 125, 150; *matalik
na kaibigan* (best friend), 72; *nanay*
(mother), 71 *ninang* (sponsor), 72;
pamangkin (nieces/nephews), pamilya (family), 145; 80; *tiya* (aunt),
71, 125 *tiyo* (uncle), 80, 125
Filipino Repatriation Act (1935), 130
Filipino Senior Center, 111
Filipino Task Force on AIDS, 108
Filipino values: *awa* (mercy or pity),
19, 64; *bahala na* (leave it to God),
14, 19, 63, 72; *damay* (sympathy),

19; *galang* (respect), 19; *hiya* (shy
or embarrassed), 19; *kasunduan*
(agreement), 122; *lingkod* (serve),
19, 182; *maintindihin* (understanding), 19; *makisama* (get along with
others), 15; *matulungin* (helpfulness), 69; *naawa* (mercy or pity),
65; *nahihiya* (shy or embarrassed),
65; *nakokonsensiya* (consciencitized), 65; *opo* (yes, sir/ma'am);
pagbigay (giving), 19, 65, 80; *paggalang sa dunong ng nakakatanda*
(respect for the wisdom of elders),
124, 134, 147, 182; *pagtulong*
(help), 80; *panata* (vow), 109;
pangako (promise), 122; *pasalamat* (thankful), 19, 69; *patawad*
(forgiveness), 19; *po* (sir/ma'am),
124; *tulong* (help or contribution),
19, 65, 122; *utang na loob* (debt
of gratitude),19, 80, 109, 122. *See
also* Filipino, traits
Filipino Wesley Methodist Church, 53
Filipino World War II veterans, 4,
14, 107, 111, 115, 147, 149–64,
174–77, 180–81, 183; *See also
veteranos*
Filipinos for Affirmative Action, 179
Filipinos: Forgotten Asian Americans,
130
financial contribution, 11
First California Volunteers, 42
First Presbyterian Church, Pasig, 2
Flores de Mayo, 50
Florida, 8, 156
Floro, Tatang (Idelfonso Bagasala),
149–50, 158–59, 161, 174–75
folk Catholicism, 87
food, 10, 13, 82–87, 95, 100, 115;
assistance, 84; industry, 84; metha-
phor, 84; preparation, 84
foodbank, 120

Foreign Direct Investment (FDI), 66
Fort Bragg, North Carolina, 166
Franciscans, 21, 41–42, 131
Fremont, 26, 112
Friere, 127, 146
Full Gospel Assembly, 111
Fundamentalist teaching, 117
fund-raising, 10

Gaa, Willie, 172
gateway cities, 104
gawa (act), 64, 72, 80
Gawad Kalinga, 78
gays and lesbians, 11
generation: first, 7, 10, 22, 93,124,
    179; gap, 124; second, 7, 10, 93,
    124; third, 10
Geneva Street, 4
Geneva United Methodist Church, 4,
    173
gentrification, 104
German Lutherans, 4
Germany, 154
globalization, 10–11, 34
God's Message, 117
Golden Gate University, 28, 32,
    69–70
Goldilocks, 26, 90
Gomez, Mariano, 129
Good Friday, 16
Gordon, Larry, 136, 142
Gramsci, 127
Gran Oriente Filipino, 49
Grand Evangelical Mission (GEM),
    58, 88, 93, 99, 116
Greater East Asia Co-Prosperity
    Sphere, 152
green card, 24–25. *See also* U.S. per-
    manent resident
Gross National Product (GNP), 67
Growing Up American, 5
Guingona, Michael, 119

Habitat for Humanity, 78
Hacienda Luisita, 170
Haile, Vera, 134
Hanna, Edward, 48
Hart, James, 42
Hatcher, Terri, 179
Hawaii, 22, 130–31, 152, 156
Hayward, 26
Hearst, William Randolph, 146
hegemonic, 3, 146, 151, 177
hermano mayor, 95–97, 116
Hermoso, Vic, 109
Hiroshima, 153
Hispanic, 26, 35, 83
Hispanicization, 90
Holy Angels Church, 51
Holy Child and Saint Martin Episco-
    pal Church, 58, 176
Holy Name Society, 115
holy persons, 18
Holy Supper, 88
Holy Thursday, 16
Holy Week, 16
Home Bound, 5
homeland security, 135
homeland, 2, 4, 6, 12, 25, 65, 71–72,
    80, 109, 124, 173, 175
hometown, 4, 7, 12, 17, 65, 71, 78,
    80, 174, 181–82; association, 6,
    106, 110–11, 116, 122; connec-
    tion, 109; fund-raising, 109
homosexuality, 108
Hong Kong, 20–21
Honolulu, 26, 70
household income, 68, 81
housing assistance, 75
Huerta, Dolores, 132
human rights, 7, 132, 151, 165, 167,
    170–71, 173
Hurricane Katrina, 78, 109

identity, 105

Iglesia Evangelica Metodista En Las
Islas Filipinas, 168
Iglesia Filipina Independiente, 44,
168–70, 172. *See also* Aglipayan
Church; Philippine Independent
Church
Iglesia ni Cristo (INC), 2, 15, 18, 44,
46, 57–58, 60–61, 70, 88, 99–101,
126–27, 129, 159; Daly City lo-
cale, 13, 30–31, 84, 93–95, 113,
116–20
Iglesia Unida Ekyumenical, 168
Ileto, Reynaldo, 128, 146
illegal immigration amnesty, 24
Illinois, 156
Ilocano, 33, 106, 135
Ilocano National Association, 109
Ilonggo, 106
Imagine, 3
Immigrant Rights Commission, San
Francisco, 3, 123, 133, 177, 180
Immigration and Customs Enforce-
ment (ICE), 25
Immigration and Naturalization Act,
155
Immigration and Naturalization Ser-
vice (INS), 25, 113, 155
immigration: Chinese, 21; debacle,
181; debate, 6; discriminatory, 21;
policy, 6
independent church, 44, 46, 53, 57–59
Indian: migration, 14, Muslim, 87
Indian American, 3
indigenous church, 35, 44
indio, 129
influence, 4, 8–9
INS Raid-Free Zone, 24
Integrated National Police (INP),
166. *See also* Philippine National
Police
integration, 4–5, 181; sociocultural, 5
Inter-American Development, Bank,

66, 69
interfaith, 165, 170–172
intergenerational: cohesion, 2, 10, 12,
140, 181; community center, 133;
gathering, 171; groups, 172; harmony, 126; networks, 165; respect,
13, 124, 127; worship, 171
International Hotel (I-Hotel), 25, 27
International Social Survey Program,
15
International Swimming Hall of Fame,
133
Iraq War, 168
Irish American, 95
Irish Catholic, 2, 114; Protestants, 4
Italian Catholics, 4, 86
Itliong, Larry, 54

Jack London Square, 100
Jaime Cardinal Sin, 18, 185n5
Japan, 152, 154
Japanese Americans, 2, 14
Japanese Imperial Army, 153
Japantown, 14
Jehovah's Witness, 3, 40, 55, 187n14
Jema'ah Islamiyah, 168
Jesuit Foundation, 28
Jesuits, 41–42
Jesus Christ, 17, 53, 55, 73, 79, 128,
187n2a
Jesus Is Lord Movement, 50
Jewish, 86
Jollibee, 26, 90–91
Journal of Democracy, 101
Journal of International Development,
102
*Journal of the American Academy of
Religion*, 85
Joy Luck Club, 125

Kadiwa, 126
ka'it ano (anything), 14

Kapangpangan, 33, 106, 135, 178
kapatiran (brotherhood/sisterhood), 144
kapwa (other), 83
kasamahan (community organization), 2, 9–10, 12, 14, 19, 34–35, 57–62, 65, 69, 79, 83–84, 93, 98–99, 101, 106, 108–9, 113, 118, 121, 124, 126,128, 131, 133–34, 145–48, 172, 182, 185n5. *See also* bonding Filipinization
Kentucky Fried Chicken (KFC), 182
Kim, Juree, 123
King Philip of Spain, 82
Klatt, Carol, 119
Knights of Rizal, 49
Knowing the Enemy, 169
Kobiaa, Samuel, 174
Korean Americans, 2
kwento (stories), 100

La Salle, 185n2
La Salle Alumni association, 112
labor movement, 132
labor union, 54
Lantos, Tom, 173
Lapu-lapu, 83
Latin America, 66–67, 86, 104, 127
Latino American, 3, 5
Latinos, 29, 76, 84, 104, 180
Lau, Diana, 123, 133
leadership structure, 134, 136–39
League of Filipino Students (LFS), 171–73
Lee, Debbie, 176
Lee, Sammy, 133
Legazpi, Miguel Lopez de, 41, 82–83
Legion of Mary, 51
Legionarios del Trabajo, 49, 131
Lennon, John, 3
Lent, 89
Lenten, 16, 73

Lesbian, Gay, Bisexual, and Transgendered (LGBT), 108
liberation theology, 127
Life, 133
life sharing, 144
Lions Club, 7, 112
Little Saigon, 14
Livermore, 100, 118
Liwanag Cultural Center, 171
Locating Filipino Americans, 5
Los Angeles, 26, 70
Los Angeles Times, 150
Louisiana, 5
Lowe, Lisa, 125
Lutheran Church in the Philippines, 168
Luzon, 110, 149; Indios, 26

Mabalon, Dawn, 130–31, 146
MacArthur, Arthur, 36
MacArthur, Douglas, 149, 152–53, 174–75
Macau, 20
Madrid, 82, 84
Magellan, Ferdinand, 82–83
Malay, 84; migration 14
Manalo, Eraño, 57
Manalo, Felix, 44, 46, 57
Manalo, Teofilo, 133
Manifest Destiny, 22
Manila, 20, 31, 38–42, 53, 77, 83, 112, 114–15, 118–19, 169, 185n5
Manila Bay, 22
Manila-Acapulco Galleon Trade, 20, 46
Manilatown, 15, 24–25, 27
Manilatown Center, 25
Manilatown Heritage Foundation, 121
manongs, 22, 24–25
Marcos dictatorship, 138, 168
Marcos, Ferdinand, 165–167, 185n5

Maria Elena Yuchengco Philippine
    Studies Program, 132
Marian devotion, 9
Marin, 26, 70, 104
Marinduque Association, 110
Market Street, 7
martial law, 23, 138, 165
Marx, 127, 139, 146, 148
Marxist, 138, 143
Maryland, 8
Masonic, 46, 49, 131, 147
McCoy, Alan, 132
McKinley, William, 22, 37, 46, 52–53
McKinnon, William, 42
medical mission, 116
melting pot, 5, 181
Memorial Day, 100
Methodist Church, 39–40, 131
Methodist Episcopal Church, 38, 44
Mexican Catholics, 54
Mexican migrants, 66
Mexico, 20, 66, 69, 80, 82
Middle East, 104
middle-class, 140–41
militarization, 165
military: aid, 166, 173; assistance,
    166, 170, 175; base, 152
Milpitas, 27, 77
Mindanao, 110, 166
minority populations, 5
Mint Mall, 27
misa de gallo, 82, 115, 120. *See also*
    Simbang gabi
Mission District, 4, 132
Mission Dolores Basilica, 51,108
Missionaries of the Immaculate Heart,
    42
Mitty, John J., 130
mobilization, 143–44, 181
modernization, 68
Moncadistas, 53–54
Moncado, Hilario Camino, 53

Monterey, California, 21
Moro uprising, 166
Morro Bay, 20
Most Holy Redeemer Catholic
    Church, 108
Mother of Perpetual Help, 114, 158
Mount Pinatubo disaster, 109
multicultural: San Francisco, 13;
    theory, 5–6
multiculturalism, 181

Naga Metropolitan Society, 110
Nagasaki, 153
Napa, 26,
National Association of Filipino-
    American United Methodists, 111
National Council of Churches in the
    Philippines (NCCP), 168–71, 173
national holiday, 16
Nationality Act of 1940, 153
Native American, 3
naturalization, 153, 155, 160
Nazareno of Quiapo, 110, 114, 158;
    See also Feast of the Black Naza-
    rene
Nebraska, 156
neutralization, 169
Nevada, 8
New Jersey, 156
New People's Army (NPA), 138, 166,
    168, 170
New York, 8, 21, 26, 84, 156
New York Times, 151
Nezhukumatathil, Aimee, 84
Nob Hill, 133
Nona, Sister, 136–137, 145
nonassimilation, 5
nonimmigrant visa, 24
novena, 82
Nuestra Señora de Peñafrancia, 111
Nueva Vizcaya Organization of Cali-
    fornia, 109

Oakland, 25, 69, 71, 100, 119, 133; Raiders, 8
Obet, Father, 136, 138
obispo maximo (supreme bishop), 44
Office of Ethnic Minorities, 140
Official Development Assistance (ODA), 66
Old Saint Mary's Cathedral, 48
Olympic Games (1948), 133
opiate of the people, 138
Otis, Elwell, 41–42
Our Lady of Antipolo Society, 51
Our Lady of Mercy, 51
Our Lady of Peñafrancia, 17
Our Lady of Perpetual Help, 50–51
Our Lady of the Abandoned, 17

Pacific Asian North American Religion (PANA), 171
Pacific Heights, 4
Pacific Islanders, 26
Pacifica, 31, 178
Paco Church, 42
padala (send), 63, 182
Pagsambang Bayan (People's Worship), 171, 173
Palace Hotel, 21
Palawan, 109
Pamayanan Ng Tagumpay, 119
Pampanga, 179
Pan-Asian Americanization, 176
Pangasinan, 78
Parent-Teacher Association (PTA), 7
parish intergenerational interest groups, 134, 142–45, 148, 183
parish organizations, 115, 125
parol (Christmas lantern), 18
Pasalamat (Thanksgiving), 88
Pasiguenans of Northern California, 110
Pasugo, 117
Pasyon (Passion of Christ), 149

Pasyon and Revolution, 128–29
Patriot Act, 3, 113
patron saint, 110
Pawican, Andy, 169–70, 175
Peace Corps, 10
Pearl Harbor, 152
pensionados, 22
People Power, 33–34, 138, 179, 185n5, 186n1
Pew Charitable Trusts, 28
philanthropy, 103
Philippine: archipelago, 110; dialect, 33; economy, 24; elections, 23; heritage, 135; independent churches, 168; insurrection, 22; national hero, 21; presidents, 167, 170; Protestant churches, 168; revolutionaries, 22; seminary and convent, 33
Philippine Airlines, 25, 72
Philippine Commission on Filipinos Overseas, 186n6
Philippine Commonwealth Act, 151
Philippine Commonwealth Army, 149, 151–53, 155, 163. *See also* Commonwealth Army of the Philippines
Philippine Constabulary (PC), 165–67
Philippine Constitution, 185n5
Philippine Consulate General of San Francisco, 23, 110–11, 132
Philippine Independence Day, 89
Philippine Independent Church, 44, 58, 70, 129. *See also* Aglipayan Church; Iglesia Filipina Independiente
Philippine International Aid, 112
Philippine Methodist Church, 46
Philippine Military Academy (PMA), 165
Philippine National Historical Institute, 186n7

Philippine National Police (PNP), 167, 174. *See also* Integrated National Police
Philippine Presbyterian Mission, 39
Philippine Revolution of 1896, 41, 153
Philippine Scouts, 150, 152–55, 163
Philippine-American War, 39, 42, 146, 165
Philippine-based restaurants, 90
Philippines, 2, 4, 36–38
pinsan (cousin), 72
Pistahan, 89
Pledge of allegiance, 174
political advocacy, 10
political organizing, 127
Portola Valley, 1
power relations, 145
praying then sending, 12, 64–65
Presbyterian Ellinwood Bible Training School, 44
Presbyterians, 40
Presbytery, 1
professional associations, 111
protest, 14
psychological stressors, 124
Public Law, 160, 162–164
public: office, 4; schools 8
Putnam, Robert, 13, 101–3, 111, 121

Quezon City, 112, 119
Quezonian Association, 78
Quiapo Church, 114

racial discrimination, 53
rainbow society, 181
Ramento, Alberto, 169–70, 172, 175
Ramirez, Candice, 123
Ramos, Fidel V., 146, 167
Recio, Dioscoro, 23
Recollects, 41
Red Cross, 7, 118, 158
Red Ribbon, 26, 90

Redemptorists, 42
regional association, 109–10
The Religion and Immigration Project (TRIP), 28–29
religious: authorities, 18; conversion, 13; diversity, 17, icon, 17; organizations, 110; persons, 18; power, 18; practices, 16; socialization, 10; theme, 31; worship, 3
Religious of the Virgin Mary (RVM), 114
remittance channel, 76
remittances, 64–69, 74–76
Rescission Acts, 154–55
resident minister, 118
Resus, Jerry, 1–2, 105–6
retirement, 73
rhetorics, 102
Richmond District, 23, 133
Rico, Bayani, 176
Rizal, Jose, 21, 129, 180
Rizalistas, 46
Rodgers, James, 53
Roman: Catholic, 70, 83, 89; Catholicism, 11
Romualdez, Diane, 162
Roosevelt, Franklin Delano, 151–52, 154–55, 175
Roosevelt, Theodore, 44
rosary: crusades, 9 session, 16
RosettaStone, 9
Russell, Charles, 40
Russian, 26

Sagado, Mark, 162
Sagisi, Jaymee Faith, 163
Saint Andrew's Church, 50
Saint Augustine's Catholic Church, 13, 31, 50, 124, 134–45, 147
Saint Boniface Catholic Church, 29, 50, 63–65, 78, 149–50, 157
Saint Charles Borromeo, 51

Saint Francis and Grace United Methodist Church, 3, 56, 105, 108–9, 169, 187n17
Saint Ignatius Church, 30, 133
Saint James Presbyterian Church, 1, 3, 54, 105, 108
Saint Joseph Church, 48, 51, 133
Saint Mary's Church, Stockton, 130
Saint Patrick's Catholic Church, 2–3, 13, 27, 30, 48–51, 79, 84, 89, 95–97, 99, 113–16, 120, 125, 134, 150, 157–58
Saint Patrick's Day, 78
Saint Patrick's Seminary and University, 52
Saint Rose Church, 48
Saint Thomas the Apostle Church, 78, 179
Salvation Army, 168
Salvation Army Chapel, 4
samahan (association), 121
samba (worship), 15, 19
sambahan (place of worship), 15
San Agustin, 21
San Buenaventura, Steffi, 131, 146
San Diego, 26, 70
San Francisco, 1, 13–14, 20–21; Bay, 21; Catholic church, 47–48; Catholic schools, 52, 61; congregations, 12; de Asis, 21; DJs, 8; economy, 20; language access, 25; Presidio, 22; Protestant church, 47; sanctuary, 25; society, 4; Union Square, 22; Veterans Day Parade, 150, 161
San Francisco Bay Area, 4, 6, 8, 12, 17, 22–24, 26, 28, 34, 51, 54, 61, 64–65, 70, 76, 87, 90, 98, 100, 104, 107, 109, 112, 119–20, 127, 147, 172, 175, 180–82
San Francisco Bay Area Religion and Remittance Survey, 65, 71, 74–75, 77

San Francisco Bay Bridge, 100
San Francisco Chronicle, 8, 151
San Francisco Department of Public Health, 112. *See also* San Francisco Health Department
San Francisco Filipino American Seventh-Day Adventist Church, 55
San Francisco Food Bank, 118
San Francisco General Hospital, 150
San Francisco Health Department, 84. *See also* San Francisco Department of Public Health
San Francisco Human Rights Commission (HRC), 159, 177
San Francisco International Airport (SFO), 4, 25, 79, 124, 135, 147
San Francisco Seventh-Day Adventist Church, Pacifica, 54, 107
San Francisco State University, 32, 70, 127, 150, 161, 173, 177
San Francisco Tabernacle Seventh-Day Adventist Church, 4, 56
San Jose, 26, 69, 77
San Jose State University, 150, 177
San Lorenzo Ruiz, 50, 61, 79, 110, 114
San Lorenzo Ruiz Senior Housing, 27
San Mateo, 26, 104
sandugo (blood compact), 83
Santa Ana, Manila, 17, 73
Santa Clara, 26, 70
Santa Rosa, Isaias, 169–170, 175
Santacruzan, 34, 116
Santo Niño, 17–18, 50, 79, 110, 114, 158, 174
sarili (self), 83
Schori, Katharine Jefferts, 172
Seattle Times, 151
second coming, 104
Second War Powers Act, 153
Senate Foreign Relations Committee, 173
Seniors Action Network, 115

seniors and elderly organizations, 111

September 11 (9/11), 3, 100, 103, 109, 135

Serra, Junipero, 21

Serramonte Mall, 28, 93

Seventh-Day Adventist, 16, 39–40, 44

Seventh-Day Adventist Church, 55

Shamana, Beverly, 172

Sicilian, 1

Sikatuna, Datu, 83

Sikh, 87

Silicon Valley, 24, 76

Silliman Institute, 53

simbahan (church), 15

Simbang gabi, 16, 50, 95–96, 99, 186n9. See also *misa de gallo*

sinakulo (passion play), 16

Singapore, 20, 84

Singles for Christ, 50

Sisters of Charity, 41

Small Christian Community, 139, 143–45

social: capital, 9, 13, 101, 104, 110, 117; energy, 107; injustice, 14; justice, 3, 13, 132, 139, 143; networking, 14; networks, 102; responsibility, 81; security, 73, 76, 121, 157, 162, 175; transformation, 139

socialization, 125

societal: giving, 76; institution, 35

socioeconomics of the congregation, 139–42

Solano, 26

Sonoma, 26

Sons of Saint Vincent de Paul, 41

South of Market (SoMa), 2, 25, 27, 70, 77, 95, 115, 120, 132–33, 146, 149, 157–58

South of Market Community Action Network (SOMCAN), 115, 121, 162

South of Market Mental Health, 112

South of Market Recreation Center, 157

South of Market Teen Center, 121

South San Francisco, 26, 31,140; City Council, 136; Planning Commission, 135, 142

Southeast Asian Americans, 176

Southeast Asian, 76

Southern California, 131

Spain, 20, 129

Spanish, 26; authorities, 21; colonizers, 22; empire, 20; paella, 84; Catholic religious orders, 37, 41

special noncitizen U.S. nationals, 22

spiritual: congregation, 18; invocation, 15; organizations, 110–111; sites, 7

Stanford University, 161

Stockton, 130

Strobel, Leny, 59

Student Action for Veterans Equity (SAVE), 159, 162–63

Subic Naval Base, 152

Sufis, 84

suki (favorite place/person), 15

Sunset: District, 108; neighborhood, 4

Tagalog, 1, 8, 26, 30, 33, 57, 95, 106, 124, 135, 149, 178, 183, 185n1; bible study, 182; mass, 50, 63, 114, 134; worship, 55

Taglish, 149

tago-ng-tago (TNT), 24, 113

Taiwan, 20

Tan, Amy, 125

Taylor, Gertrude, 133

Tenderloin District, 25, 70, 116, 132, 149, 157–58

terrorist organizations, 168

Texas, 156

Thanksgiving, 88, 182

Thirty-first Infantry Regiment, 152

Thomasians, 78
Thomasites, 98
Tony, Lolo, 174–175
transnational: influence, 2,10, 12,
  34–35, 59, 61, 65, 80–81,181; mi-
  gration, 10, 34, 61; relations, 59
Treaty of Paris, 41
Trias, Jasmine, 8
Tribu, 182
Truman, Harry S., 154–55

U.S. Air Force, 153
U.S. Armed Forces, 151
U.S. Armed Forces of the Far East
  (USAFFE), 149, 152–153, 155,
  174, 183
U.S. Army, 152–153
U.S. Census Bureau, 26
U.S. Census, 11, 26
U.S. citizenship, 135,149, 154. *See
  also* citizenship
U.S. Citizenship and Immigration Ser-
  vice, 74
U.S. Congress, 24, 36, 115, 135, 148,
  150–51, 153, 159–60, 166, 175
U.S. Department of Defense, 151
U.S. Department of Homeland Secu-
  rity, 25
U.S. Designated Foreign Terrorist Or-
  ganizations List, 168, 170
U.S. Embassy in Manila, 149, 155
U.S. House of Representatives, 163,
  173
U.S. Immigration Act of 1965, 23, 49
U.S. Institute of Peace, 173
U.S. permanent resident, 24. *See also*
  green card
U.S. State Department, 172–73, 179
U.S. Veterans Administration (VA),
  154–55, 163–64
undocumented, 24
UNESCO, 74

Union Church of Manila, 40
Union City, 26
Union Obrera Democratica, 44
Union Theological Seminary, 53
United Brethren, 39
United Church of Christ (UCC), 46,
  168, 170–73
United Evangelical Church, 46
United Farm Workers Union (UFW),
  132
United Kingdom, 67, 102
United Luisita Workers Union, 170
United Methodist Church (UMC), 56,
  165, 168, 170–73, 176
United Nations Development Pro-
  gramme (UNDP), 66, 69
United Nations high commissioner for
  human rights, 170
United Pilipino Organizing Network
  (UPON), 121
United Way, 7, 78, 111
University Mount Presbyterian
  Church, 1
University of California, Berkeley,
  127, 161
University of San Francisco, 22, 28,
  31, 70, 123–24,127, 132–33, 150,
  161, 177, 180
University of the Philippines alumni
  association, 112
USS *Thomas*, 97

Valencia, 162
Vallejo, 26, 69
Vatican, 3, 41, 44, 108
Velarde, Mariano "Mike," 185n5
Vera Cruz, Philip, 54, 132
veteranos, 150, 163; *See also* Filipino
  World War II veterans
Veterans benefit law, 163
Veterans Benefits Act, 163
Veterans Equity Center (VEC), 27,

121, 157
Veterans Health Care, Capital Asset, and Business Improvement Act, 163
Veterans Medical Center, 175
Victoria Manalo Draves Park, 123, 146, 180–81
Vietnamese Americans, 14
Vietnamese community, 5
Virgin Mary, 17, 38, 110, 146, 186n9
Visayan, 135
Visayas, 110
Visitacion Valley, 1
volunteer, 3, 103

wake (*lamay*), 19
War on Terror, 7, 100, 151, 165, 168, 170, 175–76
Waray, 33
Washington, D.C., 154, 159, 168, 175, 179
Washington Post, 151
Watchtower Bible and Tract Society, 40
Watsonville, California, 23
Weber, 127, 146

wedding (*kasal*), 19
West Bay Pilipino Multi-Services Center, 27, 107, 112, 116, 121, 179
West Coast, 22
Westborough Middle School, 143
Western Union, 76
White House, 154, 159
Wiseman, Christopher, 123
working visa, 24
World Bank, 69
World Council of Churches, 40, 174
World War II, 23, 49, 151, 153–55, 163, 165, 178
worship services, 58

Yangwas, Jenah Mari Paloy, 163
Young Men's Christian Association (YMCA), 53
Young Women's Christian Association (YWCA), 7
youth organizations, 125

Zamora, Jacinto, 129
Zamora, Nicolas, 39
Zhou, Min, 5–6

About the Author

Filipino American Joaquin Jay Gonzalez III, Ph.D., is Associate Professor of Politics and Director of the Maria Elena Yuchengco Philippine Studies Program at the University of San Francisco. After the 9/11 terrorist attacks, he was called to public service and appointed San Francisco Commissioner for Immigrant Rights and Mayor George Christopher Chair in Public Administration at Golden Gate University. He is the author of several books, including *Religion at the Corner of Bliss and Nirvana*; *Welcome to the Philippines*; *Philippine Labour Migration*; and *Governance Innovations in the Asia-Pacific Region*. In 2005, House Speaker Nancy Pelosi awarded Dr. Gonzalez a Special Congressional Recognition for his exemplary work on immigrant concerns.